KONG

OF SKULL ISLAND™

VOLUME **ONE**

DESIGN **KELSEY DIETERICH**   ASSOCIATE EDITOR **ALEX GALER**   EDITOR **DAFNA PLEBAN**

ROSS RICHIE CEO & Founder • **MATT GAGNON** Editor-in-Chief • **FILIP SABLIK** President of Publishing & Marketing • **STEPHEN CHRISTY** President of Development • **LANCE KREITER** VP of Licensing & Merchandising
PHIL BARBARO VP of Finance • **BRYCE CARLSON** Managing Editor • **MEL CAYLO** Marketing Manager • **SCOTT NEWMAN** Production Design Manager • **KATE HENNING** Operations Manager • **SIERRA HAHN** Senior Editor
DAFNA PLEBAN Editor, Talent Development • **SHANNON WATTERS** Editor • **ERIC HARBURN** Editor • **WHITNEY LEOPARD** Associate Editor • **JASMINE AMIRI** Associate Editor • **CHRIS ROSA** Associate Editor
ALEX GALER Associate Editor • **CAMERON CHITTOCK** Associate Editor • **MATTHEW LEVINE** Assistant Editor • **KELSEY DIETERICH** Production Designer • **JILLIAN CRAB** Production Designer
MICHELLE ANKLEY Production Designer • **GRACE PARK** Production Design Assistant • **AARON FERRARA** Operations Coordinator • **ELIZABETH LOUGHRIDGE** Accounting Coordinator • **STEPHANIE HOCUTT** Social Media Coordinator
JOSÉ MEZA Sales Assistant • **JAMES ARRIOLA** Mailroom Assistant • **HOLLY AITCHISON** Operations Assistant • **SAM KUSEK** Direct Market Representative • **AMBER PARKER** Administrative Assistant

G

ND™

WRITTEN BY
JAMES ASMUS

ILLUSTRATED BY
CARLOS MAGNO

COLORS BY
BRAD SIMPSON

LETTERS BY
ED DUKESHIRE

COVER BY
NICK ROBLES

BASED ON
KONG OF SKULL ISLAND
CREATED BY **JOE DEVITO**

SPECIAL THANKS TO
DANNIE FESTA, JOHN LEONHARDT, AND EVERYONE AT WORLD BUILDER ENTERTAINMENT.

BOOM! STUDIOS DeVito ArtWorks WORLD BUILDER ENTERTAINMENT

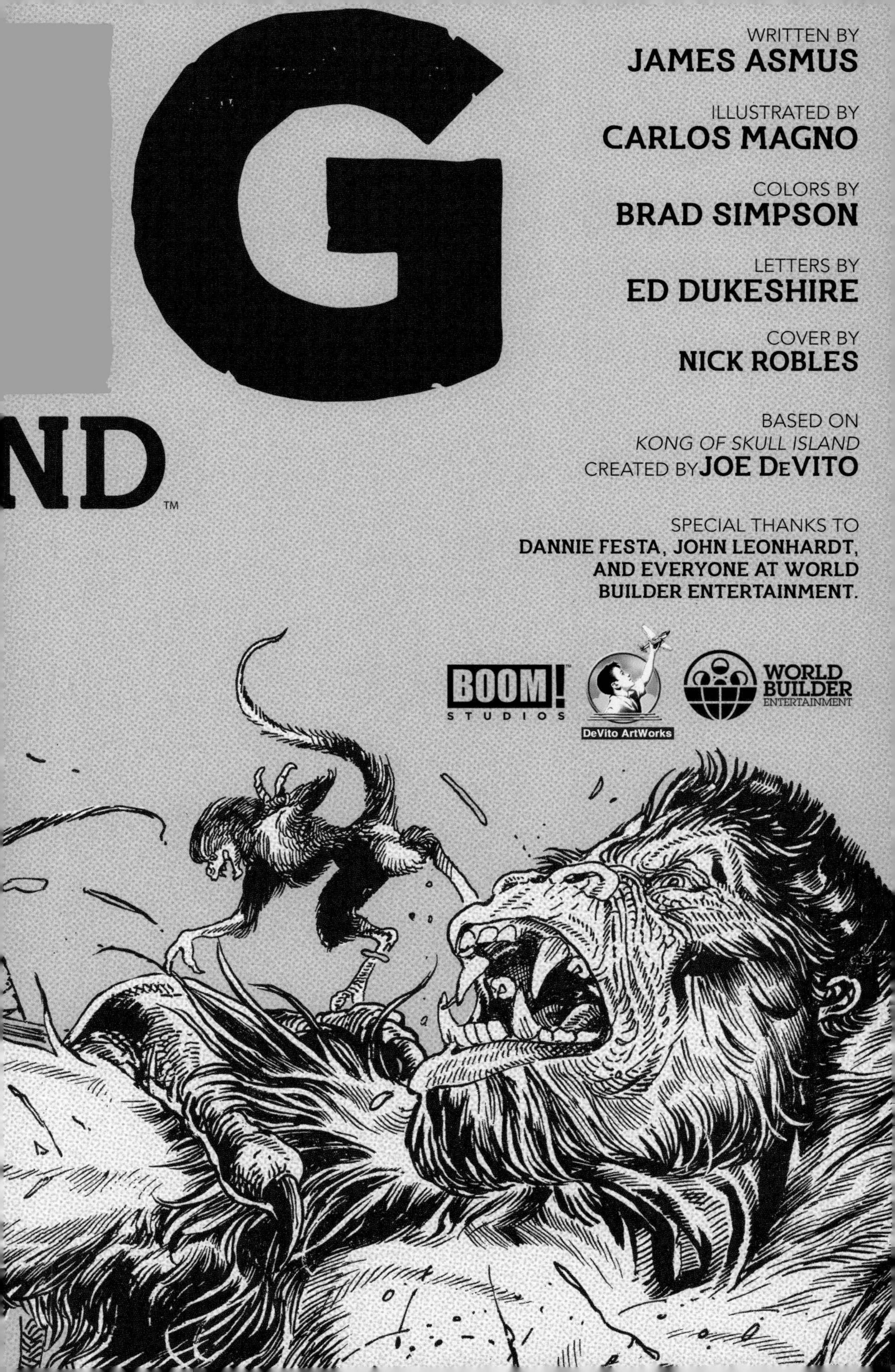

CHAPTER
ONE

WE WERE MORE *ALIKE* THAN *DIFFERENT.* AND ALREADY SO *VULNERABLE* TO THE REAL AND *DIRE THREATS* OF OUR WORLD.

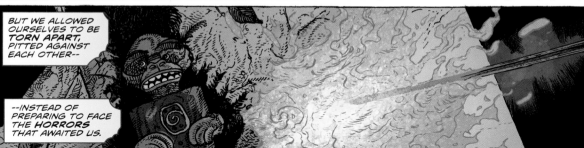

BUT WE ALLOWED OURSELVES TO BE *TORN APART,* PITTED AGAINST EACH OTHER--

--INSTEAD OF PREPARING TO FACE THE *HORRORS* THAT AWAITED US.

PERHAPS WE HAD ALLOWED OURSELVES TO BECOME TOO *DISTRACTED* TO SEE WHAT WAS COMING...

HOLD!

WHAT *IS* THIS?!

YOU *DEFILE* THE *FAMILY SEAL* OF THE *TAGU KING?!*

PLEASE--NO NEED TO *HARASS* THESE PEOPLE IN MY NAME.

AS YOU SAY, KING. MY *APOLOGIES.*

WE MAY OBSERVE DIFFERENT RITUALS, BUT WE RESPECT THE *ATU* TRADITIONS.

WE ALL HOPE FOR A *THRILLING* EXHIBITION TODAY!

SO PLEASE-- MAKE YOUR *OFFERING! EMBOLDEN* YOUR GLADIATORS!

UNLEASH YOUR--

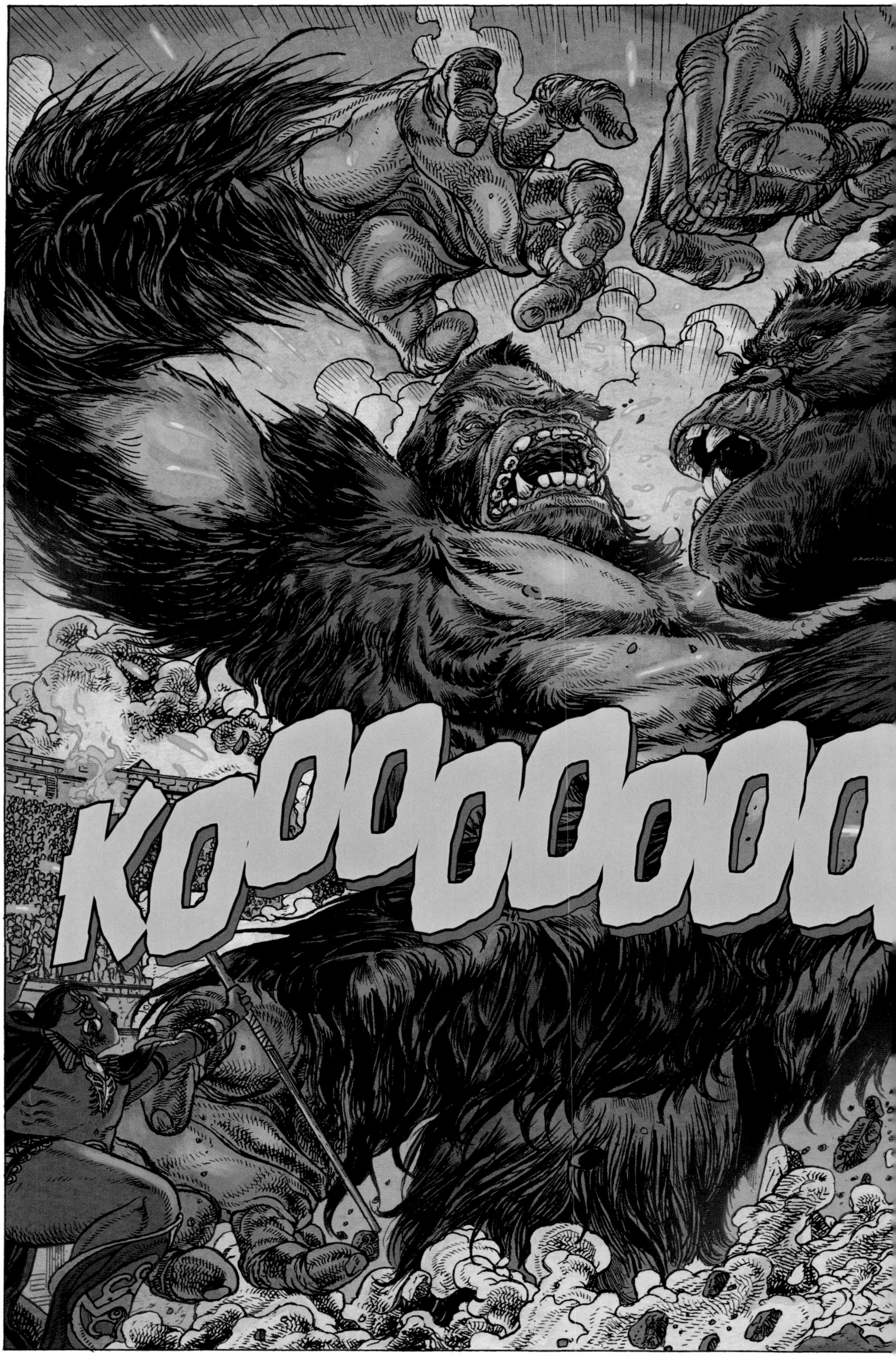
KOOOOOOOO

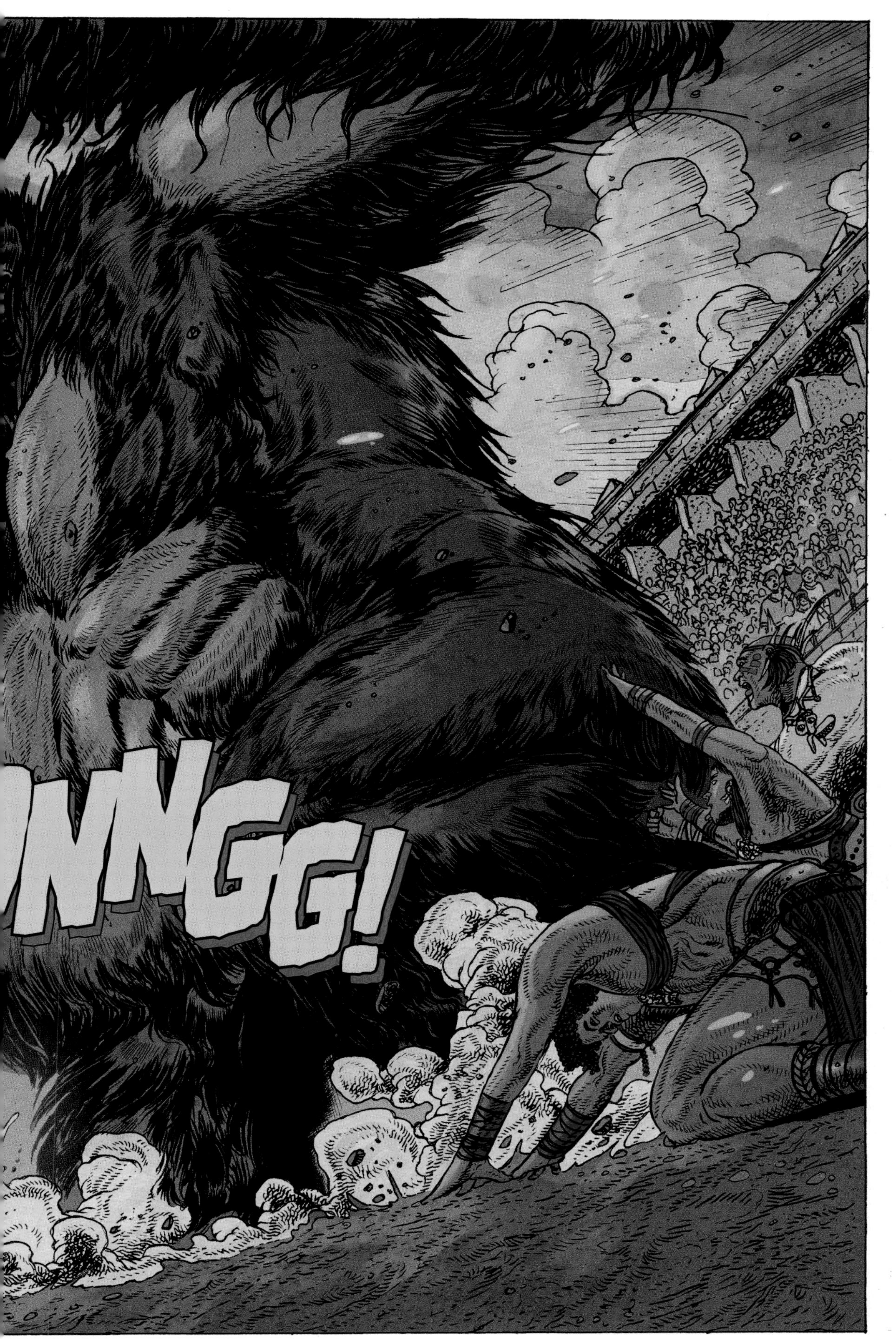
NNGG!

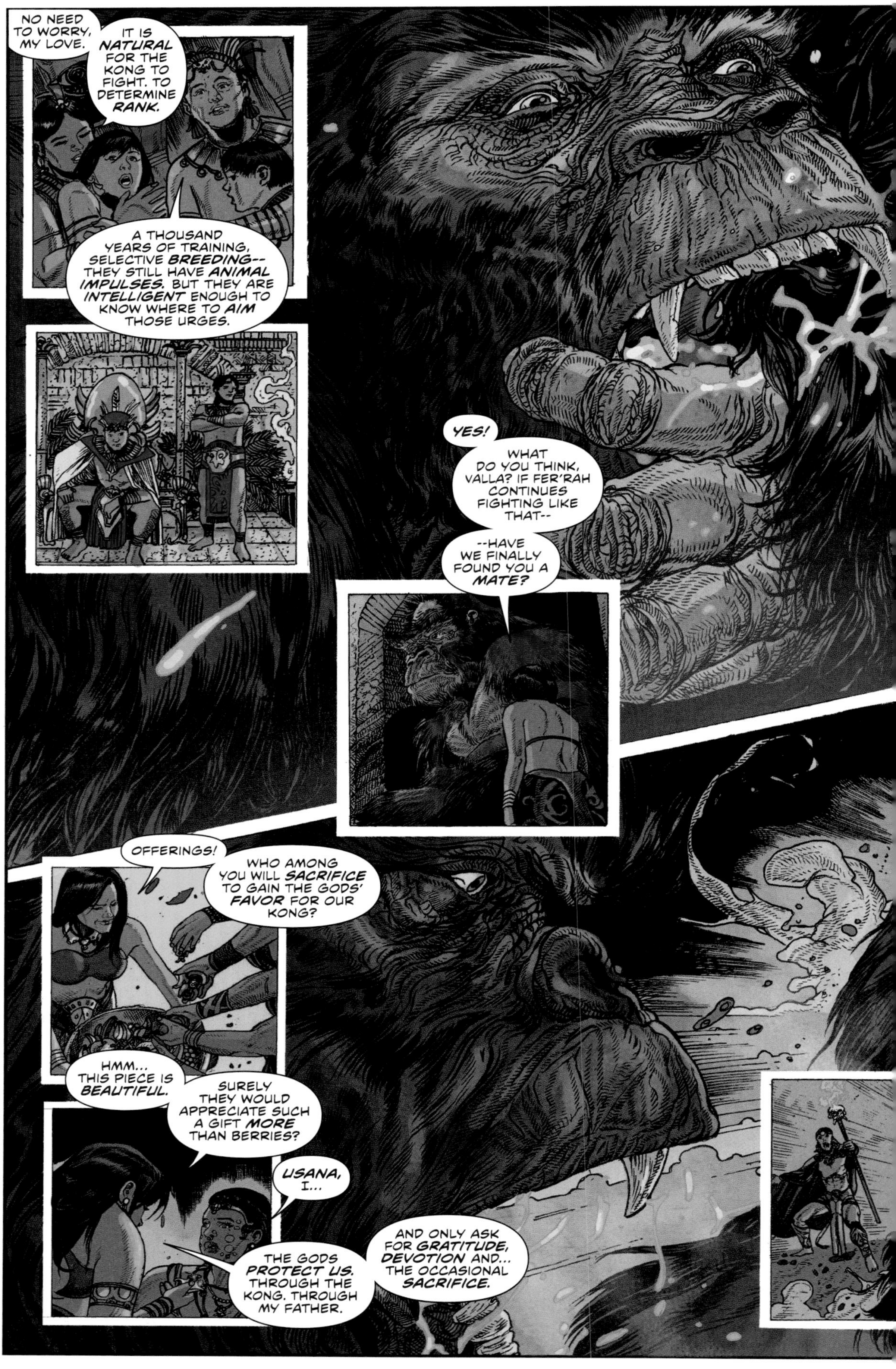
NO NEED TO WORRY, MY LOVE.
IT IS NATURAL FOR THE KONG TO FIGHT. TO DETERMINE RANK.
A THOUSAND YEARS OF TRAINING, SELECTIVE BREEDING-- THEY STILL HAVE ANIMAL IMPULSES. BUT THEY ARE INTELLIGENT ENOUGH TO KNOW WHERE TO AIM THOSE URGES.
YES!
WHAT DO YOU THINK, VALLA? IF FER'RAH CONTINUES FIGHTING LIKE THAT--
--HAVE WE FINALLY FOUND YOU A MATE?
OFFERINGS!
WHO AMONG YOU WILL SACRIFICE TO GAIN THE GODS' FAVOR FOR OUR KONG?
HMM... THIS PIECE IS BEAUTIFUL.
SURELY THEY WOULD APPRECIATE SUCH A GIFT MORE THAN BERRIES?
USANA, I...
THE GODS PROTECT US. THROUGH THE KONG. THROUGH MY FATHER.
AND ONLY ASK FOR GRATITUDE, DEVOTION AND... THE OCCASIONAL SACRIFICE.

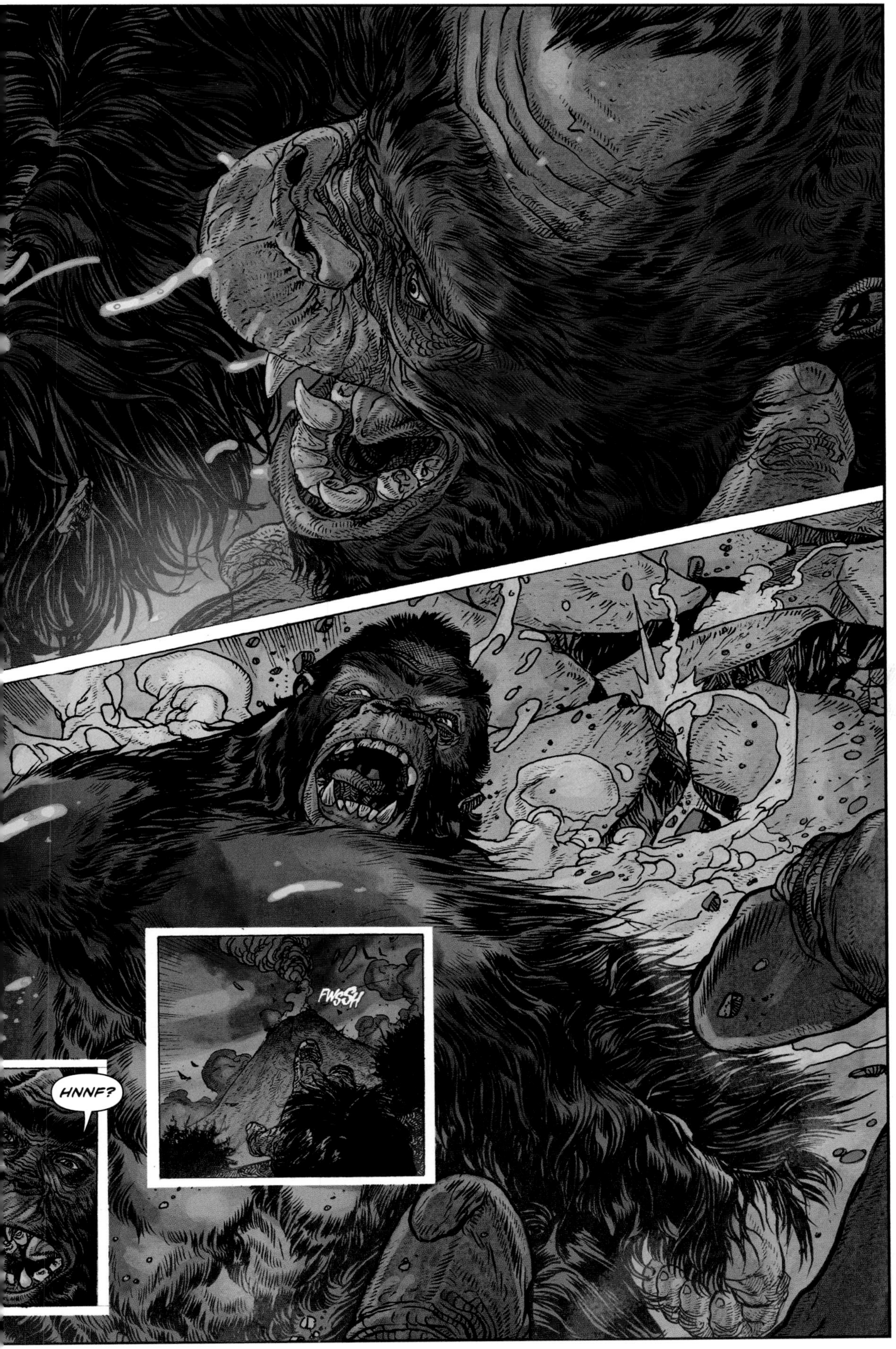
FWSSH
HNNF?

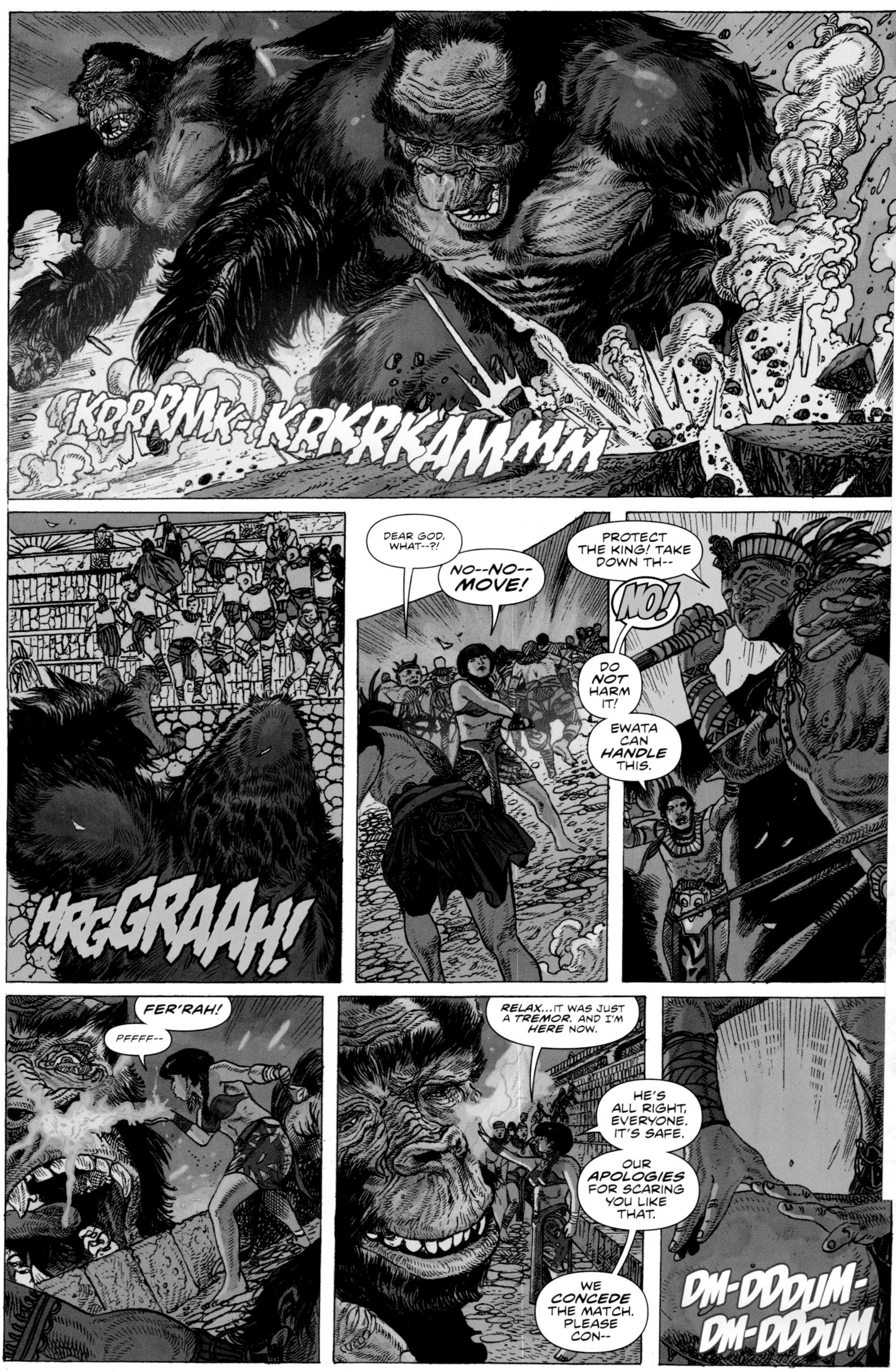
KRRRMK-KRKRKAMMMM
HRGGRAAH!
DEAR GOD, WHAT--?!
NO--NO--MOVE!
PROTECT THE KING! TAKE DOWN TH--
NO!
DO NOT HARM IT!
EWATA CAN HANDLE THIS.
FER'RAH!
PFFFF--
RELAX...IT WAS JUST A TREMOR. AND I'M HERE NOW.
HE'S ALL RIGHT, EVERYONE. IT'S SAFE.
OUR APOLOGIES FOR SCARING YOU LIKE THAT.
WE CONCEDE THE MATCH. PLEASE CON--
DM-DDDUM-DM-DDDUM

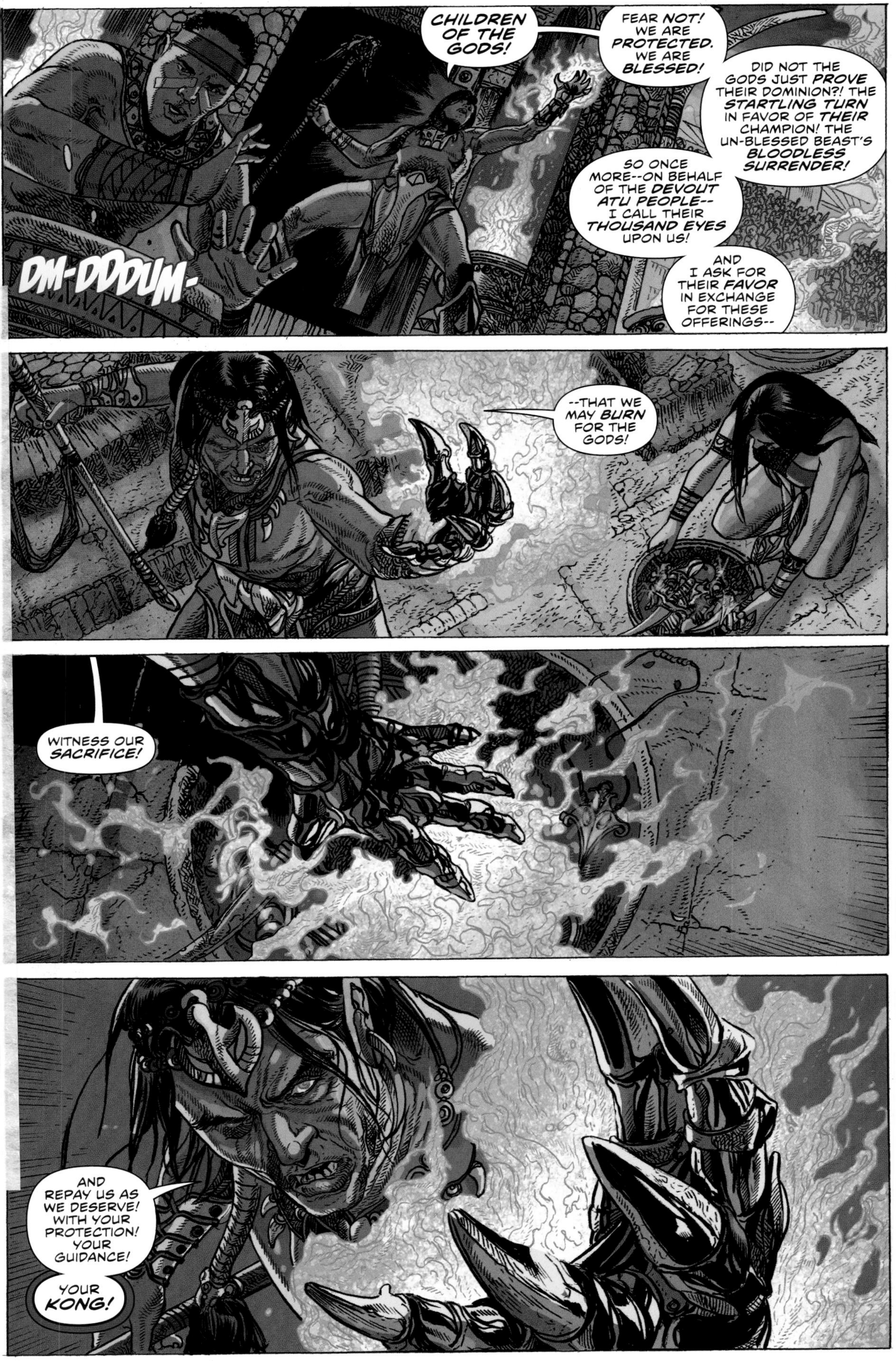
CHILDREN OF THE GODS!
FEAR NOT! WE ARE PROTECTED. WE ARE BLESSED!
DID NOT THE GODS JUST PROVE THEIR DOMINION?! THE STARTLING TURN IN FAVOR OF THEIR CHAMPION! THE UN-BLESSED BEAST'S BLOODLESS SURRENDER!
SO ONCE MORE--ON BEHALF OF THE DEVOUT ATU PEOPLE-- I CALL THEIR THOUSAND EYES UPON US!
AND I ASK FOR THEIR FAVOR IN EXCHANGE FOR THESE OFFERINGS--
DM-DDDUM-
--THAT WE MAY BURN FOR THE GODS!
WITNESS OUR SACRIFICE!
AND REPAY US AS WE DESERVE! WITH YOUR PROTECTION! YOUR GUIDANCE!
YOUR KONG!

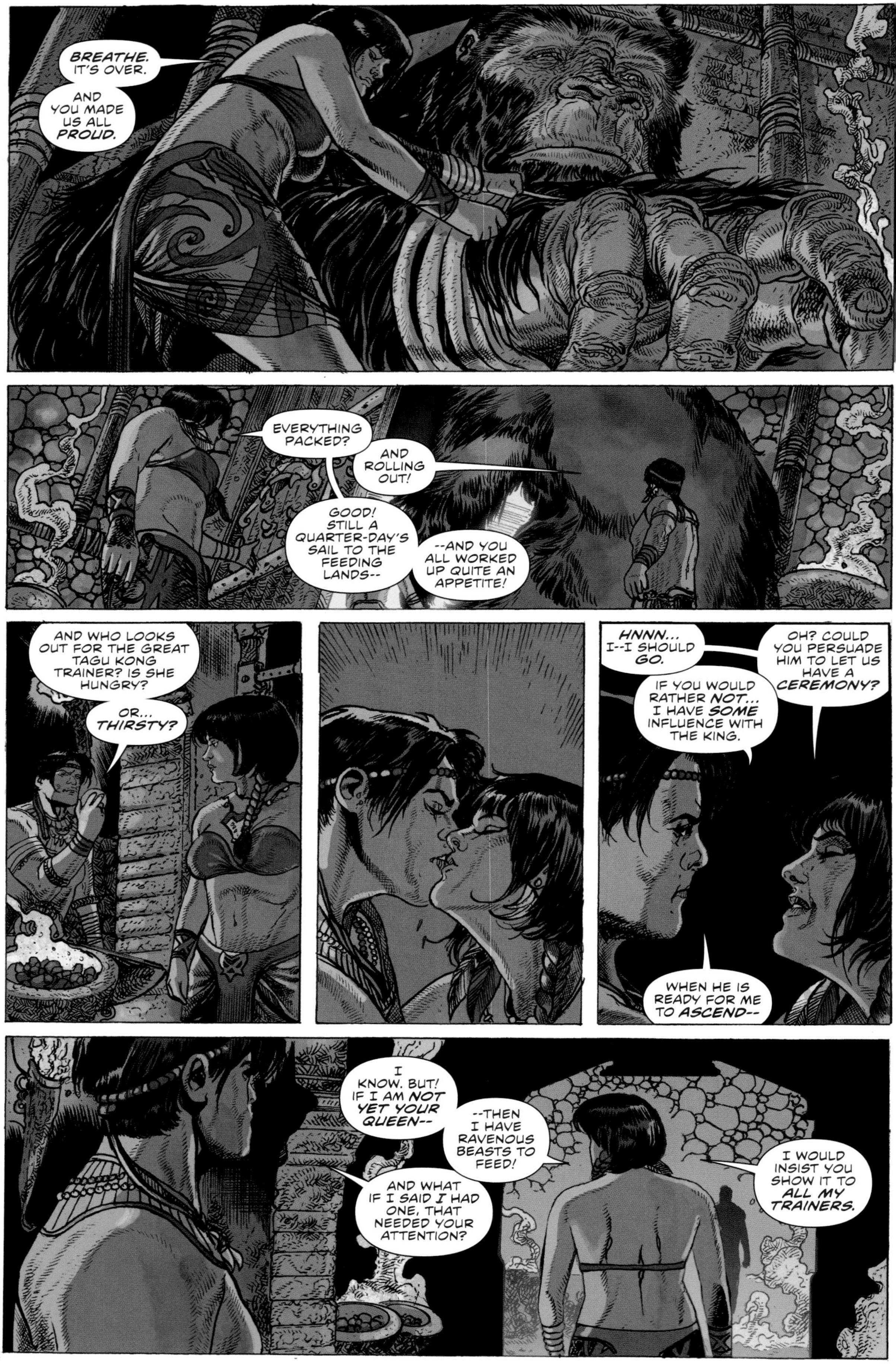
BREATHE. IT'S OVER.
AND YOU MADE US ALL PROUD.
EVERYTHING PACKED?
AND ROLLING OUT!
GOOD! STILL A QUARTER-DAY'S SAIL TO THE FEEDING LANDS--
--AND YOU ALL WORKED UP QUITE AN APPETITE!
AND WHO LOOKS OUT FOR THE GREAT TAGU KONG TRAINER? IS SHE HUNGRY?
OR... THIRSTY?
HNNN... I--I SHOULD GO.
IF YOU WOULD RATHER NOT... I HAVE SOME INFLUENCE WITH THE KING.
OH? COULD YOU PERSUADE HIM TO LET US HAVE A CEREMONY?
WHEN HE IS READY FOR ME TO ASCEND--
I KNOW. BUT! IF I AM NOT YET YOUR QUEEN--
--THEN I HAVE RAVENOUS BEASTS TO FEED!
AND WHAT IF I SAID I HAD ONE, THAT NEEDED YOUR ATTENTION?
I WOULD INSIST YOU SHOW IT TO ALL MY TRAINERS.

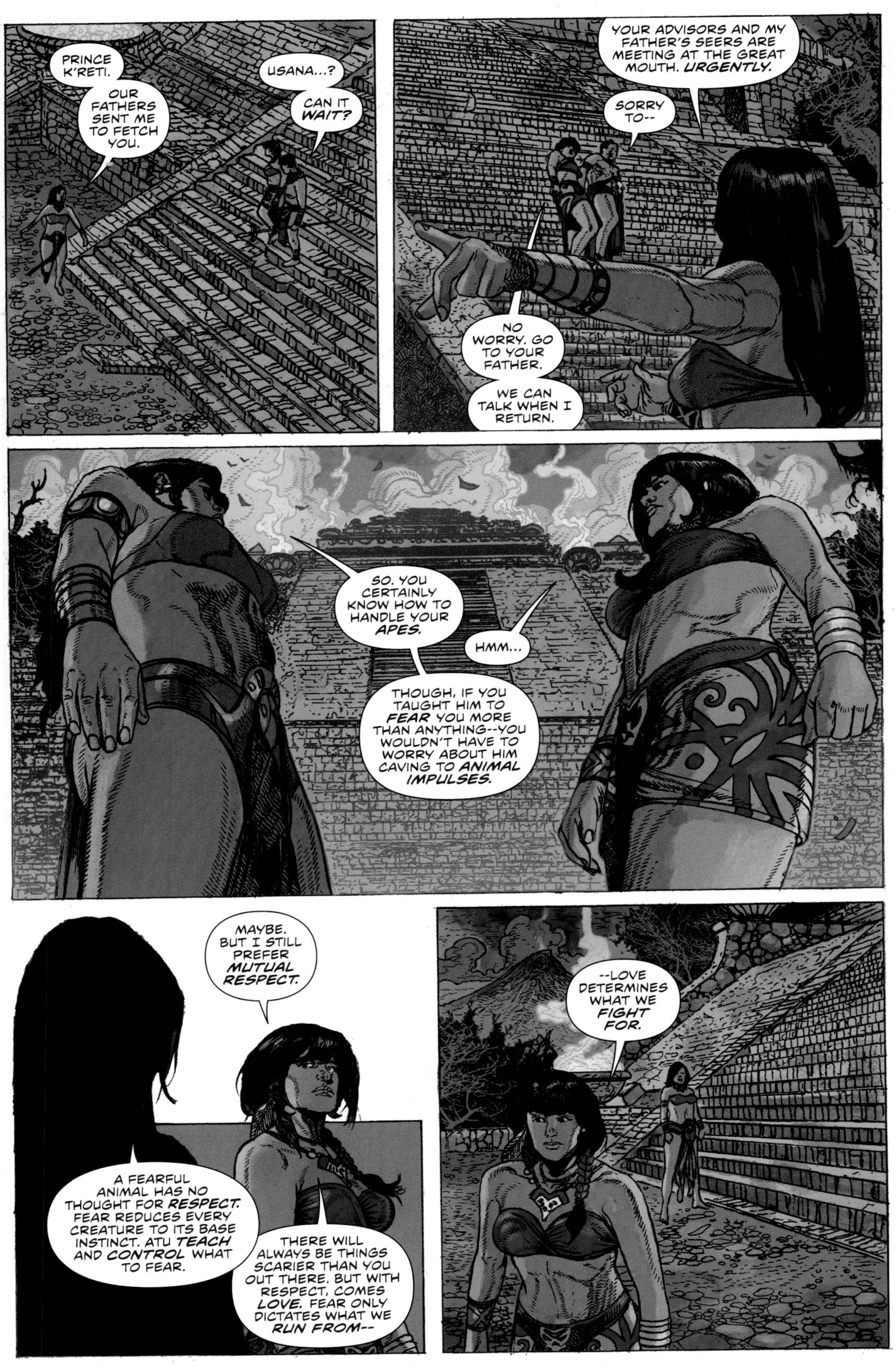
PRINCE K'RETI.
OUR FATHERS SENT ME TO FETCH YOU.
USANA...?
CAN IT WAIT?
YOUR ADVISORS AND MY FATHER'S SEERS ARE MEETING AT THE GREAT MOUTH. URGENTLY.
SORRY TO--
NO WORRY. GO TO YOUR FATHER.
WE CAN TALK WHEN I RETURN.
SO. YOU CERTAINLY KNOW HOW TO HANDLE YOUR APES.
HMM...
THOUGH, IF YOU TAUGHT HIM TO FEAR YOU MORE THAN ANYTHING--YOU WOULDN'T HAVE TO WORRY ABOUT HIM CAVING TO ANIMAL IMPULSES.
MAYBE. BUT I STILL PREFER MUTUAL RESPECT.
A FEARFUL ANIMAL HAS NO THOUGHT FOR RESPECT. FEAR REDUCES EVERY CREATURE TO ITS BASE INSTINCT. ATU TEACH AND CONTROL WHAT TO FEAR.
THERE WILL ALWAYS BE THINGS SCARIER THAN YOU OUT THERE. BUT WITH RESPECT, COMES LOVE. FEAR ONLY DICTATES WHAT WE RUN FROM--
--LOVE DETERMINES WHAT WE FIGHT FOR.

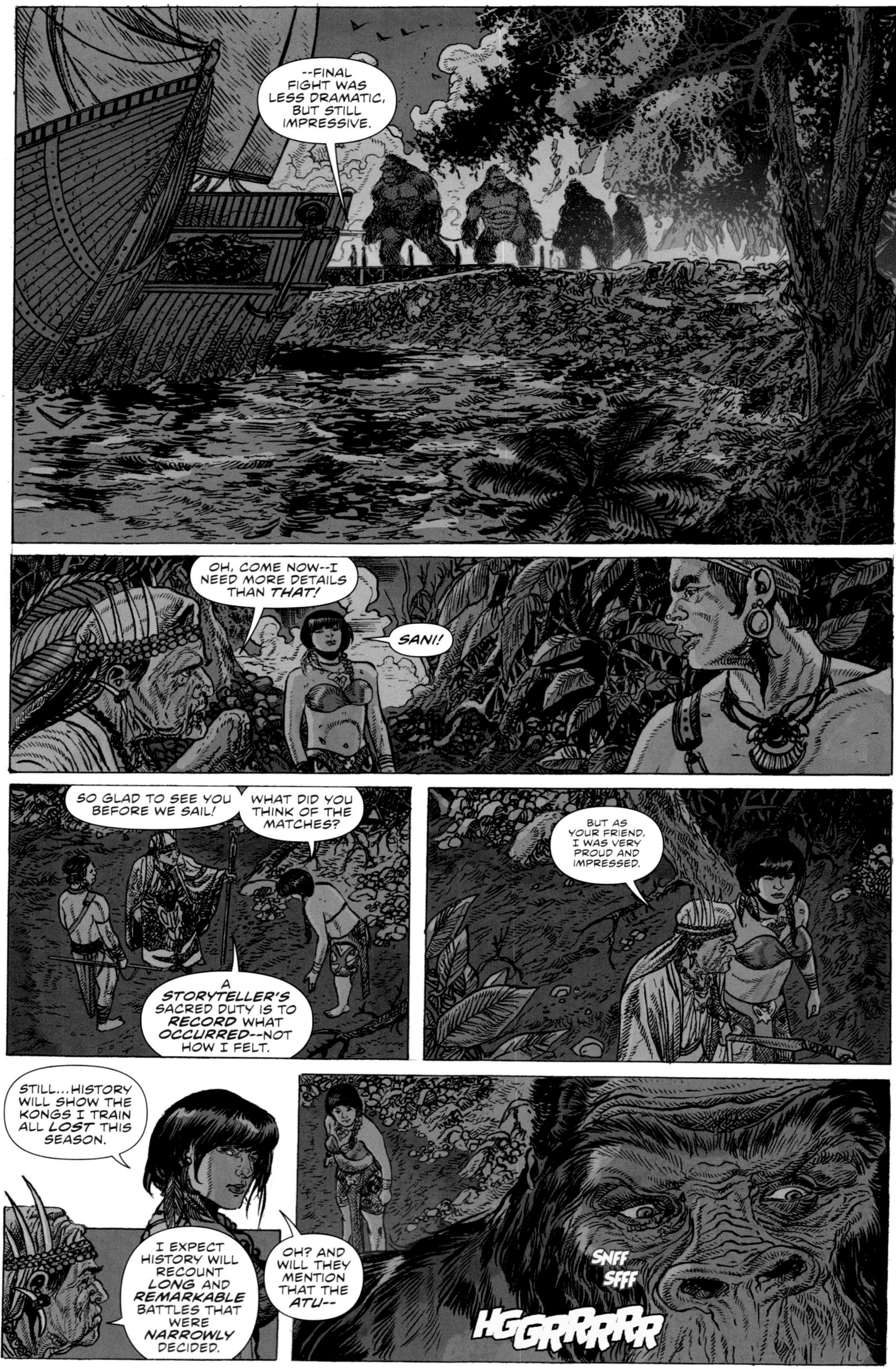
--FINAL FIGHT WAS LESS DRAMATIC, BUT STILL IMPRESSIVE.
OH, COME NOW--I NEED MORE DETAILS THAN *THAT!*
SANI!
SO GLAD TO SEE YOU BEFORE WE SAIL!
WHAT DID YOU THINK OF THE MATCHES?
A ***STORYTELLER'S*** SACRED DUTY IS TO ***RECORD*** WHAT ***OCCURRED***--NOT HOW I FELT.
BUT AS YOUR FRIEND, I WAS VERY PROUD AND IMPRESSED.
STILL...HISTORY WILL SHOW THE KONGS I TRAIN ALL *LOST* THIS SEASON.
I EXPECT HISTORY WILL RECOUNT ***LONG*** AND ***REMARKABLE*** BATTLES THAT WERE ***NARROWLY*** DECIDED.
OH? AND WILL THEY MENTION THAT THE ***ATU***--
SNFF
SFFF
HGGRRRRRR

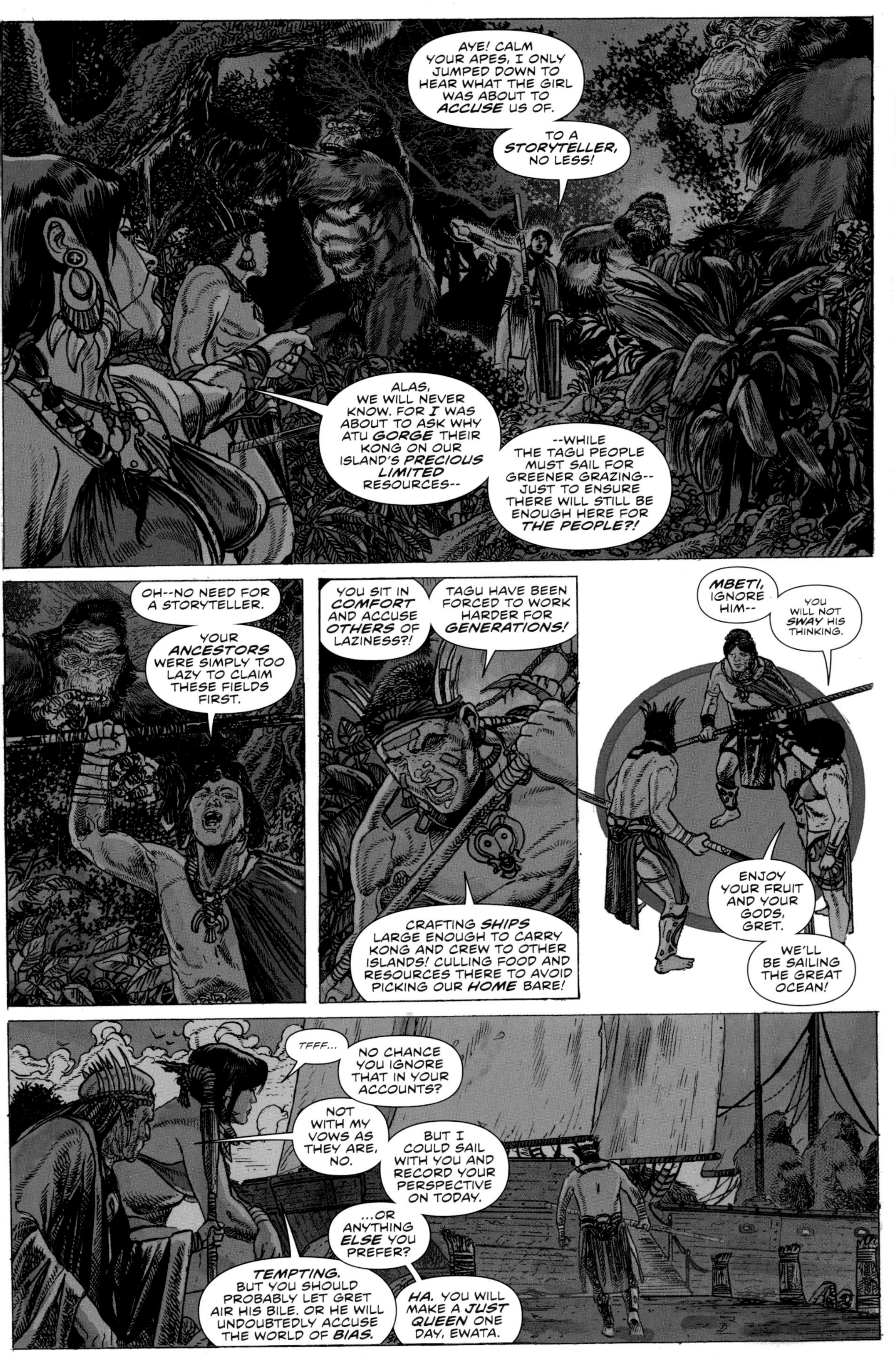
AYE! CALM YOUR APES, I ONLY JUMPED DOWN TO HEAR WHAT THE GIRL WAS ABOUT TO ACCUSE US OF.
TO A STORYTELLER, NO LESS!
ALAS, WE WILL NEVER KNOW. FOR I WAS ABOUT TO ASK WHY ATU GORGE THEIR KONG ON OUR ISLAND'S PRECIOUS LIMITED RESOURCES--
--WHILE THE TAGU PEOPLE MUST SAIL FOR GREENER GRAZING--JUST TO ENSURE THERE WILL STILL BE ENOUGH HERE FOR THE PEOPLE?!
OH--NO NEED FOR A STORYTELLER.
YOUR ANCESTORS WERE SIMPLY TOO LAZY TO CLAIM THESE FIELDS FIRST.
YOU SIT IN COMFORT AND ACCUSE OTHERS OF LAZINESS?!
TAGU HAVE BEEN FORCED TO WORK HARDER FOR GENERATIONS!
CRAFTING SHIPS LARGE ENOUGH TO CARRY KONG AND CREW TO OTHER ISLANDS! CULLING FOOD AND RESOURCES THERE TO AVOID PICKING OUR HOME BARE!
MBETI, IGNORE HIM--
YOU WILL NOT SWAY HIS THINKING.
ENJOY YOUR FRUIT AND YOUR GODS, GRET.
WE'LL BE SAILING THE GREAT OCEAN!
TFFF...
NO CHANCE YOU IGNORE THAT IN YOUR ACCOUNTS?
NOT WITH MY VOWS AS THEY ARE, NO.
BUT I COULD SAIL WITH YOU AND RECORD YOUR PERSPECTIVE ON TODAY.
...OR ANYTHING ELSE YOU PREFER?
TEMPTING. BUT YOU SHOULD PROBABLY LET GRET AIR HIS BILE. OR HE WILL UNDOUBTEDLY ACCUSE THE WORLD OF BIAS.
HA. YOU WILL MAKE A JUST QUEEN ONE DAY, EWATA.

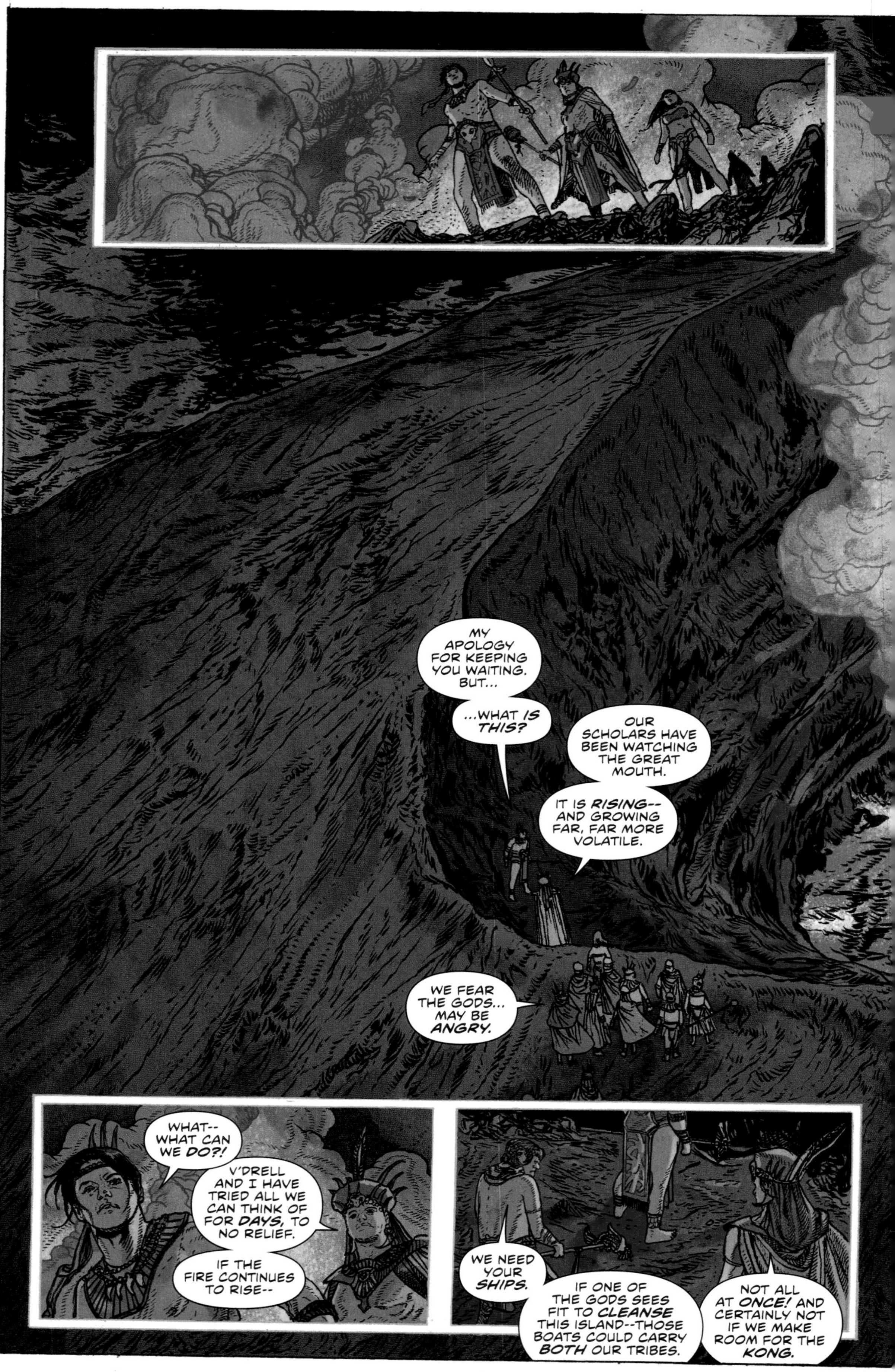

MY APOLOGY FOR KEEPING YOU WAITING. BUT...
...WHAT *IS* *THIS?*
OUR SCHOLARS HAVE BEEN WATCHING THE GREAT MOUTH.
IT IS *RISING*--AND GROWING FAR, FAR MORE VOLATILE.
WE FEAR THE GODS... MAY BE *ANGRY.*
WHAT--WHAT CAN WE *DO?!*
V'DRELL AND I HAVE TRIED ALL WE CAN THINK OF FOR *DAYS,* TO NO RELIEF.
IF THE FIRE CONTINUES TO RISE--
WE NEED YOUR *SHIPS.*
IF ONE OF THE GODS SEES FIT TO *CLEANSE* THIS ISLAND--THOSE BOATS COULD CARRY *BOTH* OUR TRIBES.
NOT ALL AT *ONCE!* AND CERTAINLY NOT IF WE MAKE ROOM FOR THE *KONG.*

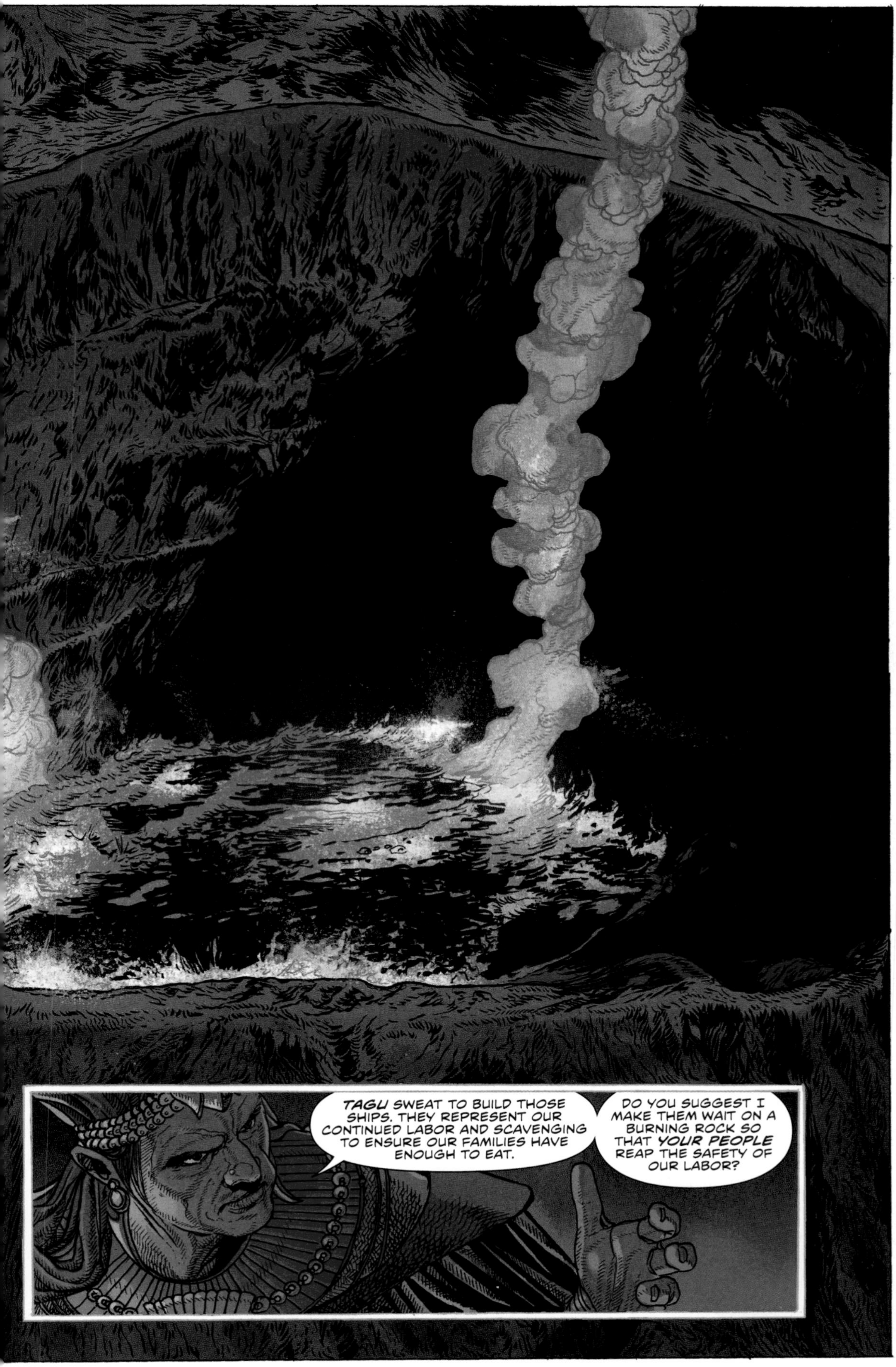
TAGU SWEAT TO BUILD THOSE SHIPS. THEY REPRESENT OUR CONTINUED LABOR AND SCAVENGING TO ENSURE OUR FAMILIES HAVE ENOUGH TO EAT.
DO YOU SUGGEST I MAKE THEM WAIT ON A BURNING ROCK SO THAT YOUR PEOPLE REAP THE SAFETY OF OUR LABOR?

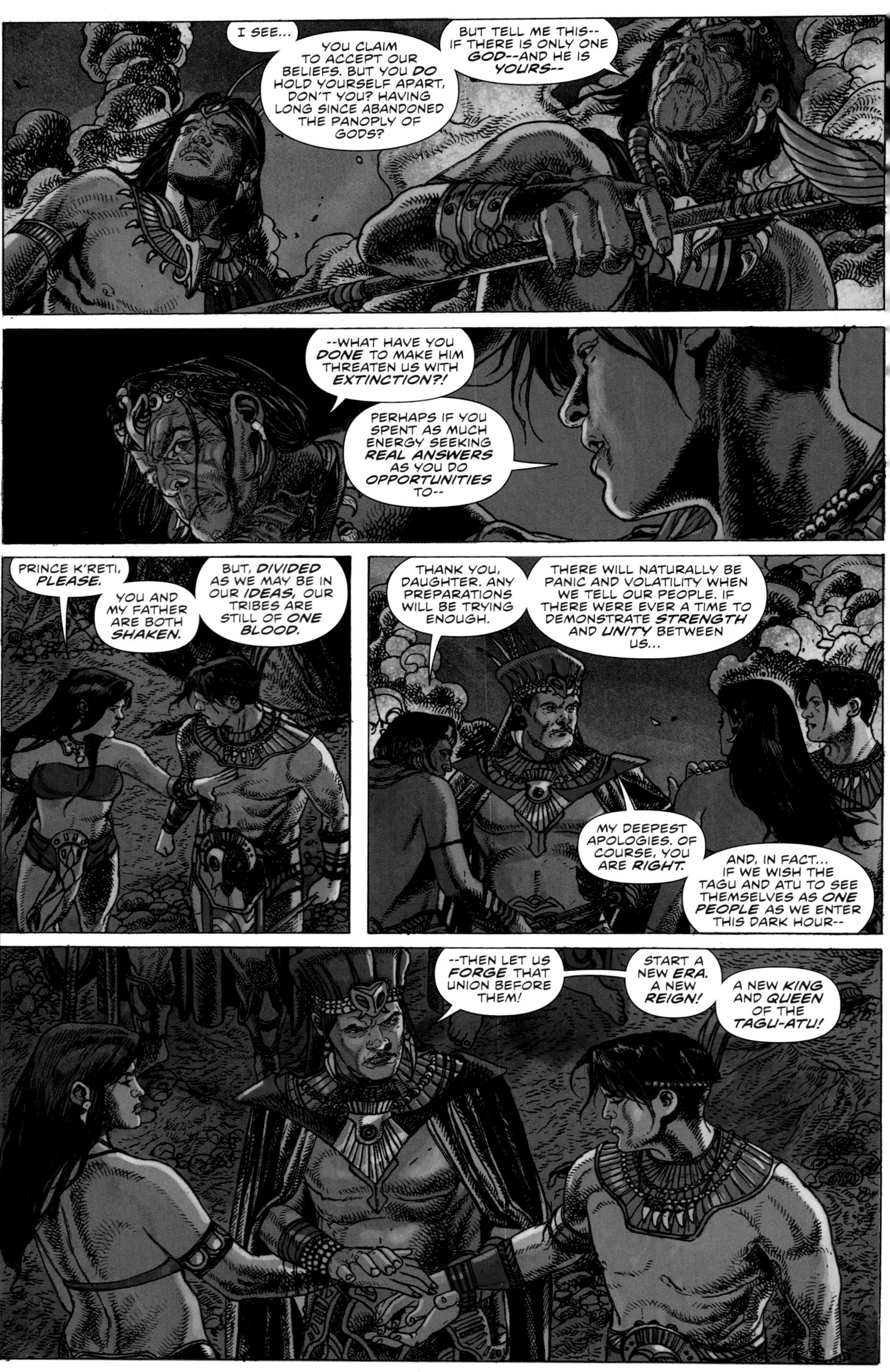

I SEE...
YOU CLAIM TO ACCEPT OUR BELIEFS. BUT YOU DO HOLD YOURSELF APART, DON'T YOU? HAVING LONG SINCE ABANDONED THE PANOPLY OF GODS?
BUT TELL ME THIS-- IF THERE IS ONLY ONE GOD--AND HE IS YOURS--
--WHAT HAVE YOU DONE TO MAKE HIM THREATEN US WITH EXTINCTION?!
PERHAPS IF YOU SPENT AS MUCH ENERGY SEEKING REAL ANSWERS AS YOU DO OPPORTUNITIES TO--
PRINCE K'RETI, PLEASE.
YOU AND MY FATHER ARE BOTH SHAKEN.
BUT, DIVIDED AS WE MAY BE IN OUR IDEAS, OUR TRIBES ARE STILL OF ONE BLOOD.
THANK YOU, DAUGHTER. ANY PREPARATIONS WILL BE TRYING ENOUGH.
THERE WILL NATURALLY BE PANIC AND VOLATILITY WHEN WE TELL OUR PEOPLE. IF THERE WERE EVER A TIME TO DEMONSTRATE STRENGTH AND UNITY BETWEEN US...
MY DEEPEST APOLOGIES. OF COURSE, YOU ARE RIGHT.
AND, IN FACT... IF WE WISH THE TAGU AND ATU TO SEE THEMSELVES AS ONE PEOPLE AS WE ENTER THIS DARK HOUR--
--THEN LET US FORGE THAT UNION BEFORE THEM!
START A NEW ERA. A NEW REIGN!
A NEW KING AND QUEEN OF THE TAGU-ATU!

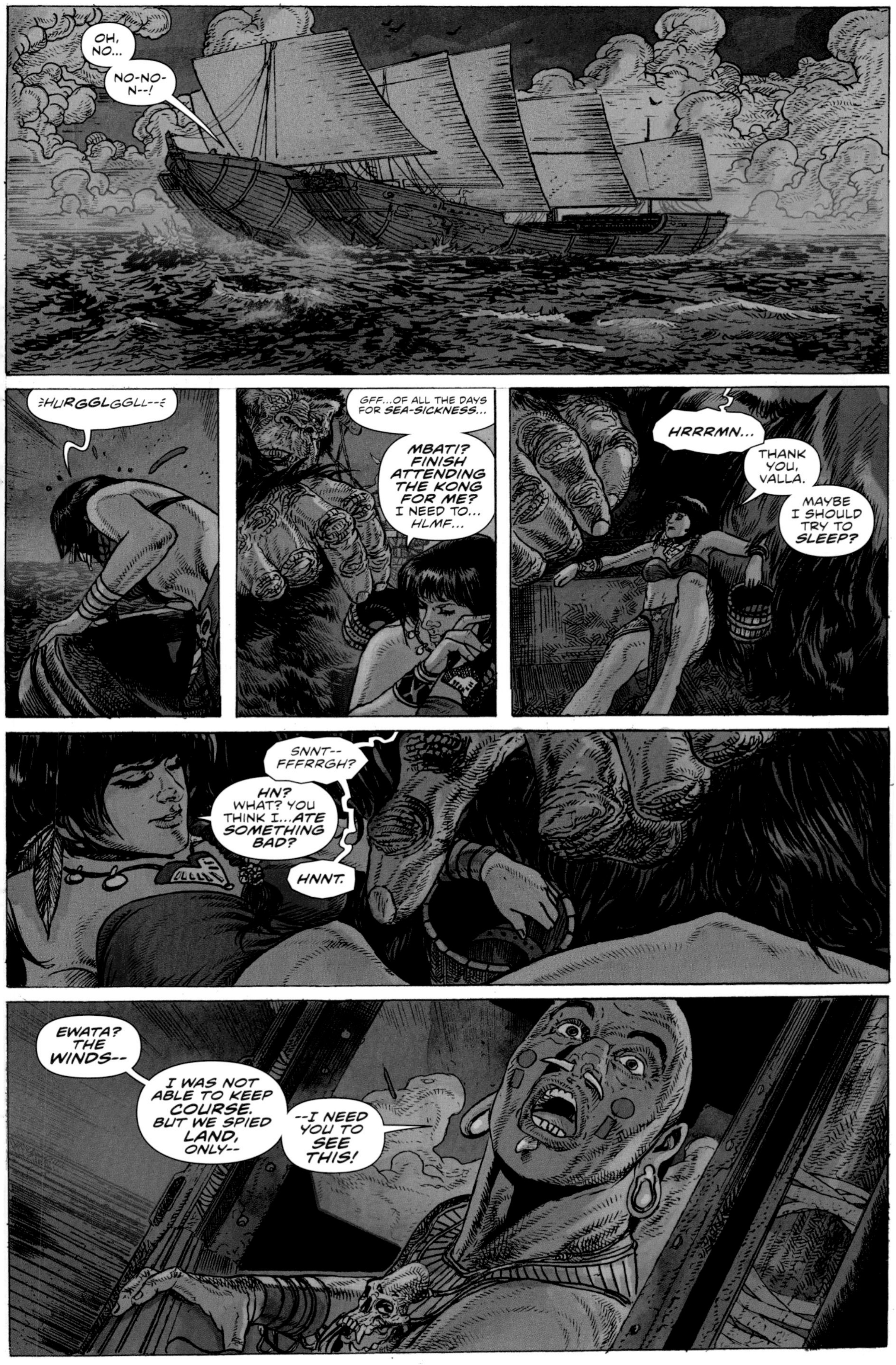
OH, NO...
NO-NO-N--!
HURGGLGGLL--
GFF...OF ALL THE DAYS FOR SEA-SICKNESS...
MBATI? FINISH ATTENDING THE KONG FOR ME? I NEED TO... HLMF...
HRRRMN...
THANK YOU, VALLA.
MAYBE I SHOULD TRY TO SLEEP?
SNNT-- FFFRRGH?
HN? WHAT? YOU THINK I...ATE SOMETHING BAD?
HNNT.
EWATA? THE WINDS--
I WAS NOT ABLE TO KEEP COURSE. BUT WE SPIED LAND, ONLY--
--I NEED YOU TO SEE THIS!

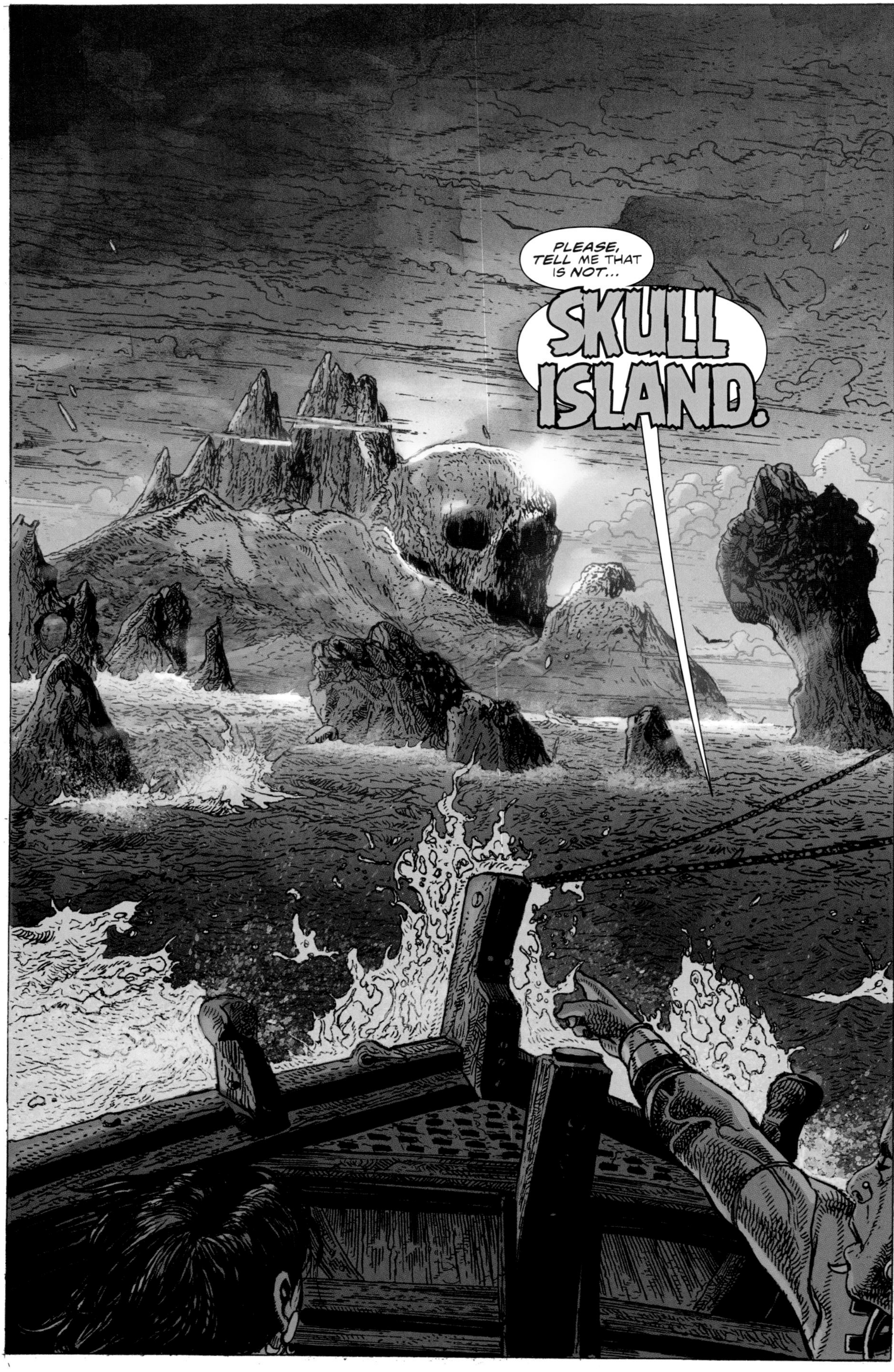
PLEASE, TELL ME THAT IS NOT...
SKULL ISLAND.

WHAT *IS* THAT PLACE?

SKULL ISLAND IS A NAME THE STORYTELLERS ONLY *WHISPER*.

A PLACE SUPPOSEDLY FILLED WITH *MONSTERS*.

BUT THE ACCOUNTS CAME FROM MEN WHO WERE *WOUNDED* AND *FEVERISH*.

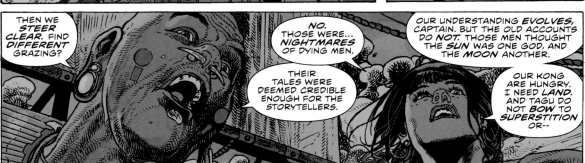

THEN WE *STEER CLEAR*. FIND *DIFFERENT* GRAZING?

NO. THOSE WERE... *NIGHTMARES* OF DYING MEN.

THEIR TALES WERE DEEMED CREDIBLE ENOUGH FOR THE STORYTELLERS.

OUR UNDERSTANDING *EVOLVES*, CAPTAIN. BUT THE OLD ACCOUNTS DO *NOT*. THOSE MEN THOUGHT THE *SUN* WAS ONE GOD, AND THE *MOON* ANOTHER.

OUR KONG ARE HUNGRY. I NEED *LAND*. AND TAGU DO NOT *BOW* TO *SUPERSTITION* OR--

DARK GODS--!?

THEY *SPOTTED* US!

COMING TOO *FAST*.

EVERYONE-- GET THE *KONG* AND PREPARE FOR--

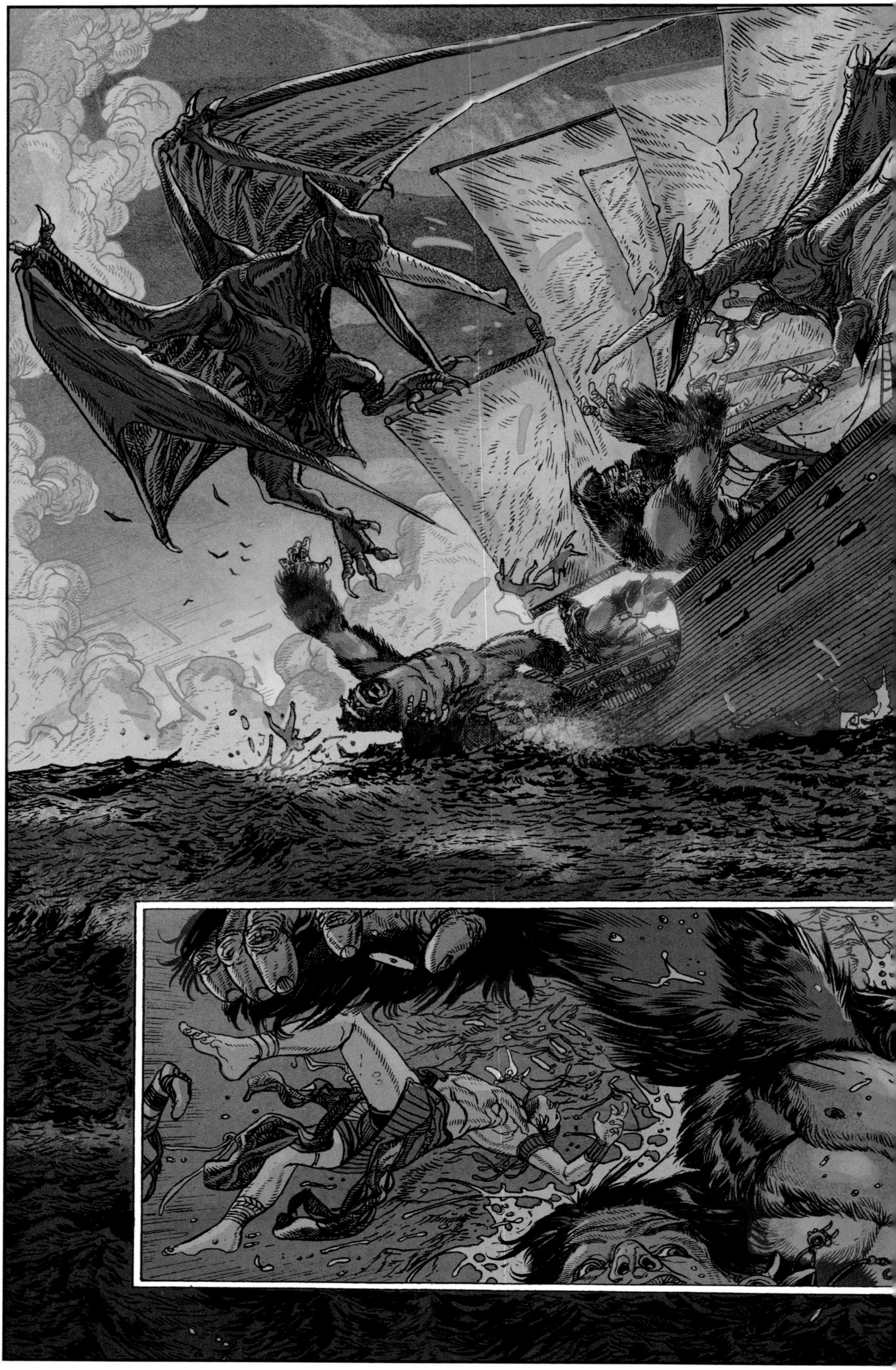

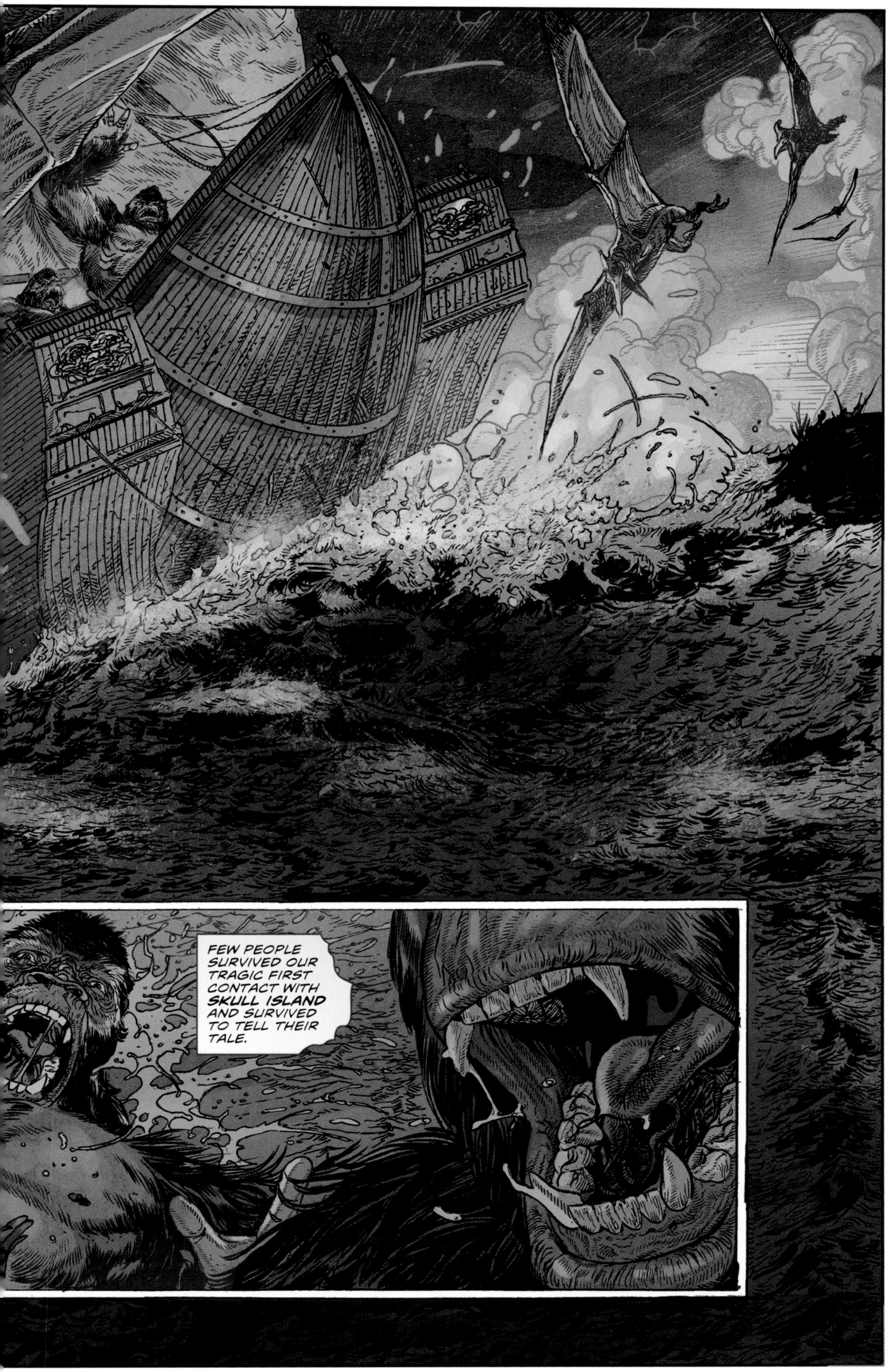
FEW PEOPLE SURVIVED OUR TRAGIC FIRST CONTACT WITH **SKULL ISLAND** AND SURVIVED TO TELL THEIR TALE.

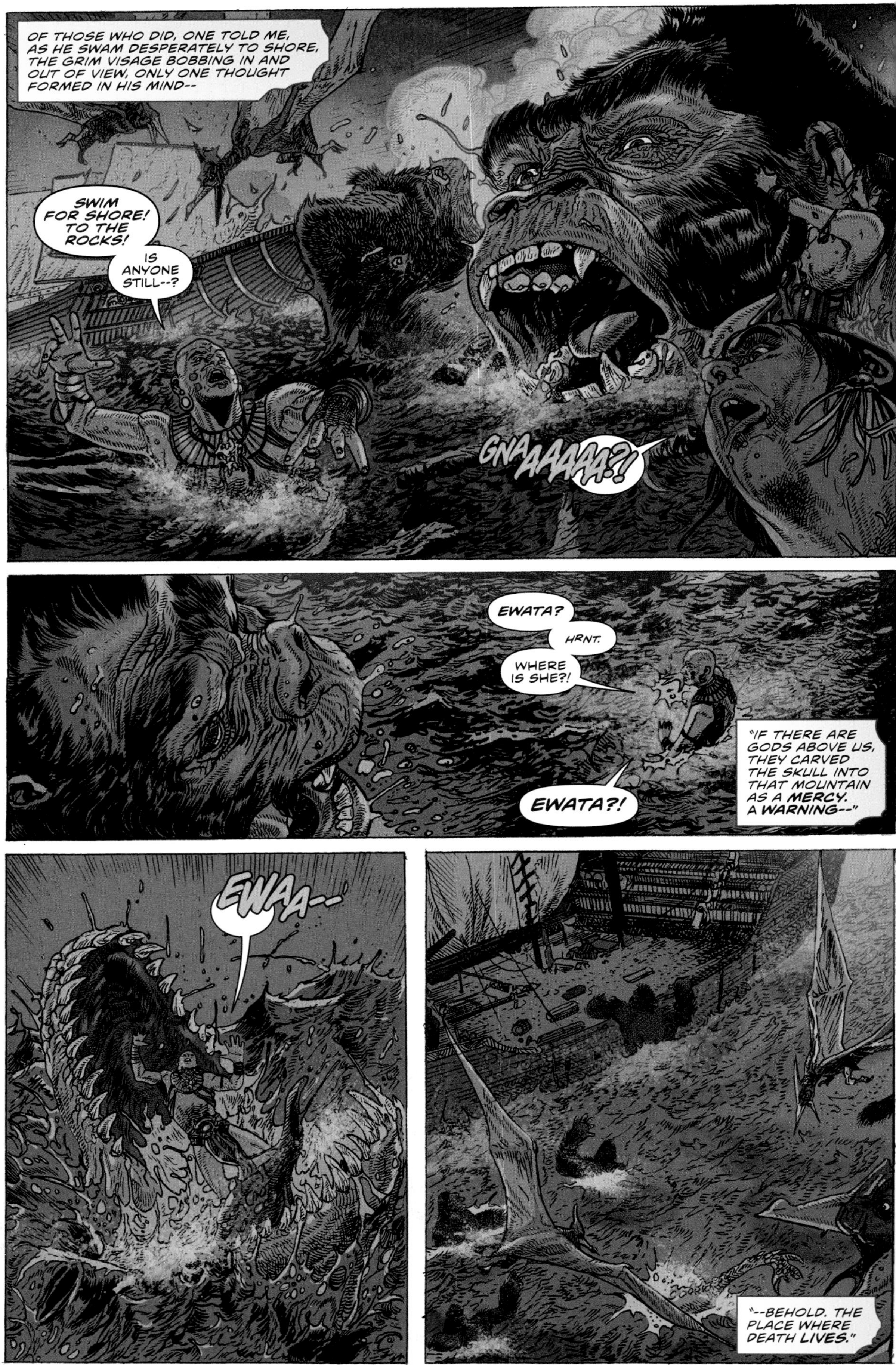
OF THOSE WHO DID, ONE TOLD ME, AS HE SWAM DESPERATELY TO SHORE, THE GRIM VISAGE BOBBING IN AND OUT OF VIEW, ONLY ONE THOUGHT FORMED IN HIS MIND--
SWIM FOR SHORE! TO THE ROCKS!
IS ANYONE STILL--?
GNAAAAAA?!
EWATA?
HRNT.
WHERE IS SHE?!
EWATA?!
"IF THERE ARE GODS ABOVE US, THEY CARVED THE SKULL INTO THAT MOUNTAIN AS A MERCY. A WARNING--"
EWAA--
"--BEHOLD. THE PLACE WHERE DEATH LIVES."

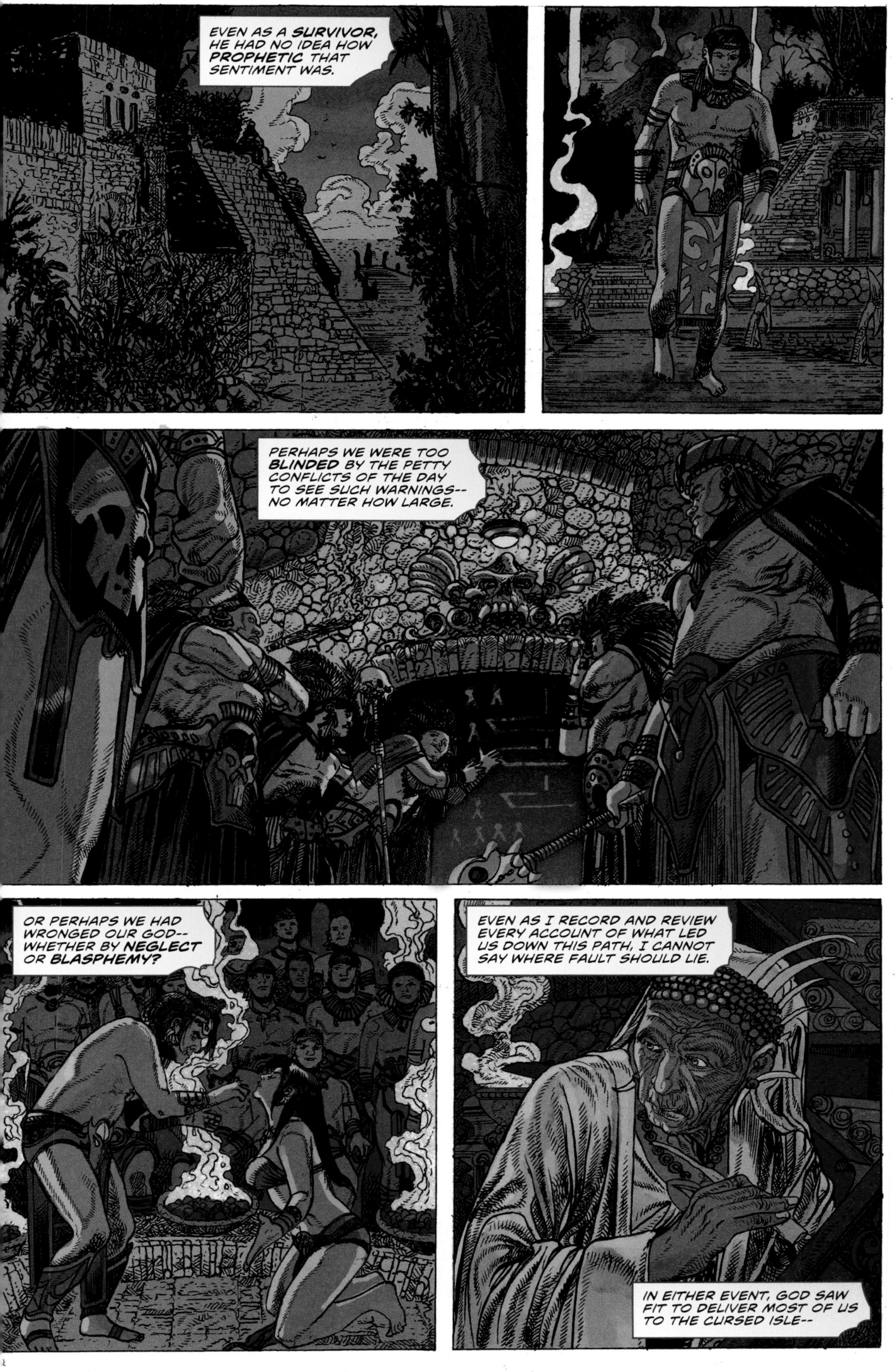
EVEN AS A SURVIVOR, HE HAD NO IDEA HOW PROPHETIC THAT SENTIMENT WAS.
PERHAPS WE WERE TOO BLINDED BY THE PETTY CONFLICTS OF THE DAY TO SEE SUCH WARNINGS-- NO MATTER HOW LARGE.
OR PERHAPS WE HAD WRONGED OUR GOD-- WHETHER BY NEGLECT OR BLASPHEMY?
EVEN AS I RECORD AND REVIEW EVERY ACCOUNT OF WHAT LED US DOWN THIS PATH, I CANNOT SAY WHERE FAULT SHOULD LIE.
IN EITHER EVENT, GOD SAW FIT TO DELIVER MOST OF US TO THE CURSED ISLE--

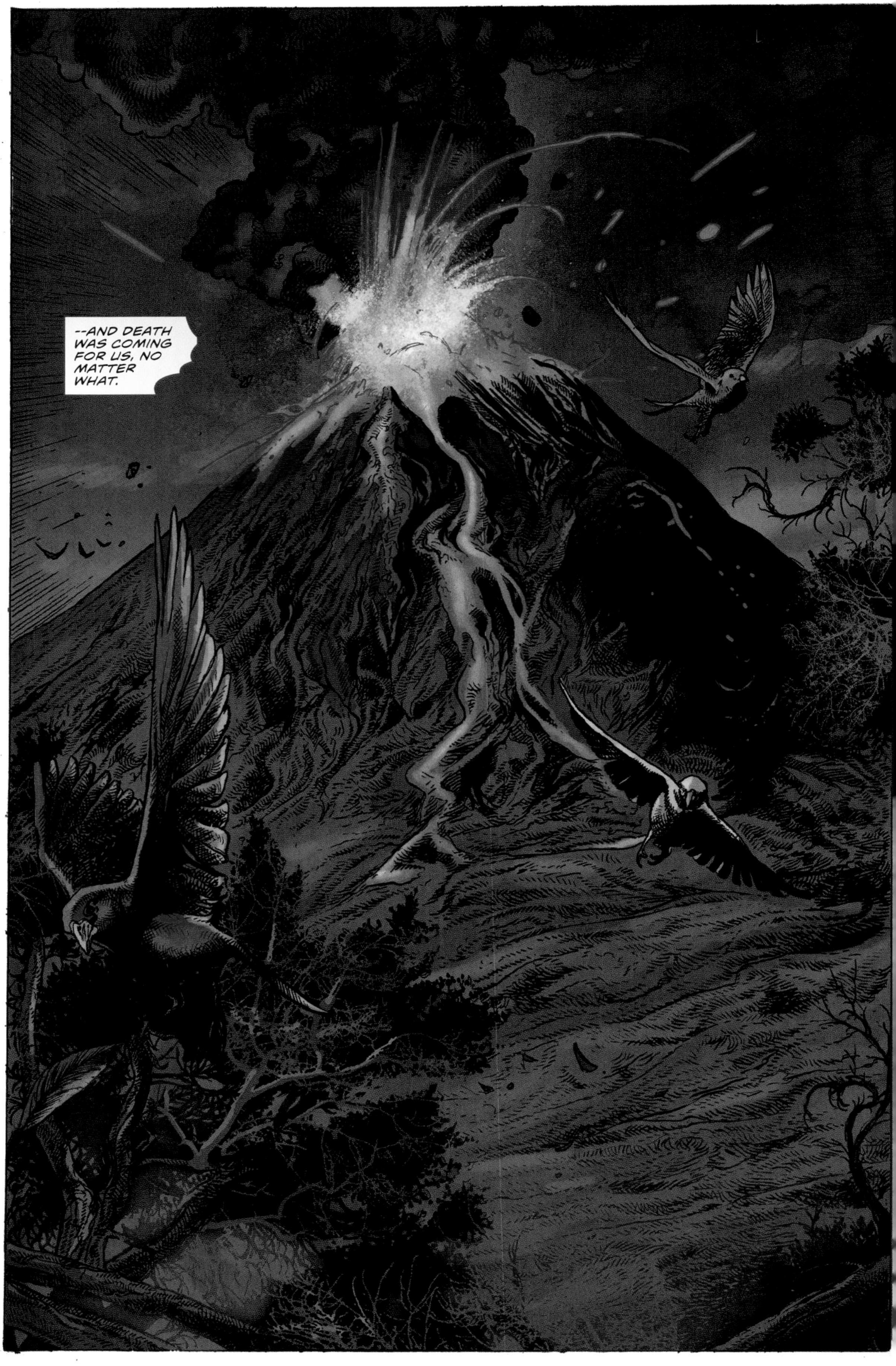
--AND DEATH WAS COMING FOR US, NO MATTER WHAT.

ISSUE ONE VARIANT COVER
NICK ROBLES

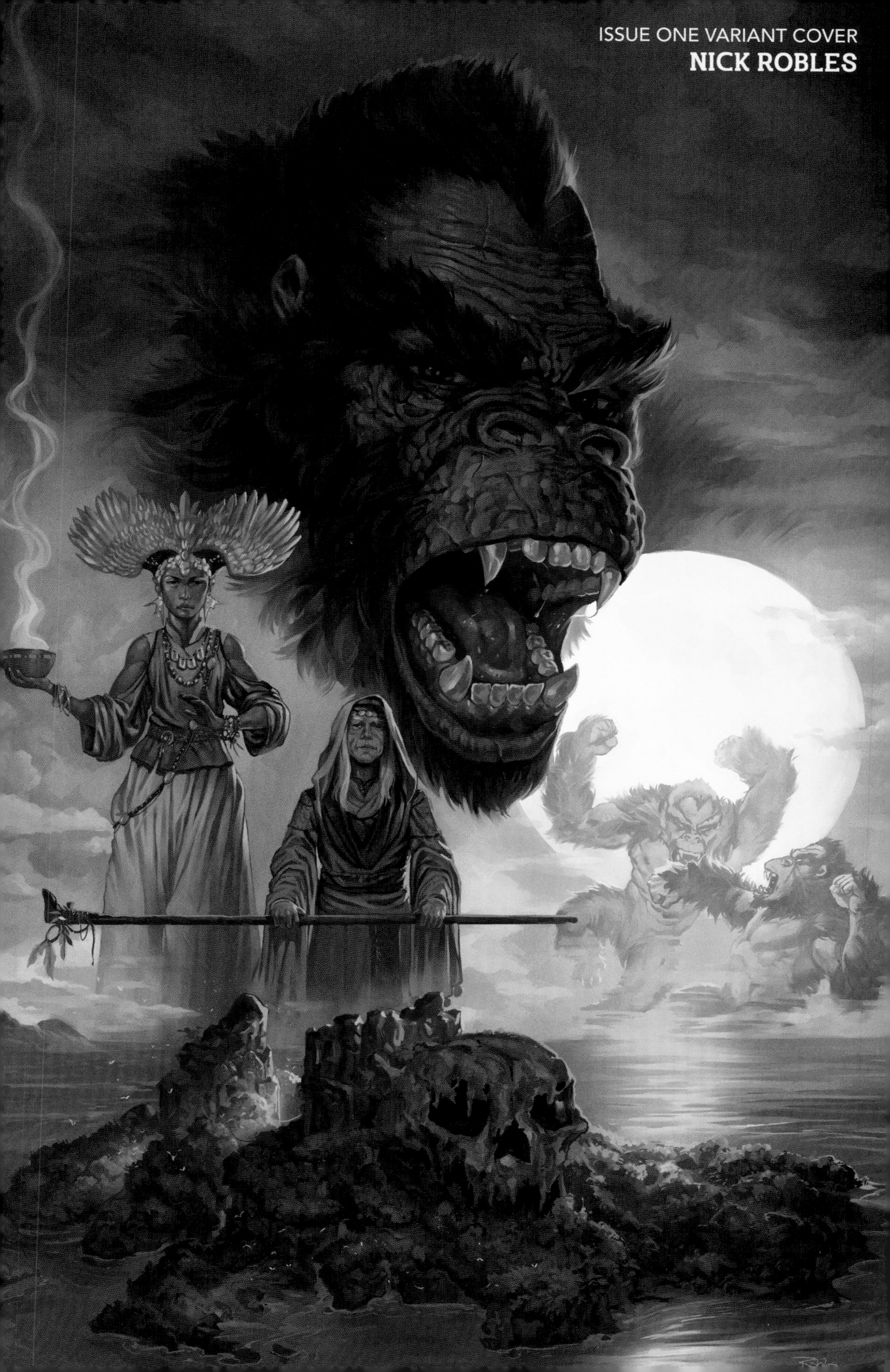

CHAPTER
TWO

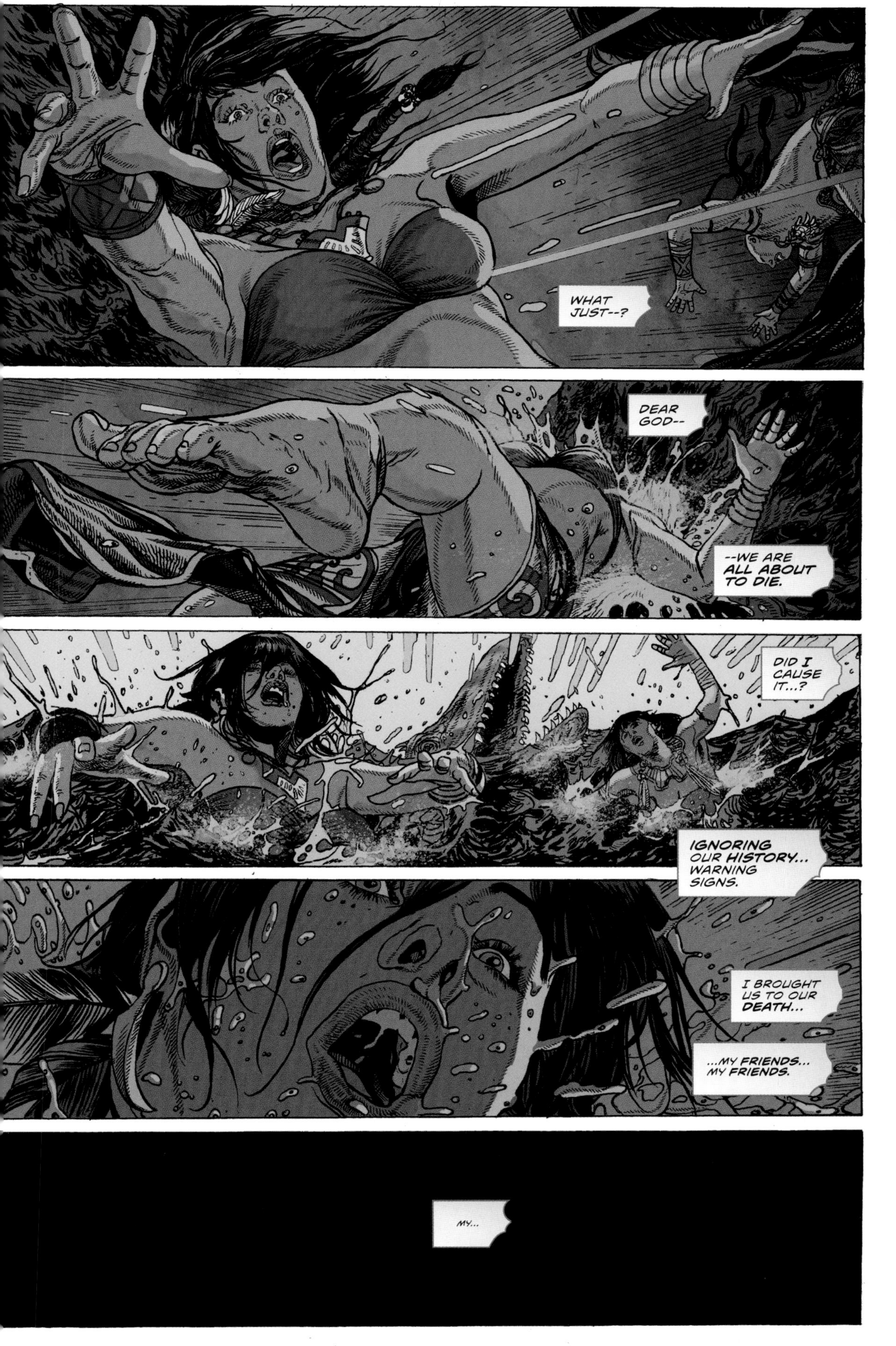
WHAT JUST--?
DEAR GOD--
--WE ARE ALL ABOUT TO DIE.
DID I CAUSE IT...?
IGNORING OUR HISTORY... WARNING SIGNS.
I BROUGHT US TO OUR DEATH...
...MY FRIENDS... MY FRIENDS.
MY...

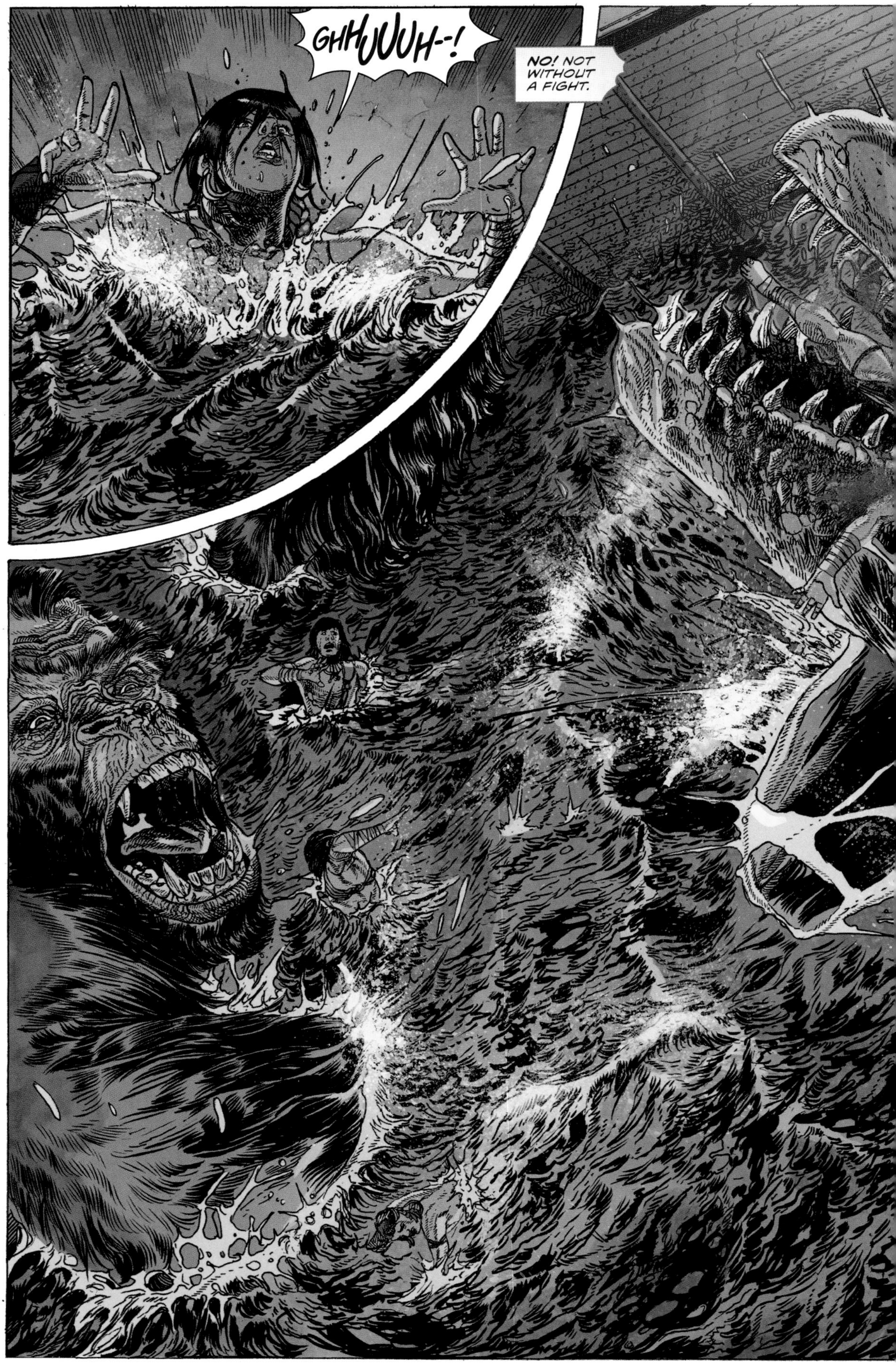

GHHUUUH--!
NO! NOT WITHOUT A FIGHT.

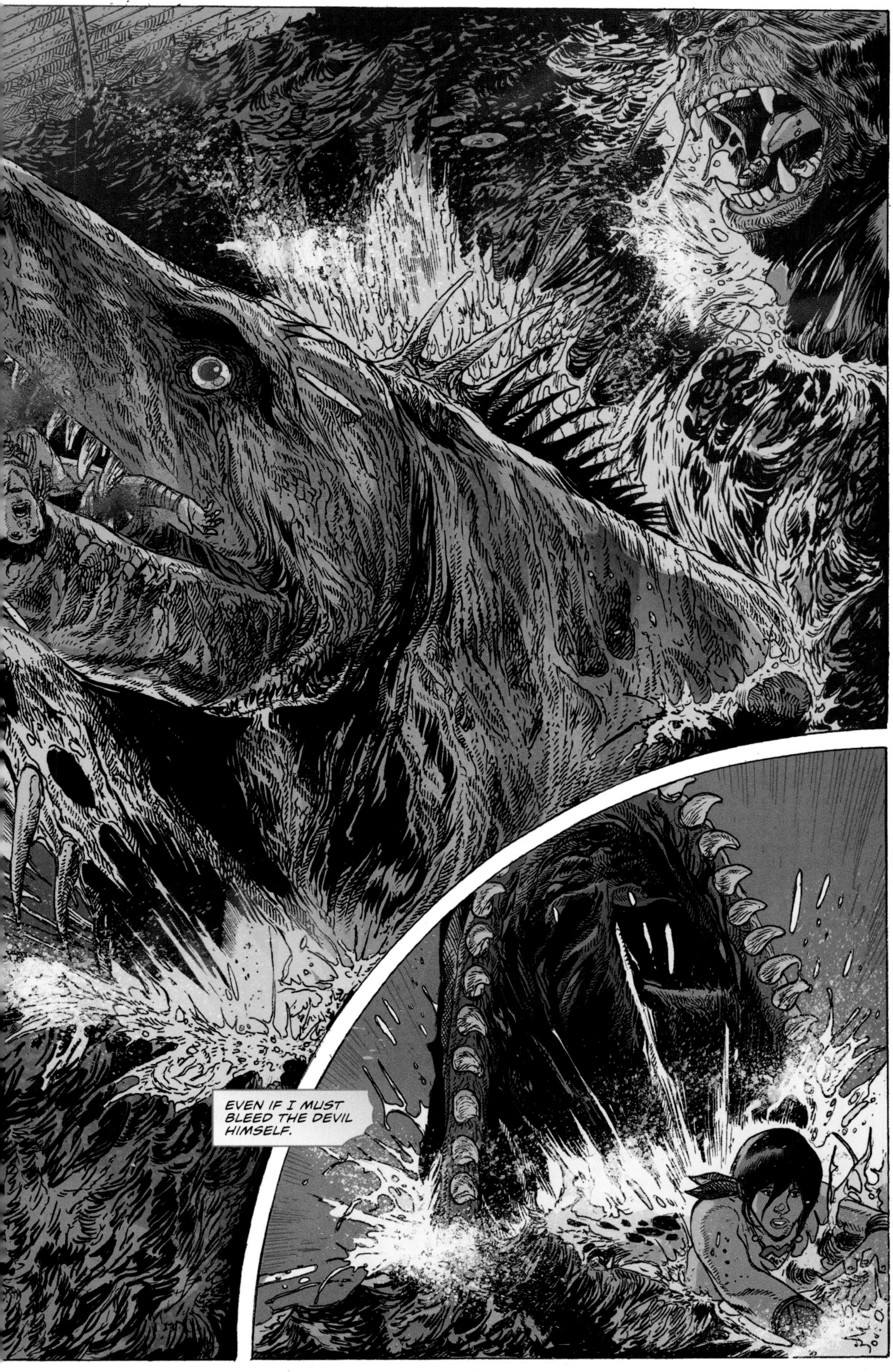
EVEN IF I MUST BLEED THE DEVIL HIMSELF.

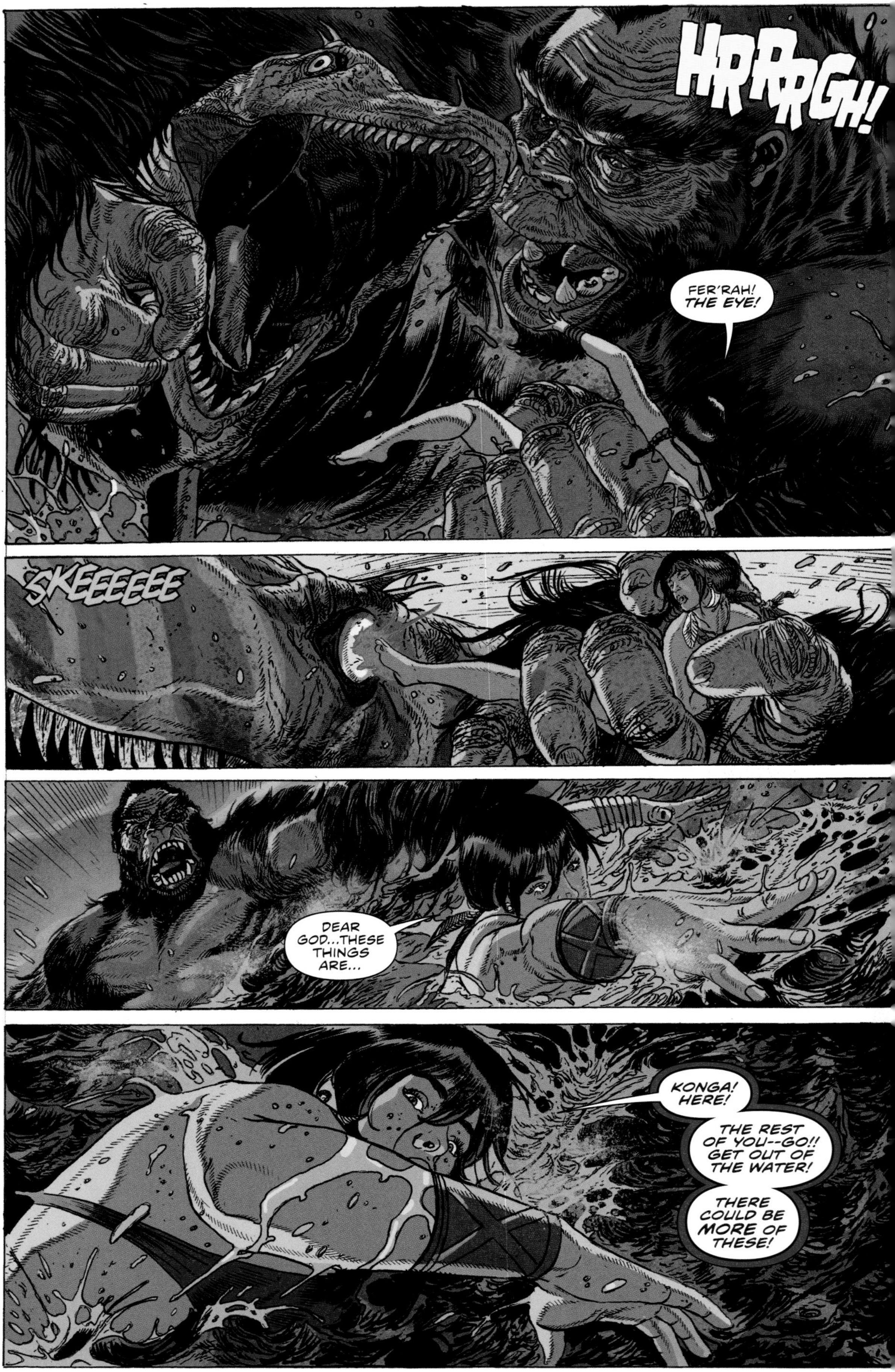
HRRRRGH!
FER'RAH! THE EYE!
SKEEEEEE
DEAR GOD...THESE THINGS ARE...
KONGA! HERE!
THE REST OF YOU--GO!! GET OUT OF THE WATER!
THERE COULD BE MORE OF THESE!

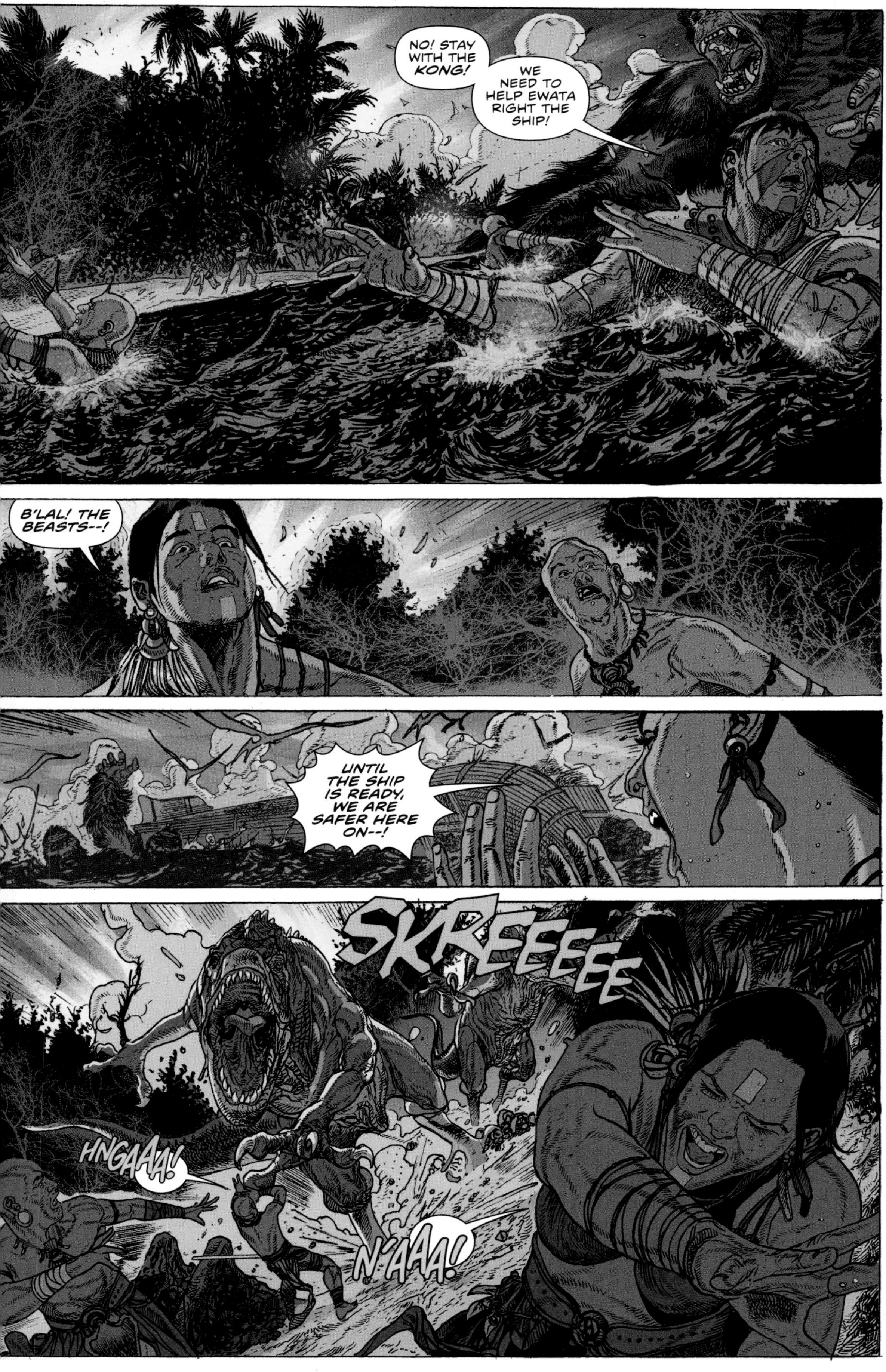
NO! STAY WITH THE KONG!
WE NEED TO HELP EWATA RIGHT THE SHIP!
B'LAL! THE BEASTS--!
UNTIL THE SHIP IS READY, WE ARE SAFER HERE ON--!
SKREEEEEE
HNGAAA!
N'AAA!

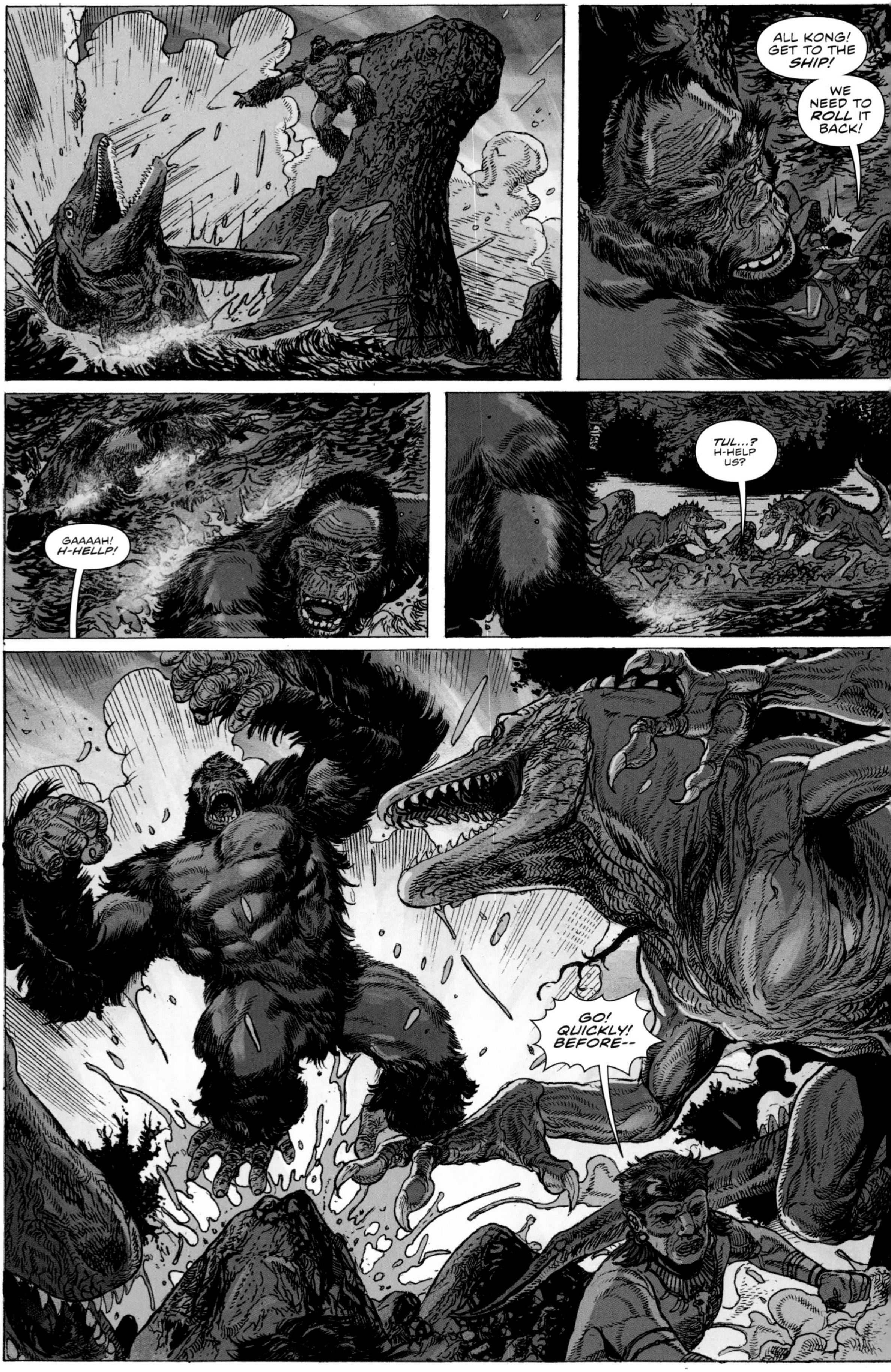
ALL KONG! GET TO THE SHIP!
WE NEED TO ROLL IT BACK!
GAAAAH! H-HELLP!
TUL...? H-HELP US?
GO! QUICKLY! BEFORE--

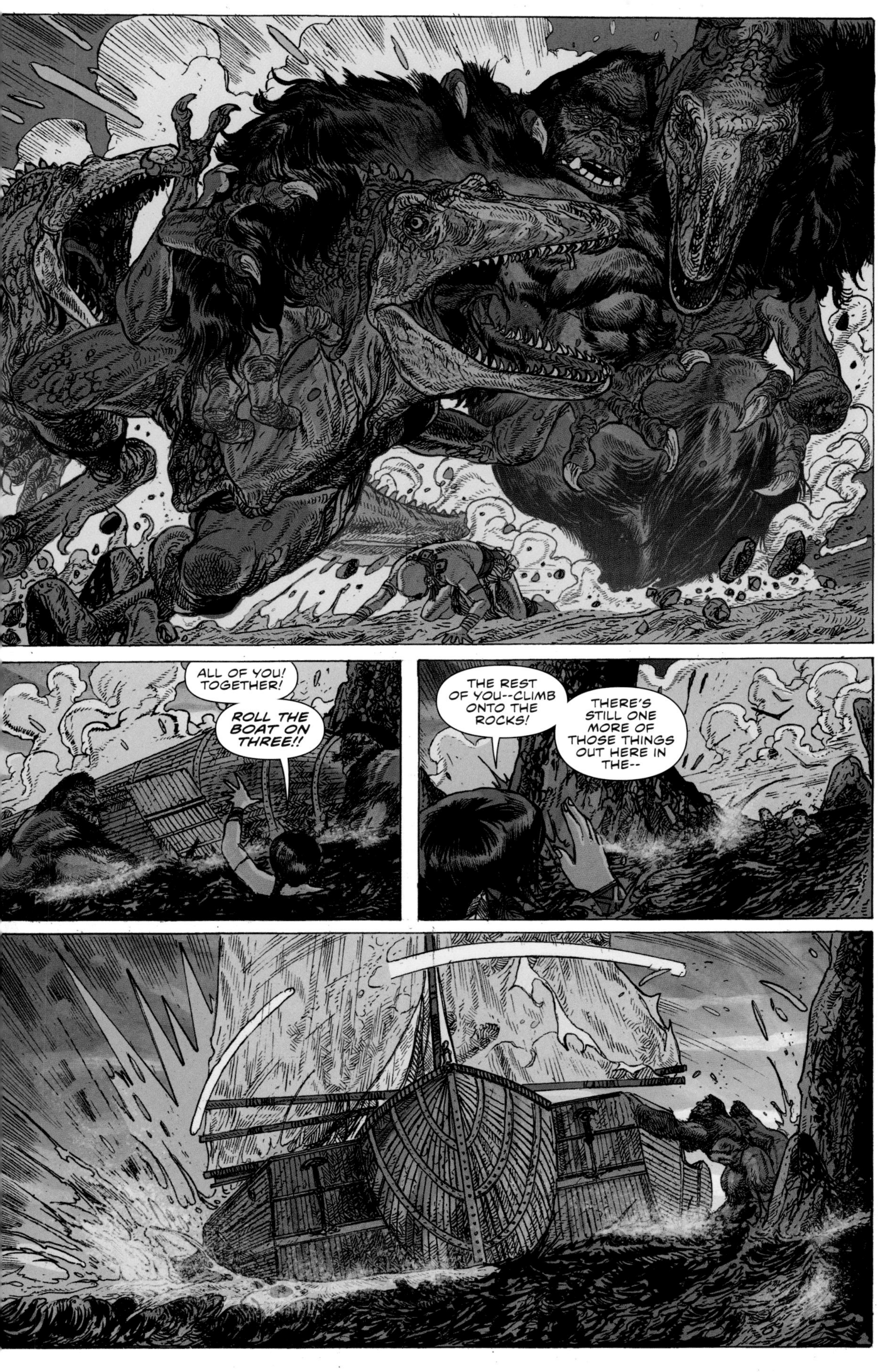
ALL OF YOU! TOGETHER!
ROLL THE BOAT ON THREE!!
THE REST OF YOU--CLIMB ONTO THE ROCKS!
THERE'S STILL ONE MORE OF THOSE THINGS OUT HERE IN THE--

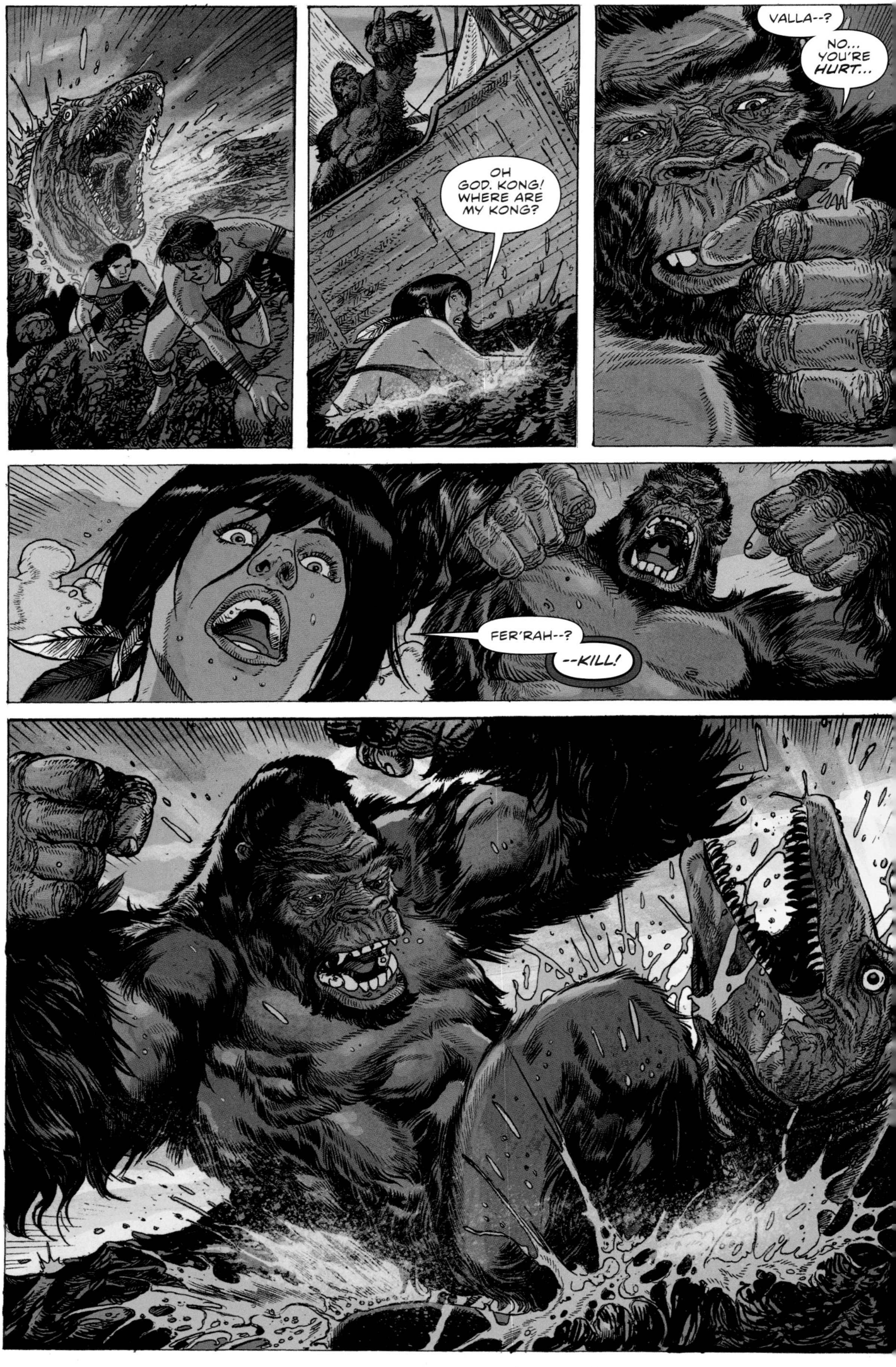
OH GOD. KONG! WHERE ARE MY KONG?
VALLA--?
NO... YOU'RE HURT...
FER'RAH--?
--KILL!

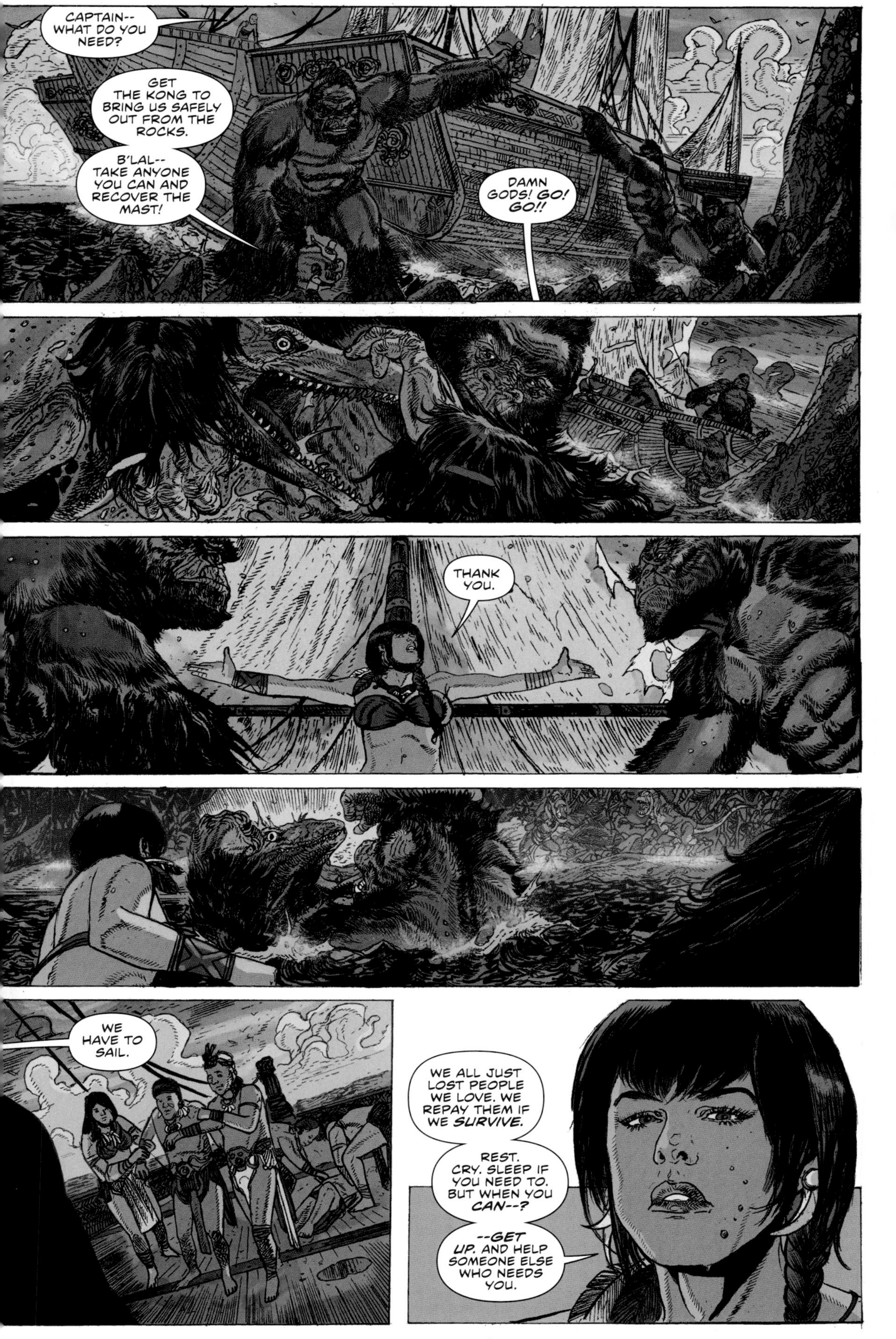

CAPTAIN-- WHAT DO YOU NEED?
GET THE KONG TO BRING US SAFELY OUT FROM THE ROCKS.
B'LAL-- TAKE ANYONE YOU CAN AND RECOVER THE MAST!
DAMN GODS! GO! GO!!
THANK YOU.
WE HAVE TO SAIL.
WE ALL JUST LOST PEOPLE WE LOVE. WE REPAY THEM IF WE SURVIVE.
REST. CRY. SLEEP IF YOU NEED TO. BUT WHEN YOU CAN--?
--GET UP. AND HELP SOMEONE ELSE WHO NEEDS YOU.

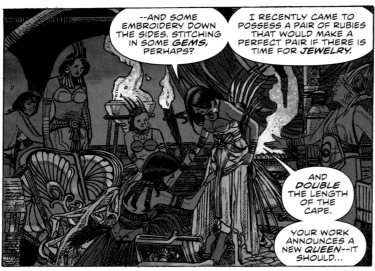

--AND SOME EMBROIDERY DOWN THE SIDES. STITCHING IN SOME *GEMS*, PERHAPS?

I RECENTLY CAME TO POSSESS A PAIR OF RUBIES THAT WOULD MAKE A PERFECT PAIR IF THERE IS TIME FOR *JEWELRY*.

AND *DOUBLE* THE LENGTH OF THE CAPE.

YOUR WORK ANNOUNCES A NEW *QUEEN*--IT SHOULD...

HNNRRMNNNRRRMNNN

...STEAL THE BREATH FROM THEIR VERY THROATS.

YES. VERY GOOD, YOUR GRACE.

BUT...

WHAT OF THE *MOUNTAIN?* THERE ARE MEN AT THE BAY LOADING SHIPS WITH OUR WINTER SUPPLIES.

SH-SHOULD WE BE PREPARING OUR *FAMILES*--

THIS *WEDDING* IS A *TRIBUTE* TO THE GODS.

AND THEY *PROTECT* THOSE WHO TOIL IN THEIR SERVICE.

WEAR THEIR *BLESSING*.

AND TAKE *COMFORT* IN THE KNOWLEDGE THAT, AS YOU UPHOLD *YOUR* RIGHTEOUS TASK FOR *TOMORROW*--

--THERE ARE *OTHERS* FORGING THE *DESTINY* THAT FOLLOWS.

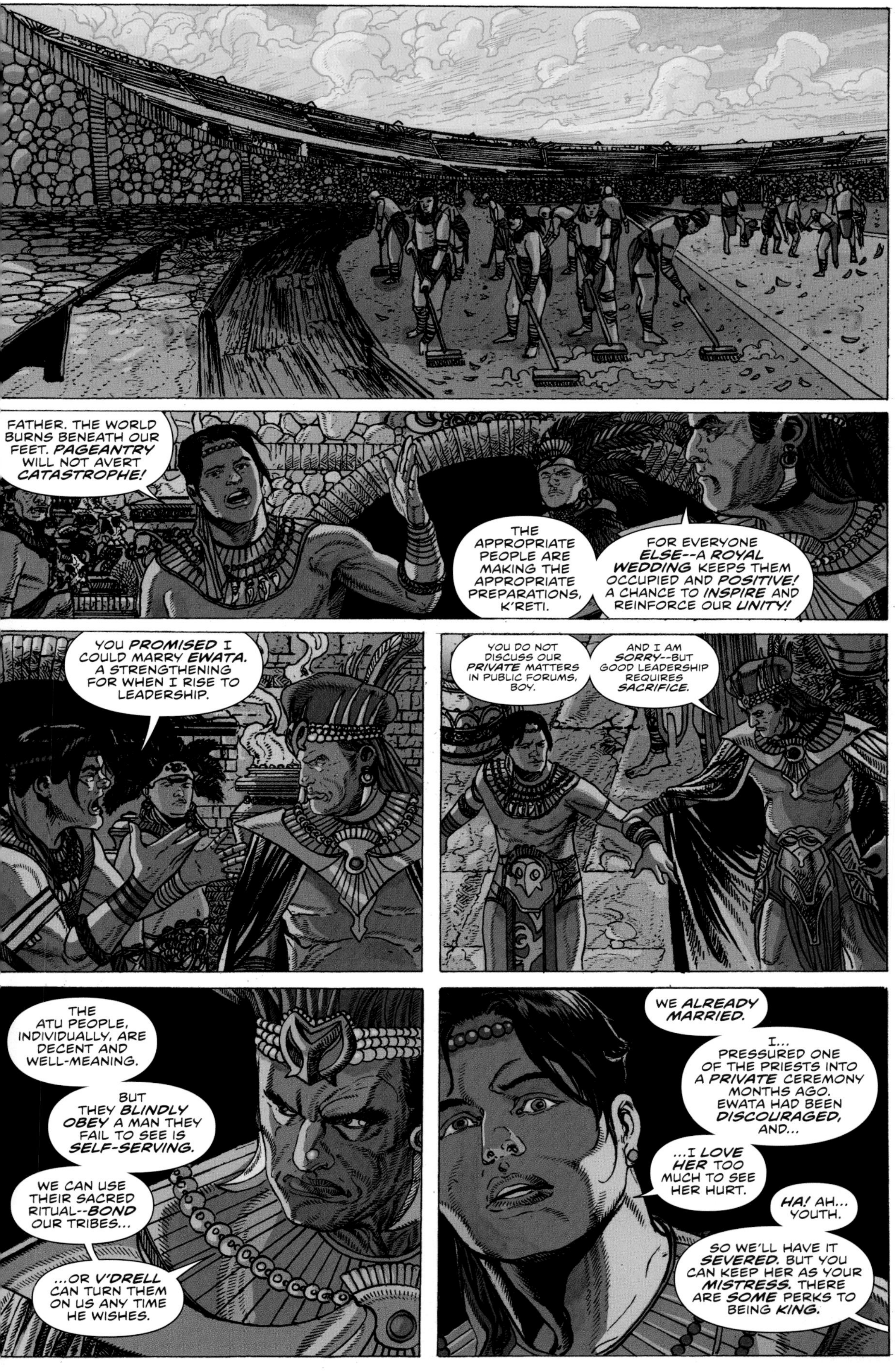
FATHER. THE WORLD BURNS BENEATH OUR FEET. PAGEANTRY WILL NOT AVERT CATASTROPHE!
THE APPROPRIATE PEOPLE ARE MAKING THE APPROPRIATE PREPARATIONS, K'RETI.
FOR EVERYONE ELSE--A ROYAL WEDDING KEEPS THEM OCCUPIED AND POSITIVE! A CHANCE TO INSPIRE AND REINFORCE OUR UNITY!
YOU PROMISED I COULD MARRY EWATA. A STRENGTHENING FOR WHEN I RISE TO LEADERSHIP.
YOU DO NOT DISCUSS OUR PRIVATE MATTERS IN PUBLIC FORUMS, BOY.
AND I AM SORRY--BUT GOOD LEADERSHIP REQUIRES SACRIFICE.
THE ATU PEOPLE, INDIVIDUALLY, ARE DECENT AND WELL-MEANING.
BUT THEY BLINDLY OBEY A MAN THEY FAIL TO SEE IS SELF-SERVING.
WE CAN USE THEIR SACRED RITUAL--BOND OUR TRIBES...
...OR V'DRELL CAN TURN THEM ON US ANY TIME HE WISHES.
WE ALREADY MARRIED.
I... PRESSURED ONE OF THE PRIESTS INTO A PRIVATE CEREMONY MONTHS AGO. EWATA HAD BEEN DISCOURAGED, AND...
...I LOVE HER TOO MUCH TO SEE HER HURT.
HA! AH... YOUTH.
SO WE'LL HAVE IT SEVERED. BUT YOU CAN KEEP HER AS YOUR MISTRESS. THERE ARE SOME PERKS TO BEING KING.

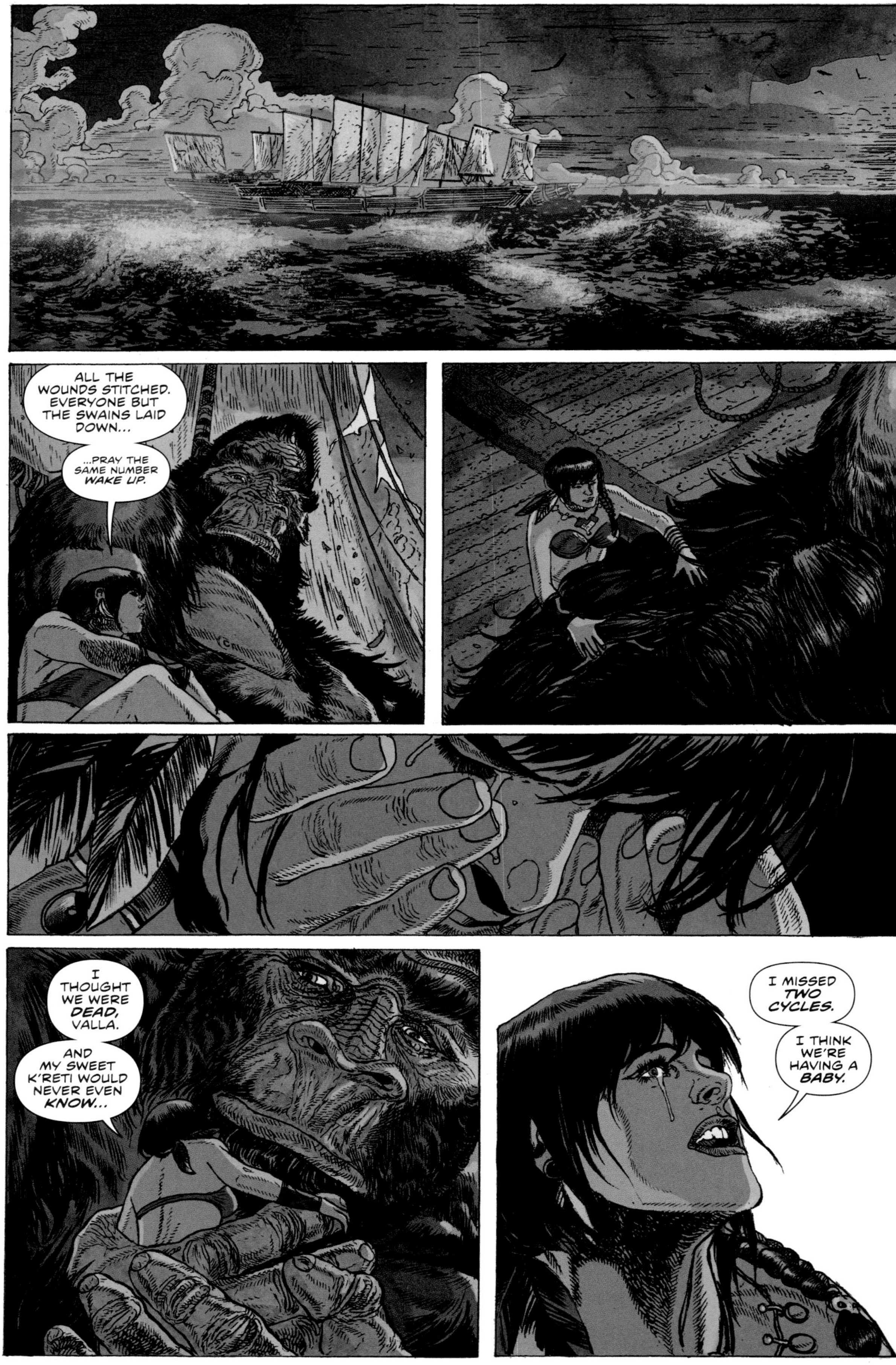
ALL THE WOUNDS STITCHED. EVERYONE BUT THE SWAINS LAID DOWN...
...PRAY THE SAME NUMBER WAKE UP.
I THOUGHT WE WERE DEAD, VALLA.
AND MY SWEET K'RETI WOULD NEVER EVEN KNOW...
I MISSED TWO CYCLES.
I THINK WE'RE HAVING A BABY.

USANA--!

K'RETI? WHAT BRINGS YOU TO THIS SIDE OF THE ISLAND?

MAY I...SPEAK WITH YOU PRIVATELY?

OF COURSE.

THIS WAY.

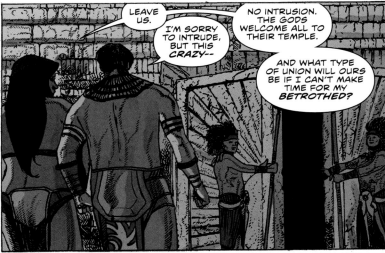

LEAVE US.

I'M SORRY TO INTRUDE, BUT THIS CRAZY--

NO INTRUSION. THE GODS WELCOME ALL TO THEIR TEMPLE.

AND WHAT TYPE OF UNION WILL OURS BE IF I CAN'T MAKE TIME FOR MY BETROTHED?

AND NOW--YOU WERE SAYING?

I FAIL TO SEE HOW A THEATRICAL MARRIAGE SAVES ANY LIVES.

SURELY THIS CAN'T BE WHAT YOU DREAMED OF FOR YOUR FUTURE.

IF WE BOTH SPOKE TO OUR FATHERS--

MINE WOULD STILL NOT BE MOVED.

MY FATHER'S FAITH IS SINCERE. IF HE BELIEVES A UNION IS THE WILL OF THE GODS--HE WILL NOT BE SWAYED.

WHAT ABOUT YOU? DO YOU SERVE THE GODS OR YOUR FATHER?

TO MY EYES, THERE IS A TRUTH GREATER THAN GODS, GREATER THAN YOUR STUDIES--THE DRIVING FORCE BEHIND BOTH THOSE THINGS.

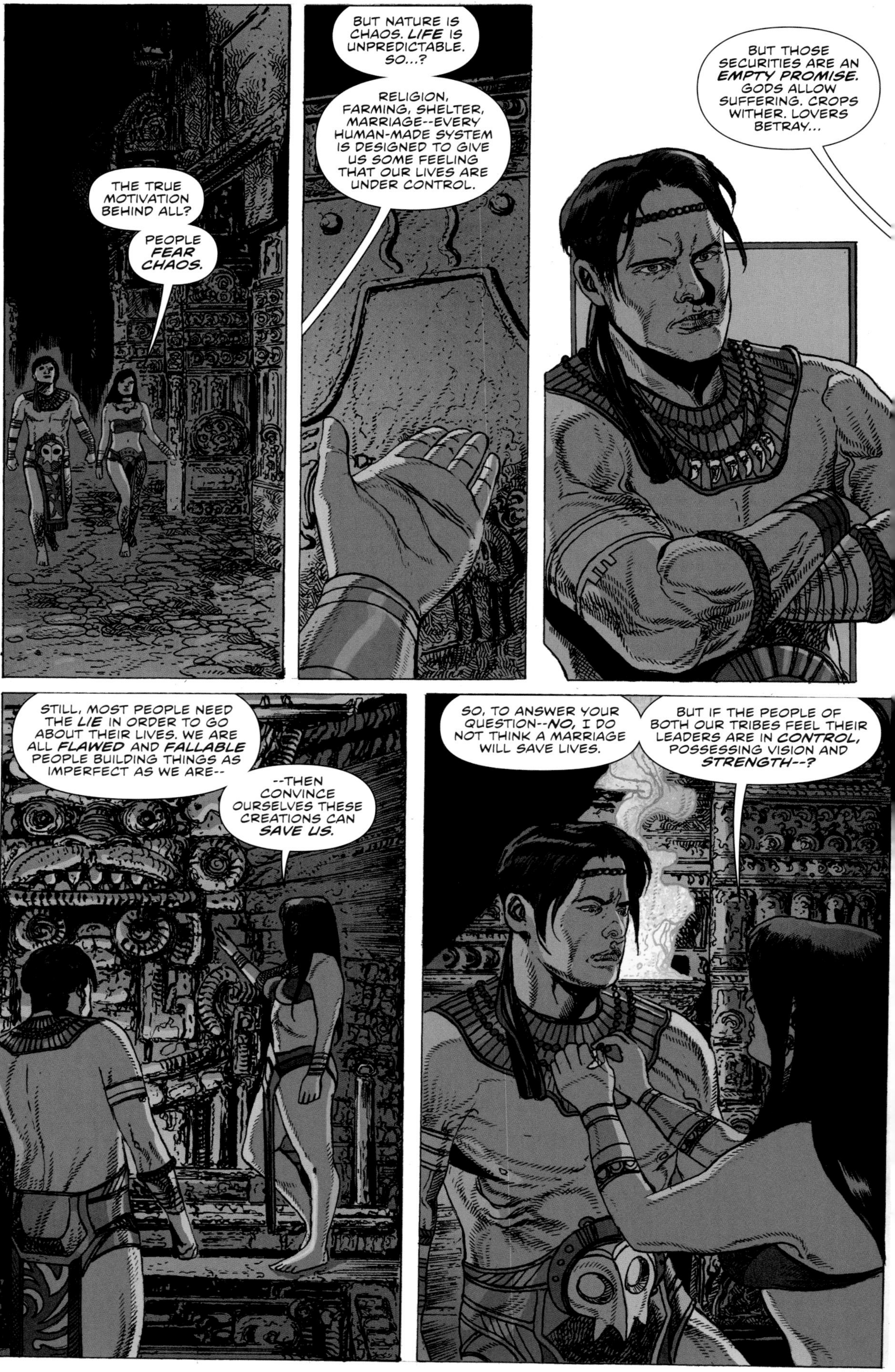

THE TRUE MOTIVATION BEHIND ALL?
PEOPLE *FEAR CHAOS.*
BUT NATURE IS CHAOS. *LIFE* IS UNPREDICTABLE. SO...?
RELIGION, FARMING, SHELTER, MARRIAGE--EVERY HUMAN-MADE SYSTEM IS DESIGNED TO GIVE US SOME FEELING THAT OUR LIVES ARE UNDER CONTROL.
BUT THOSE SECURITIES ARE AN *EMPTY PROMISE.* GODS ALLOW SUFFERING. CROPS WITHER. LOVERS BETRAY...
STILL, MOST PEOPLE NEED THE *LIE* IN ORDER TO GO ABOUT THEIR LIVES. WE ARE ALL *FLAWED* AND *FALLABLE* PEOPLE BUILDING THINGS AS IMPERFECT AS WE ARE--
--THEN CONVINCE OURSELVES THESE CREATIONS CAN *SAVE US.*
SO, TO ANSWER YOUR QUESTION--*NO,* I DO NOT THINK A MARRIAGE WILL SAVE LIVES.
BUT IF THE PEOPLE OF BOTH OUR TRIBES FEEL THEIR LEADERS ARE IN *CONTROL,* POSSESSING VISION AND *STRENGTH--?*

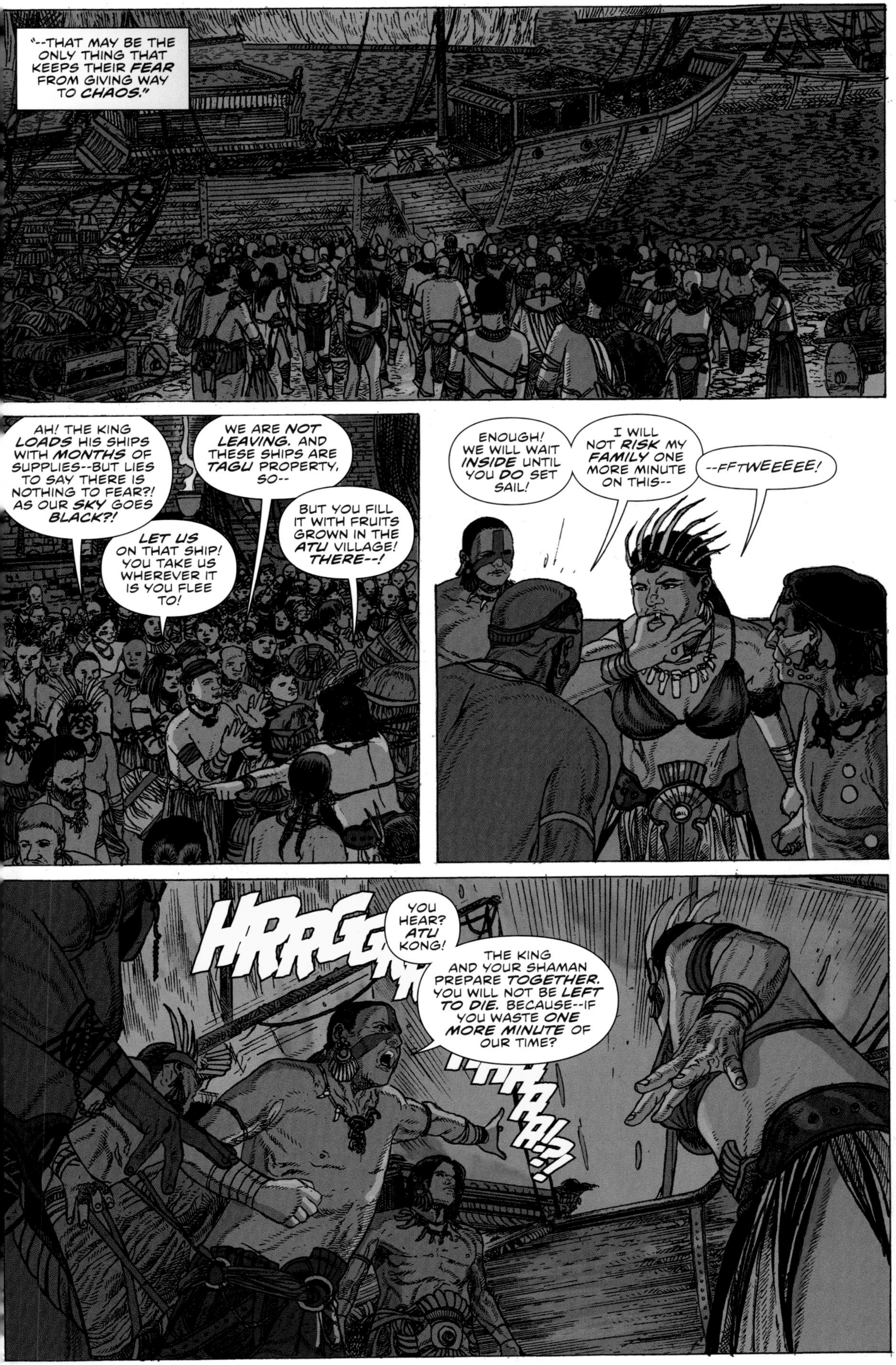
"--THAT MAY BE THE ONLY THING THAT KEEPS THEIR FEAR FROM GIVING WAY TO CHAOS."
AH! THE KING LOADS HIS SHIPS WITH MONTHS OF SUPPLIES--BUT LIES TO SAY THERE IS NOTHING TO FEAR?! AS OUR SKY GOES BLACK?!
WE ARE NOT LEAVING. AND THESE SHIPS ARE TAGU PROPERTY, SO--
LET US ON THAT SHIP! YOU TAKE US WHEREVER IT IS YOU FLEE TO!
BUT YOU FILL IT WITH FRUITS GROWN IN THE ATU VILLAGE! THERE--!
ENOUGH! WE WILL WAIT INSIDE UNTIL YOU DO SET SAIL!
I WILL NOT RISK MY FAMILY ONE MORE MINUTE ON THIS--
--FFTWEEEEE!
HRRGGHHHAA!?!
YOU HEAR? ATU KONG!
THE KING AND YOUR SHAMAN PREPARE TOGETHER. YOU WILL NOT BE LEFT TO DIE. BECAUSE--IF YOU WASTE ONE MORE MINUTE OF OUR TIME?

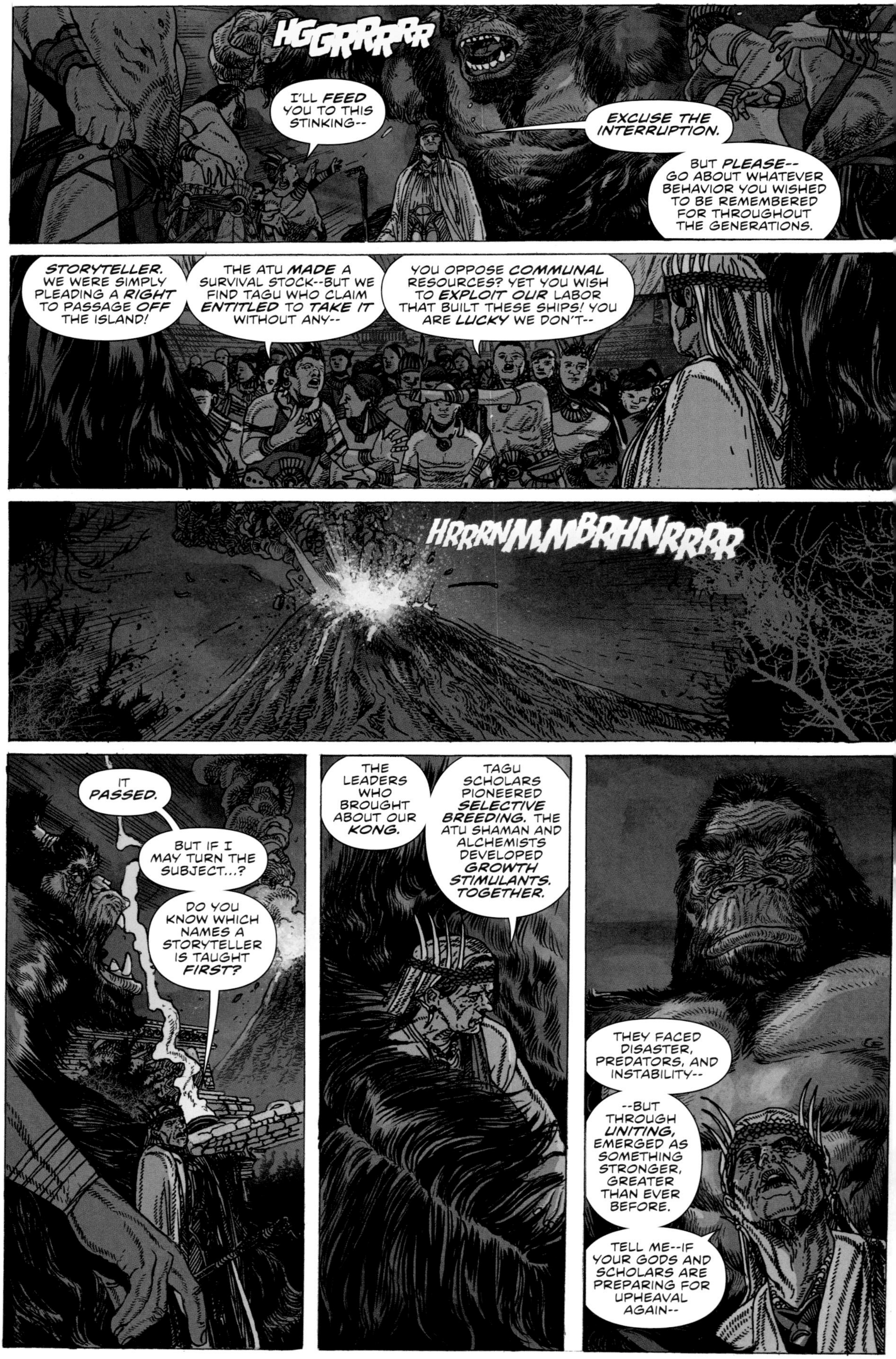
HGGRRRRRR
I'LL FEED YOU TO THIS STINKING--
EXCUSE THE INTERRUPTION.
BUT PLEASE-- GO ABOUT WHATEVER BEHAVIOR YOU WISHED TO BE REMEMBERED FOR THROUGHOUT THE GENERATIONS.
STORYTELLER. WE WERE SIMPLY PLEADING A RIGHT TO PASSAGE OFF THE ISLAND!
THE ATU MADE A SURVIVAL STOCK--BUT WE FIND TAGU WHO CLAIM ENTITLED TO TAKE IT WITHOUT ANY--
YOU OPPOSE COMMUNAL RESOURCES? YET YOU WISH TO EXPLOIT OUR LABOR THAT BUILT THESE SHIPS! YOU ARE LUCKY WE DON'T--
HRRRNMMMBRHNRRRR
IT PASSED.
BUT IF I MAY TURN THE SUBJECT...?
DO YOU KNOW WHICH NAMES A STORYTELLER IS TAUGHT FIRST?
THE LEADERS WHO BROUGHT ABOUT OUR KONG.
TAGU SCHOLARS PIONEERED SELECTIVE BREEDING. THE ATU SHAMAN AND ALCHEMISTS DEVELOPED GROWTH STIMULANTS. TOGETHER.
THEY FACED DISASTER, PREDATORS, AND INSTABILITY--
--BUT THROUGH UNITING, EMERGED AS SOMETHING STRONGER, GREATER THAN EVER BEFORE.
TELL ME--IF YOUR GODS AND SCHOLARS ARE PREPARING FOR UPHEAVAL AGAIN--

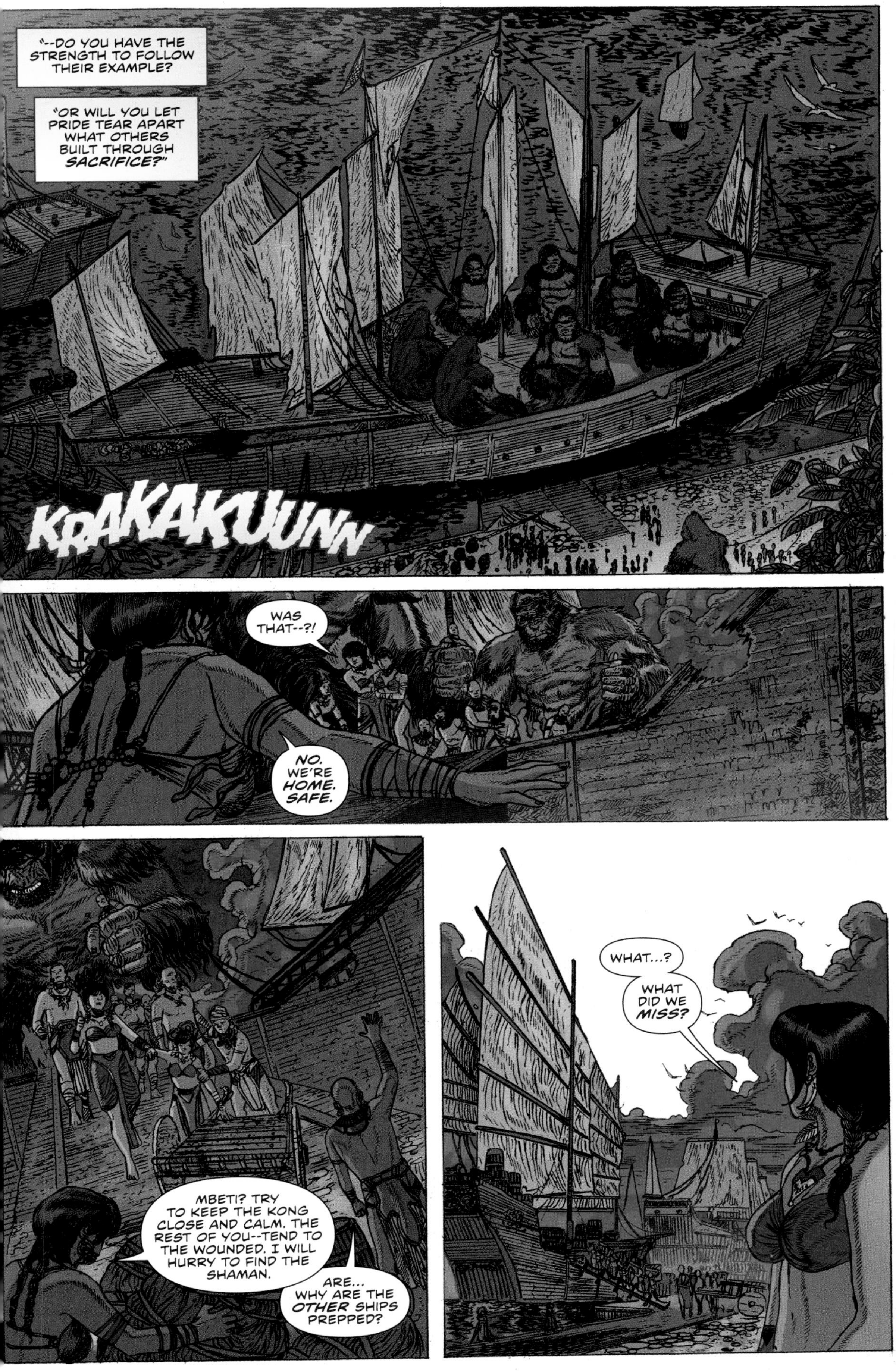
"--DO YOU HAVE THE STRENGTH TO FOLLOW THEIR EXAMPLE?
"OR WILL YOU LET PRIDE TEAR APART WHAT OTHERS BUILT THROUGH SACRIFICE?"
KRAKAKUUNN
WAS THAT--?!
NO. WE'RE HOME. SAFE.
MBETI? TRY TO KEEP THE KONG CLOSE AND CALM. THE REST OF YOU--TEND TO THE WOUNDED. I WILL HURRY TO FIND THE SHAMAN.
ARE... WHY ARE THE OTHER SHIPS PREPPED?
WHAT...?
WHAT DID WE MISS?

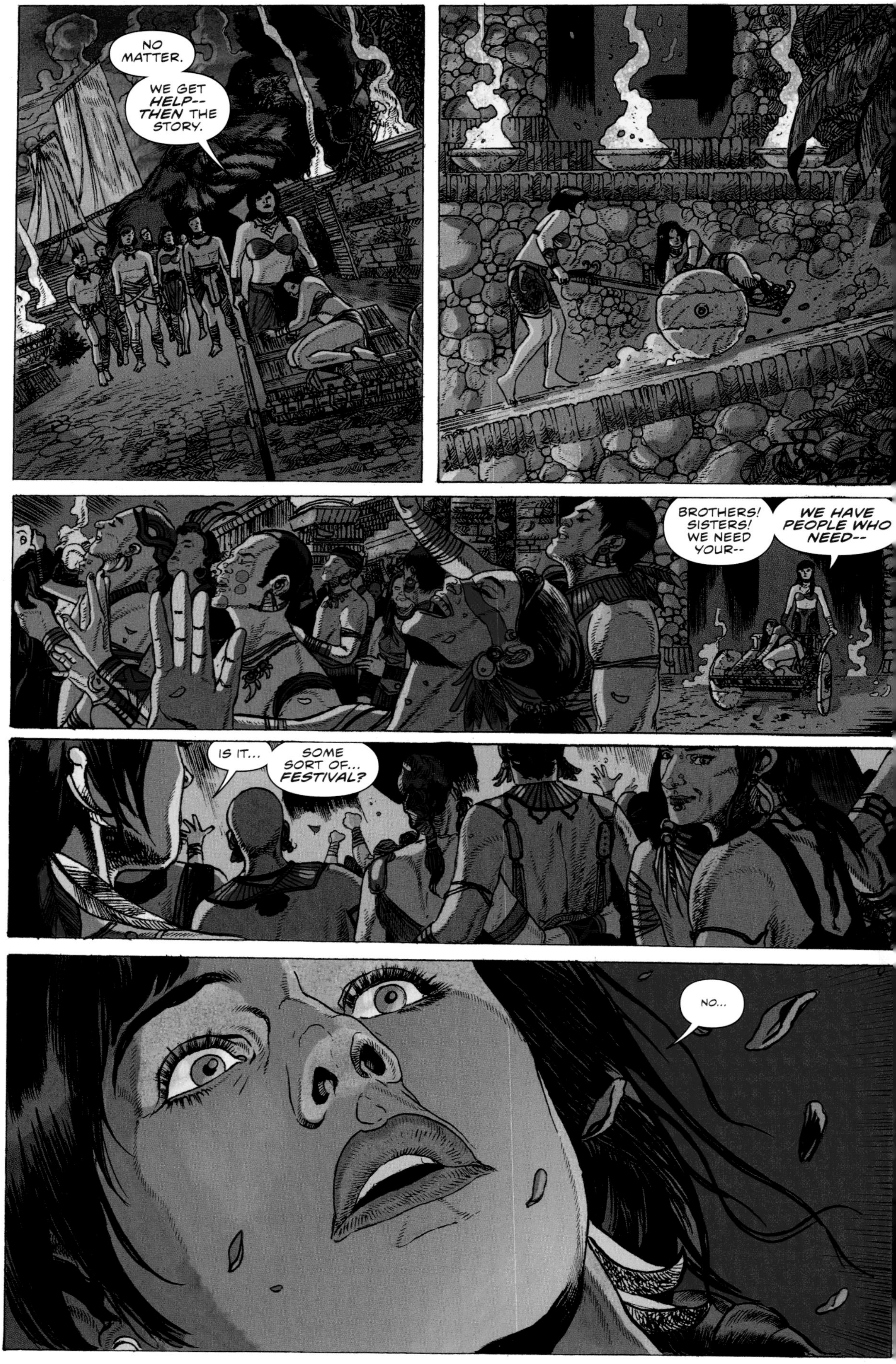
NO MATTER.
WE GET HELP-- THEN THE STORY.
BROTHERS! SISTERS! WE NEED YOUR--
WE HAVE PEOPLE WHO NEED--
IS IT...
SOME SORT OF... FESTIVAL?
NO...

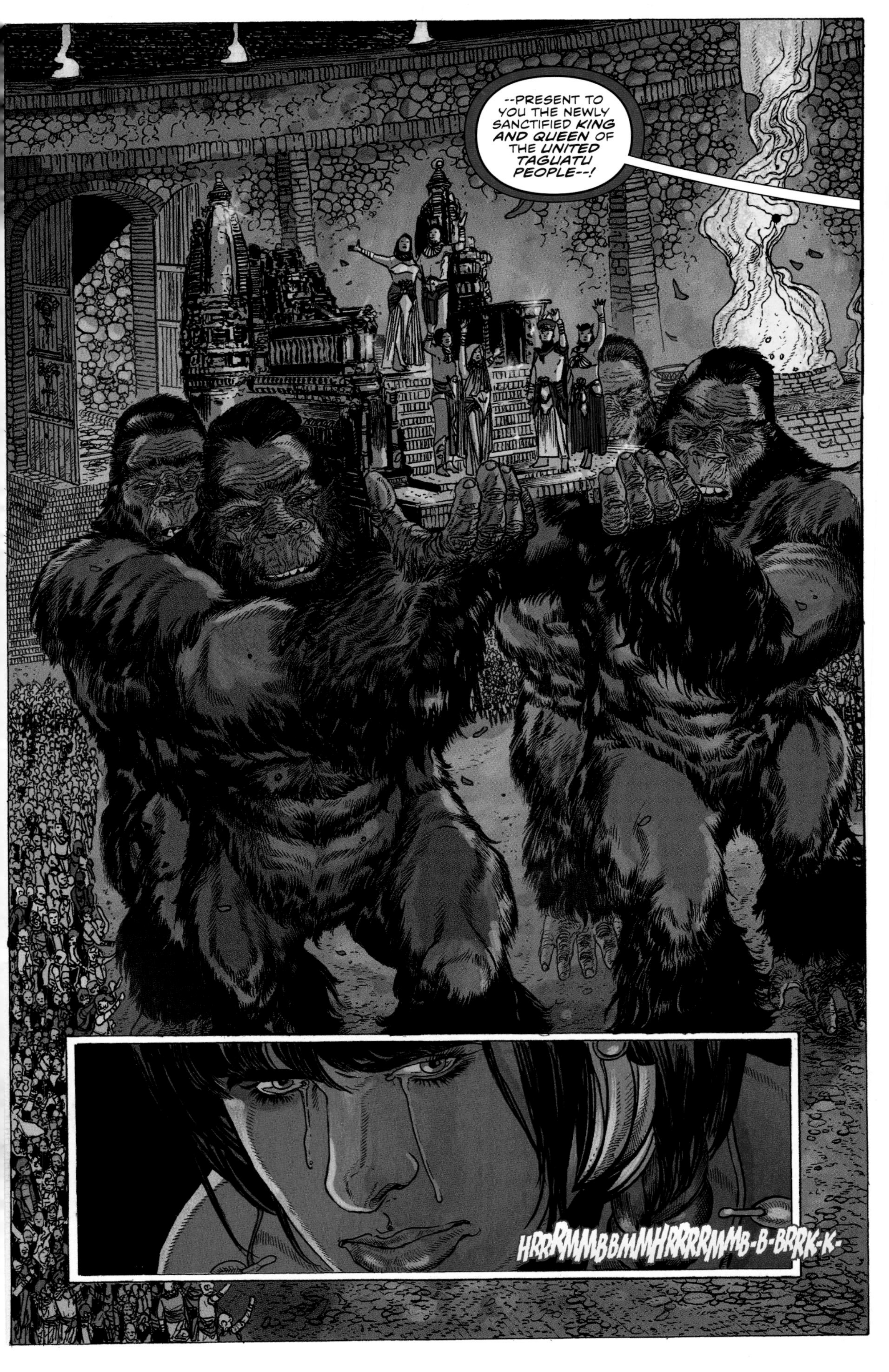
--PRESENT TO YOU THE NEWLY SANCTIFIED KING AND QUEEN OF THE UNITED TAGUATU PEOPLE--!
HRRRMMBBMMHRRRRMMB-B-BRRK-K-

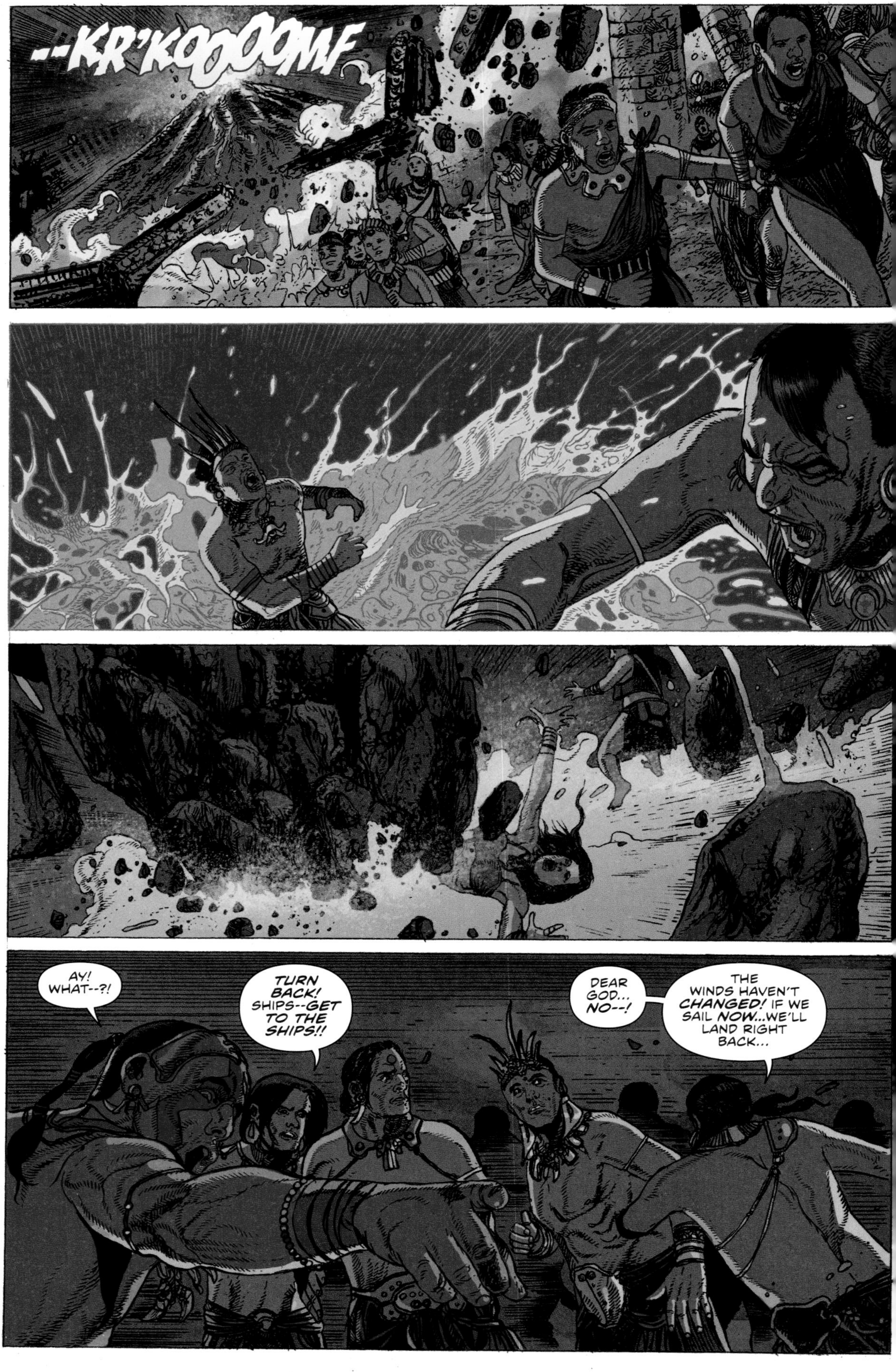
--KR'KOOOOMF
AY! WHAT--?!
TURN BACK! SHIPS--GET TO THE SHIPS!!
DEAR GOD... NO--!
THE WINDS HAVEN'T CHANGED! IF WE SAIL NOW...WE'LL LAND RIGHT BACK...

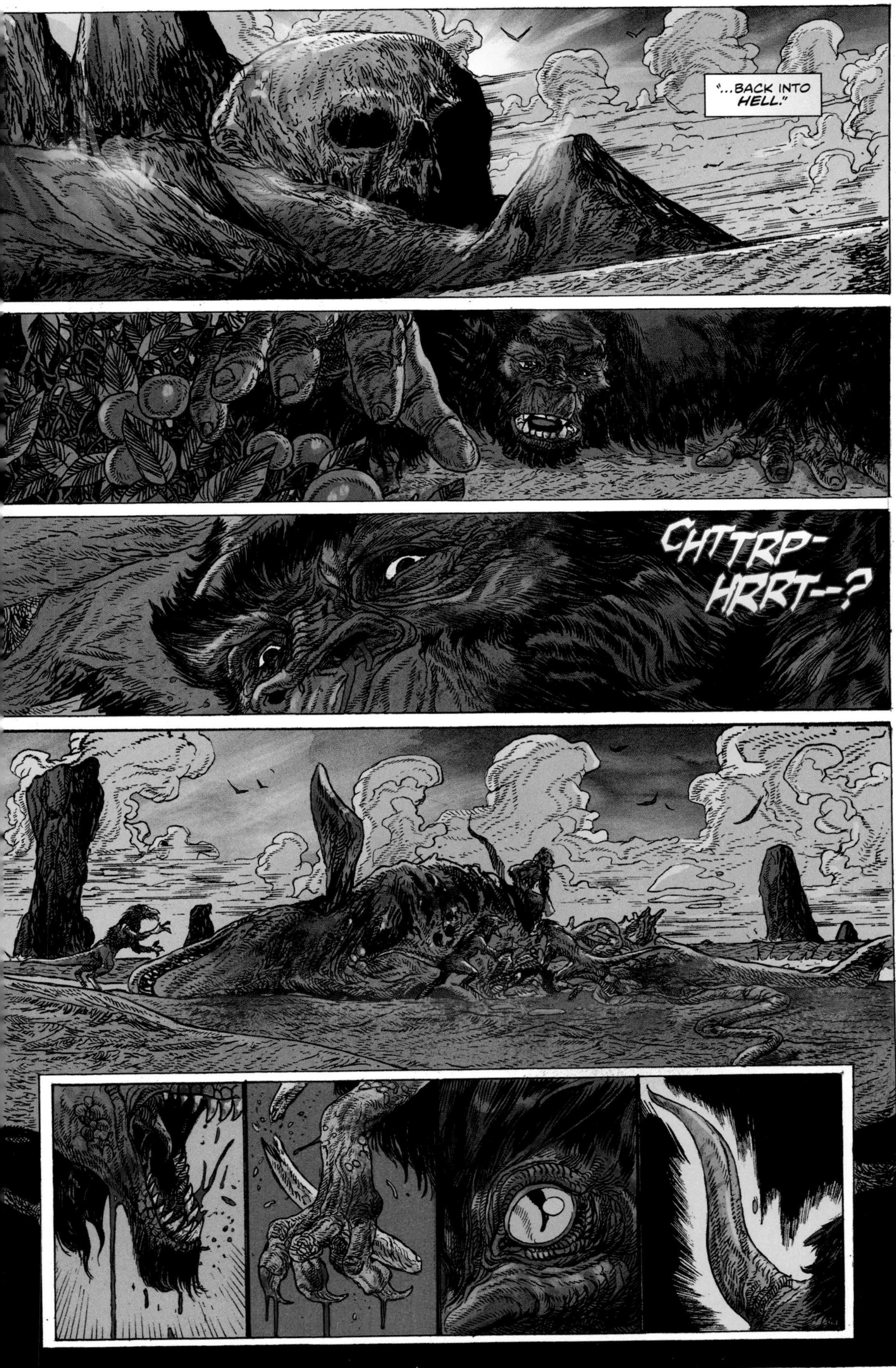
"...BACK INTO HELL."
CHTTRP-HRRT--?

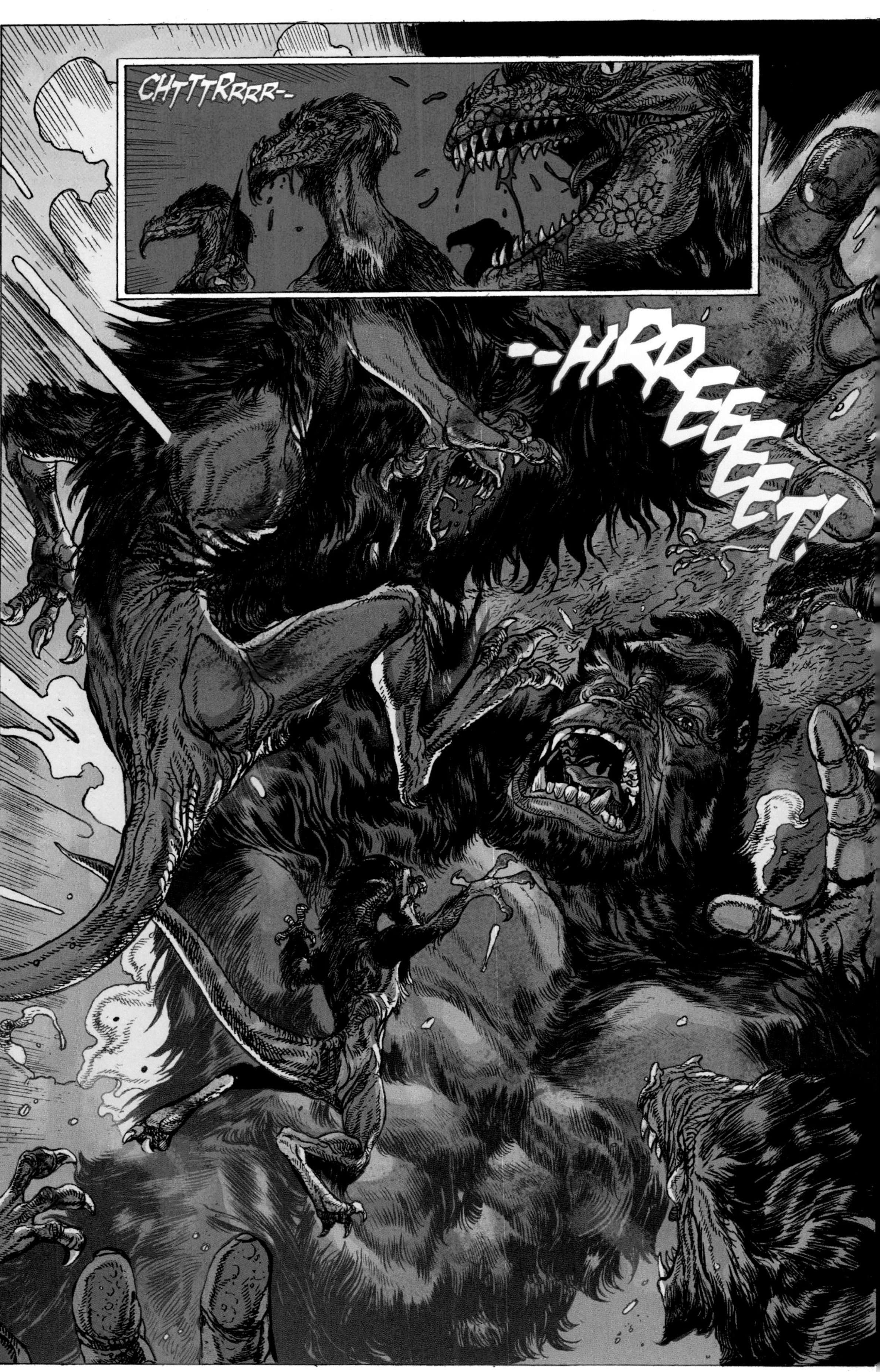
CHTTTRRRR--
--HRREEEEEET!

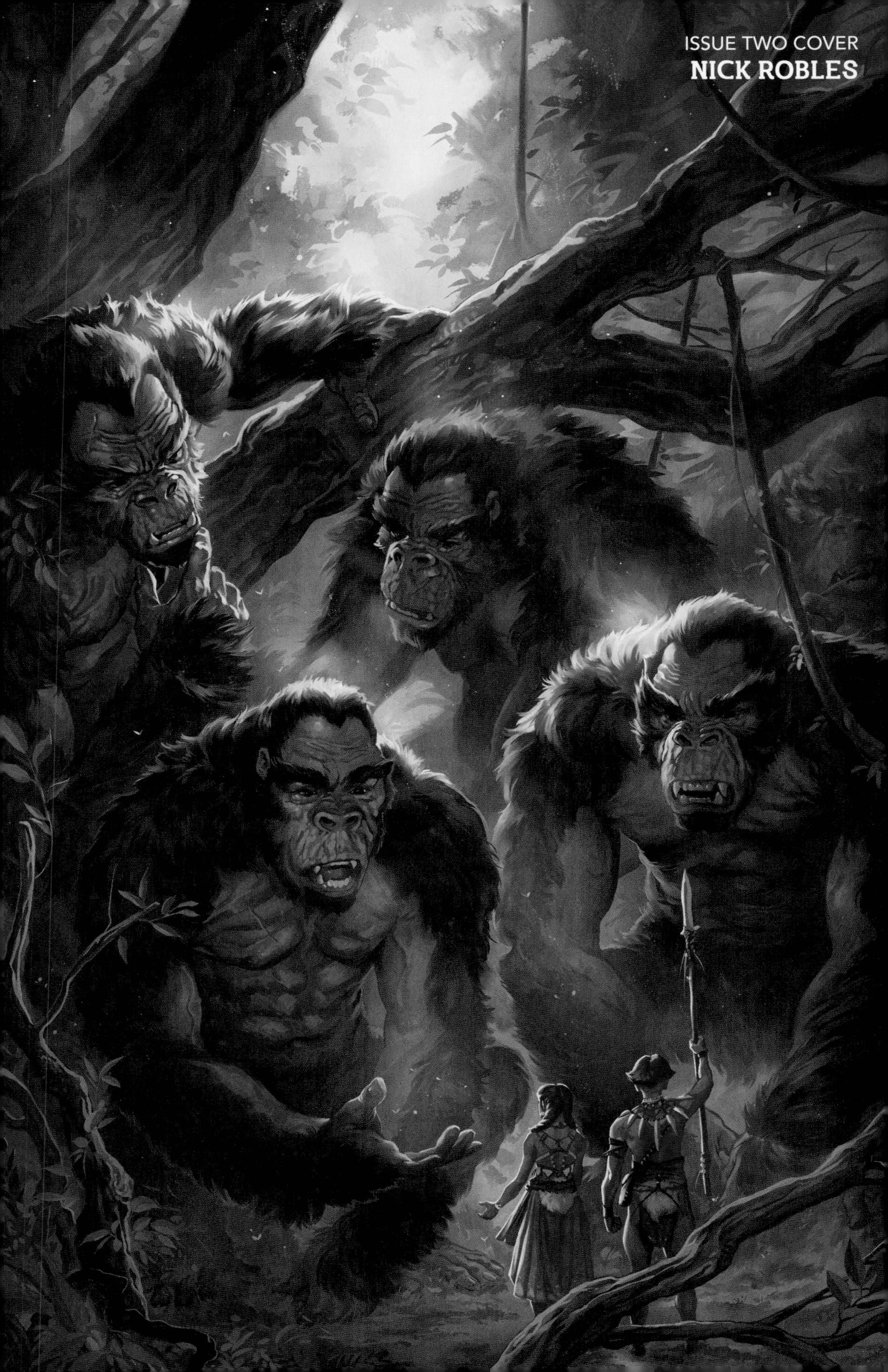

ISSUE TWO COVER
NICK ROBLES

CHAPTER
THREE

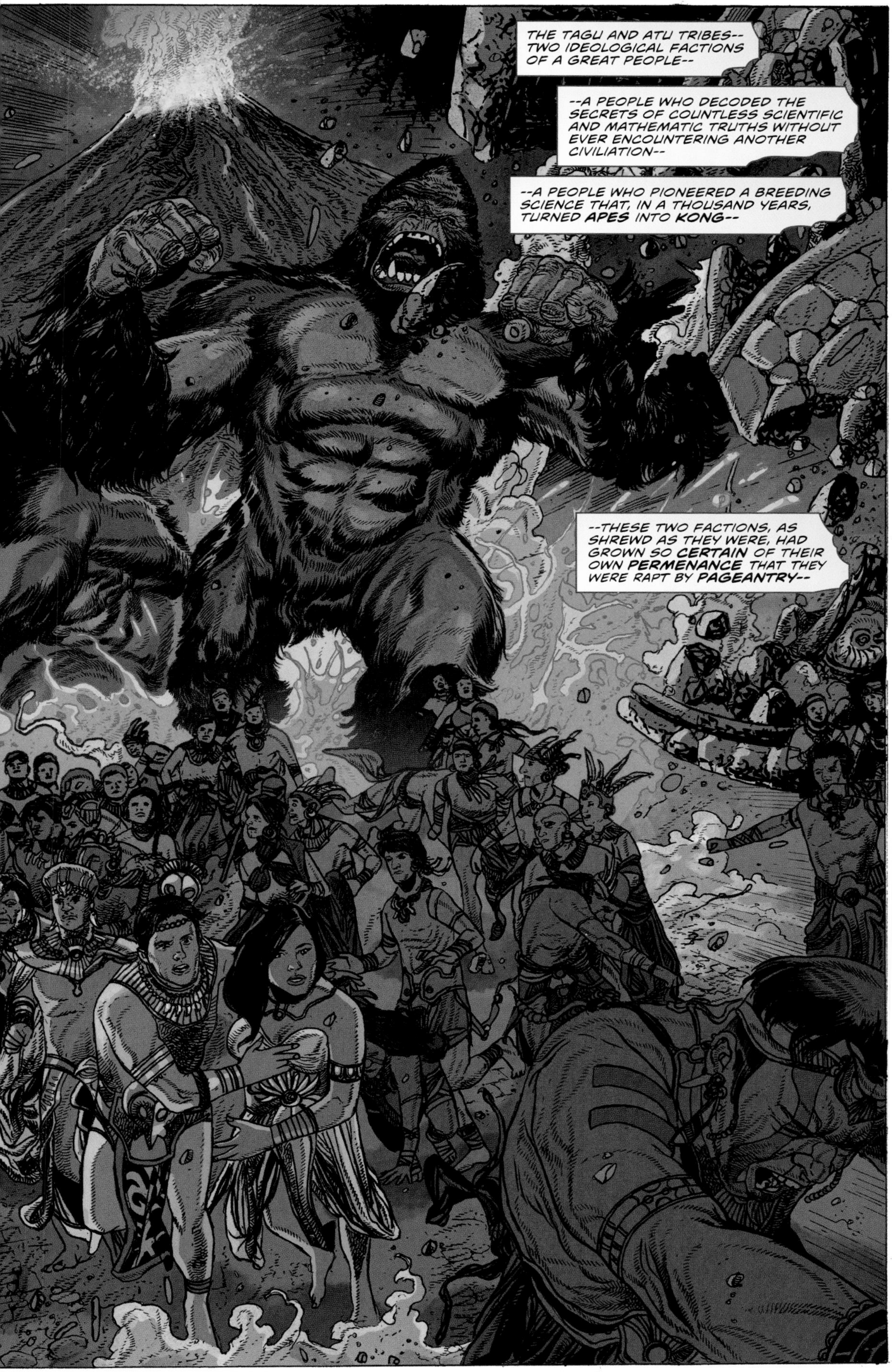
THE TAGU AND ATU TRIBES-- TWO IDEOLOGICAL FACTIONS OF A GREAT PEOPLE--
--A PEOPLE WHO DECODED THE SECRETS OF COUNTLESS SCIENTIFIC AND MATHEMATIC TRUTHS WITHOUT EVER ENCOUNTERING ANOTHER CIVILIATION--
--A PEOPLE WHO PIONEERED A BREEDING SCIENCE THAT, IN A THOUSAND YEARS, TURNED APES INTO KONG--
--THESE TWO FACTIONS, AS SHREWD AS THEY WERE, HAD GROWN SO CERTAIN OF THEIR OWN PERMENANCE THAT THEY WERE RAPT BY PAGEANTRY--

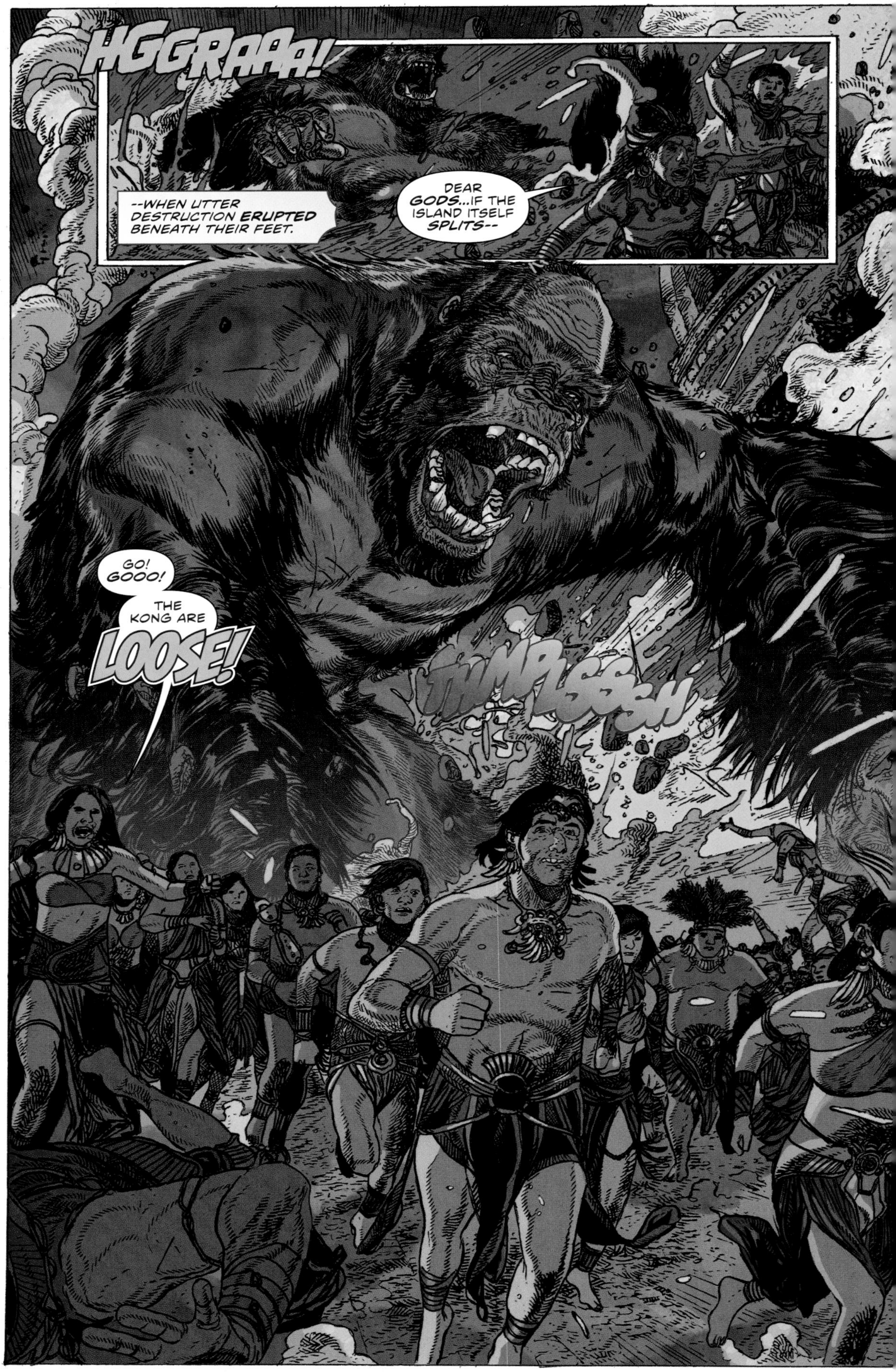
HGGRAAAA!
--WHEN UTTER DESTRUCTION ERUPTED BENEATH THEIR FEET.
DEAR GODS...IF THE ISLAND ITSELF SPLITS--
GO! GOOO!
THE KONG ARE LOOSE!
THMPLOOSH

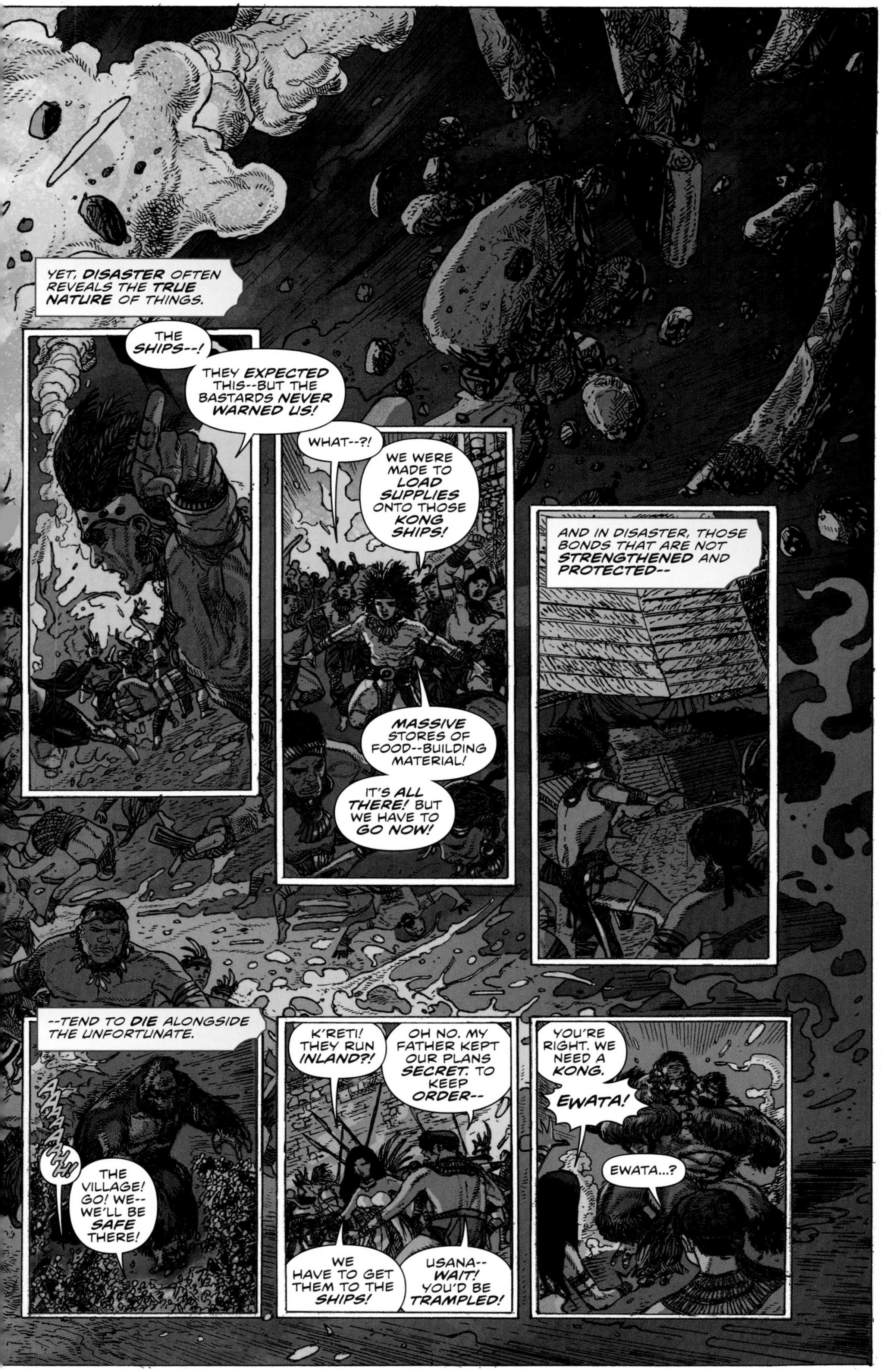

YET, DISASTER OFTEN REVEALS THE TRUE NATURE OF THINGS.
THE SHIPS--!
THEY EXPECTED THIS--BUT THE BASTARDS NEVER WARNED US!
WHAT--?!
WE WERE MADE TO LOAD SUPPLIES ONTO THOSE KONG SHIPS!
MASSIVE STORES OF FOOD--BUILDING MATERIAL!
IT'S ALL THERE! BUT WE HAVE TO GO NOW!
AND IN DISASTER, THOSE BONDS THAT ARE NOT STRENGTHENED AND PROTECTED--
--TEND TO DIE ALONGSIDE THE UNFORTUNATE.
AAAAAAHHH!
THE VILLAGE! GO! WE--WE'LL BE SAFE THERE!
K'RETI! THEY RUN INLAND?!
OH NO. MY FATHER KEPT OUR PLANS SECRET. TO KEEP ORDER--
WE HAVE TO GET THEM TO THE SHIPS!
USANA--WAIT! YOU'D BE TRAMPLED!
YOU'RE RIGHT. WE NEED A KONG.
EWATA!
EWATA...?

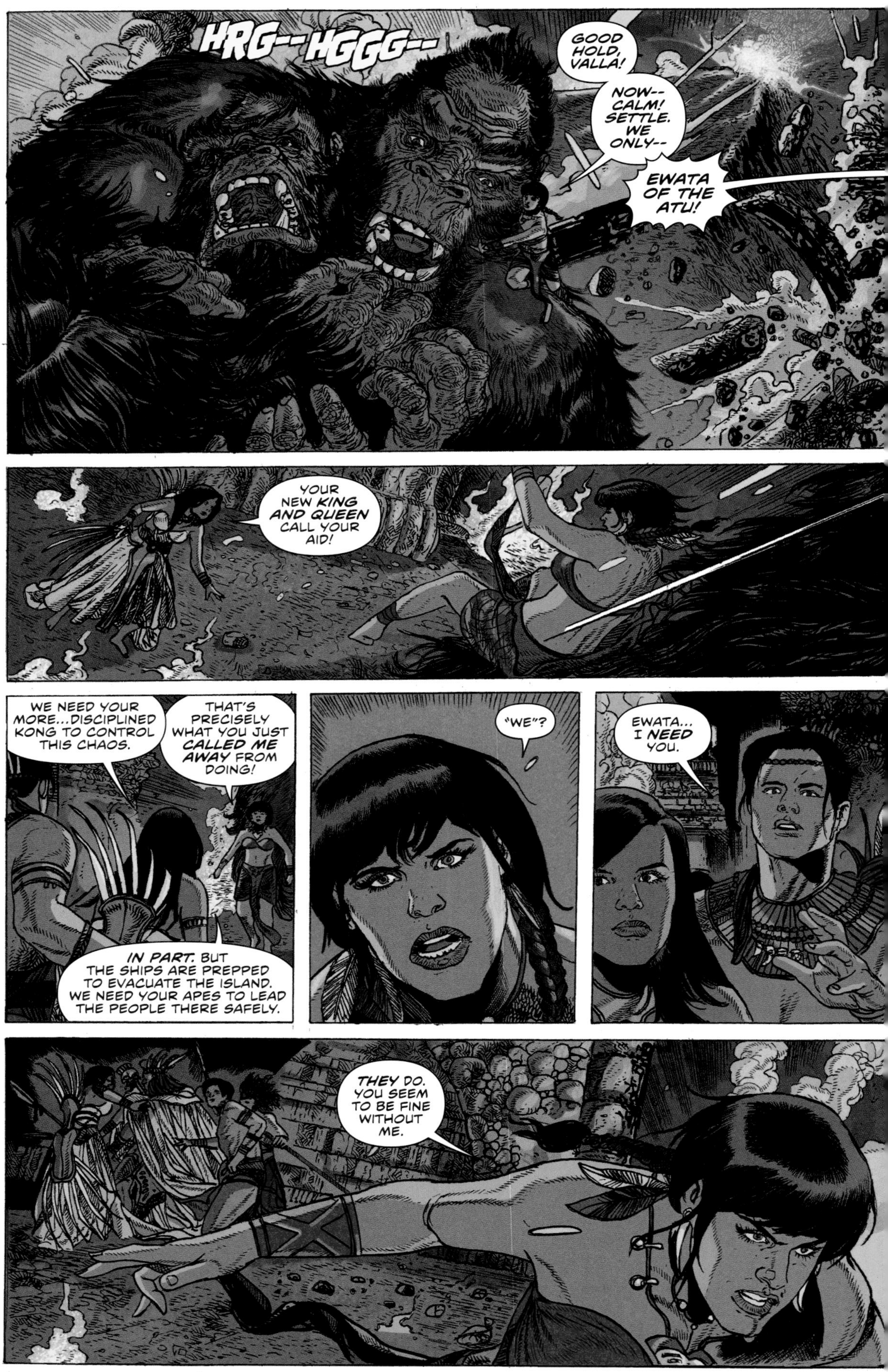
HRG--HGGG--
GOOD HOLD, VALLA!
NOW--CALM! SETTLE. WE ONLY--
EWATA OF THE ATU!
YOUR NEW KING AND QUEEN CALL YOUR AID!
WE NEED YOUR MORE...DISCIPLINED KONG TO CONTROL THIS CHAOS.
THAT'S PRECISELY WHAT YOU JUST CALLED ME AWAY FROM DOING!
IN PART. BUT THE SHIPS ARE PREPPED TO EVACUATE THE ISLAND. WE NEED YOUR APES TO LEAD THE PEOPLE THERE SAFELY.
"WE"?
EWATA... I NEED YOU.
THEY DO. YOU SEEM TO BE FINE WITHOUT ME.

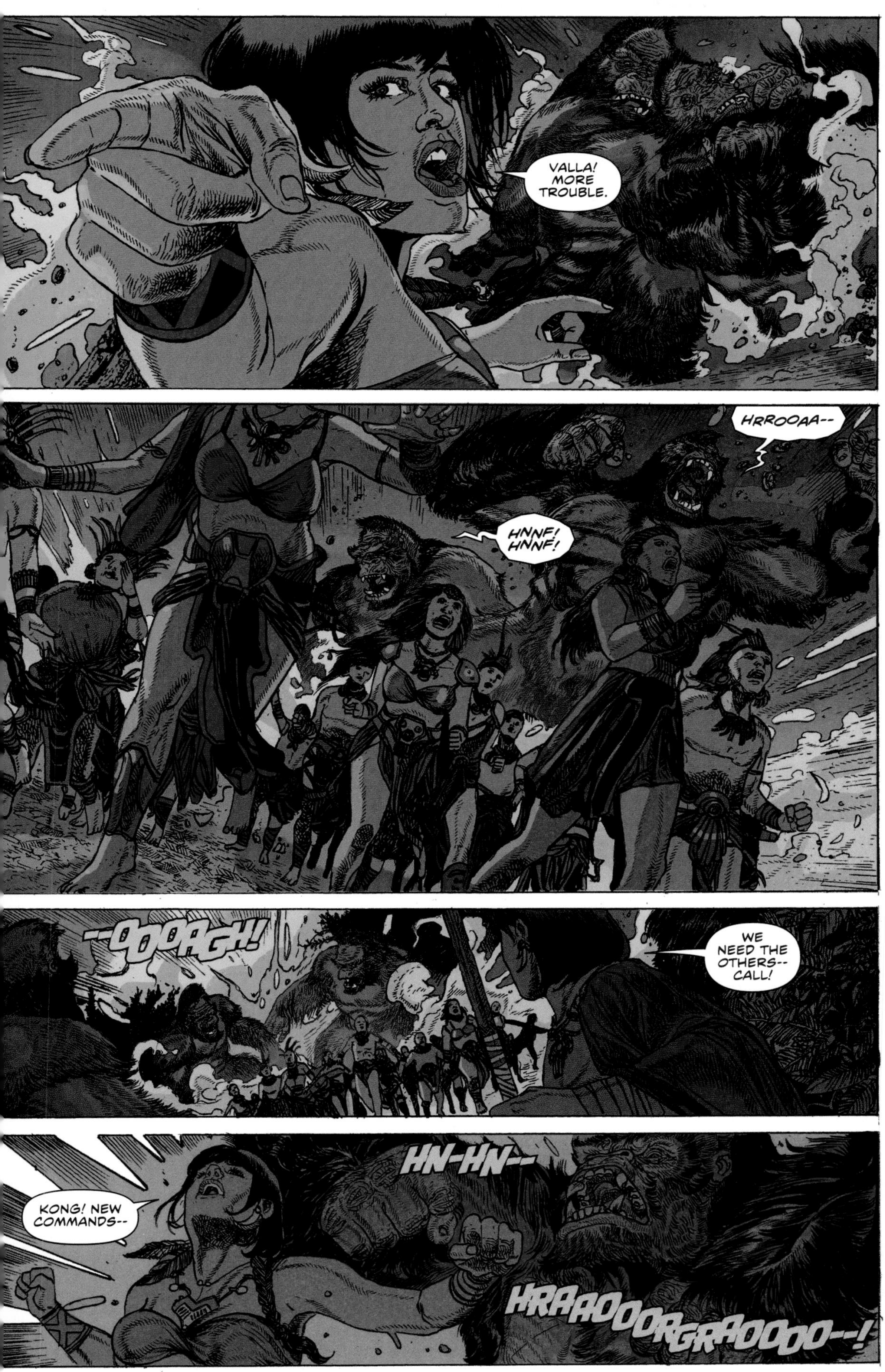
VALLA! MORE TROUBLE.
HRROOAA--
HNNF! HNNF!
--OOOAGH!
WE NEED THE OTHERS-- CALL!
KONG! NEW COMMANDS--
HN-HN--
HRAAOOORGRAOOOO--!

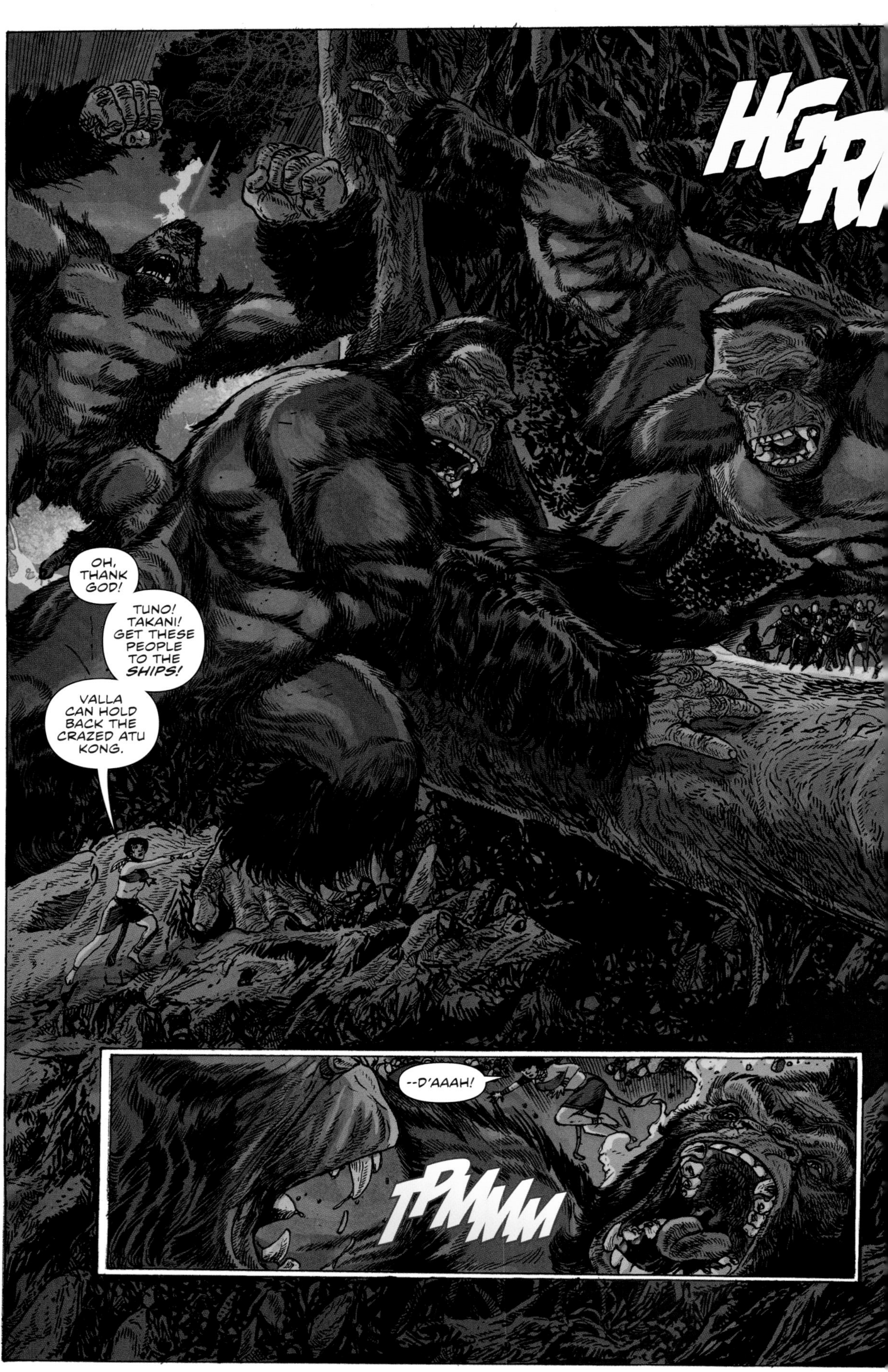
HGRR
OH, THANK GOD!
TUNO! TAKANI! GET THESE PEOPLE TO THE SHIPS!
VALLA CAN HOLD BACK THE CRAZED ATU KONG.
--D'AAAH!
TPMMM

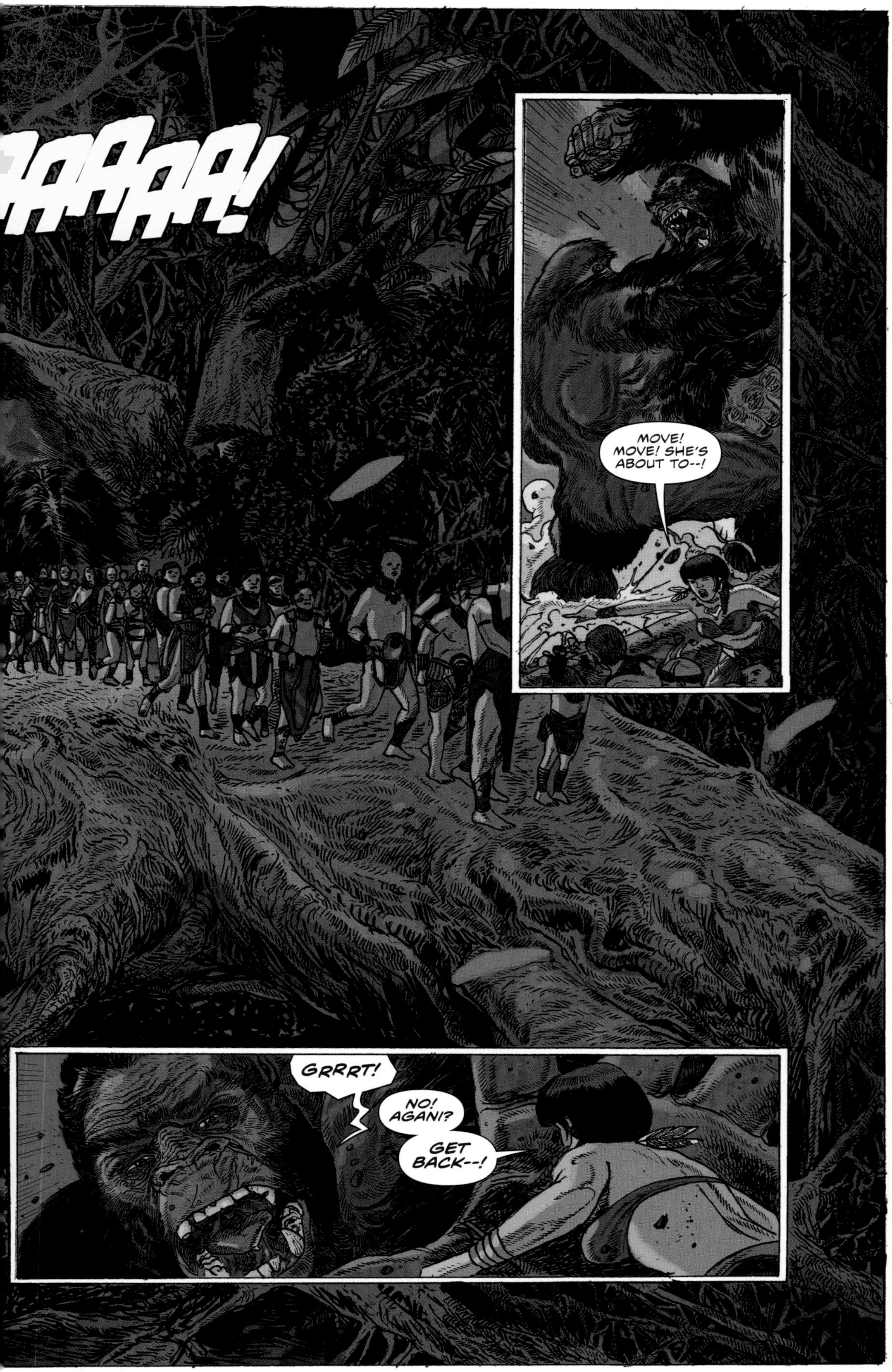
AAAAAA!
MOVE! MOVE! SHE'S ABOUT TO--!
GRRRT!
NO! AGANI?
GET BACK--!

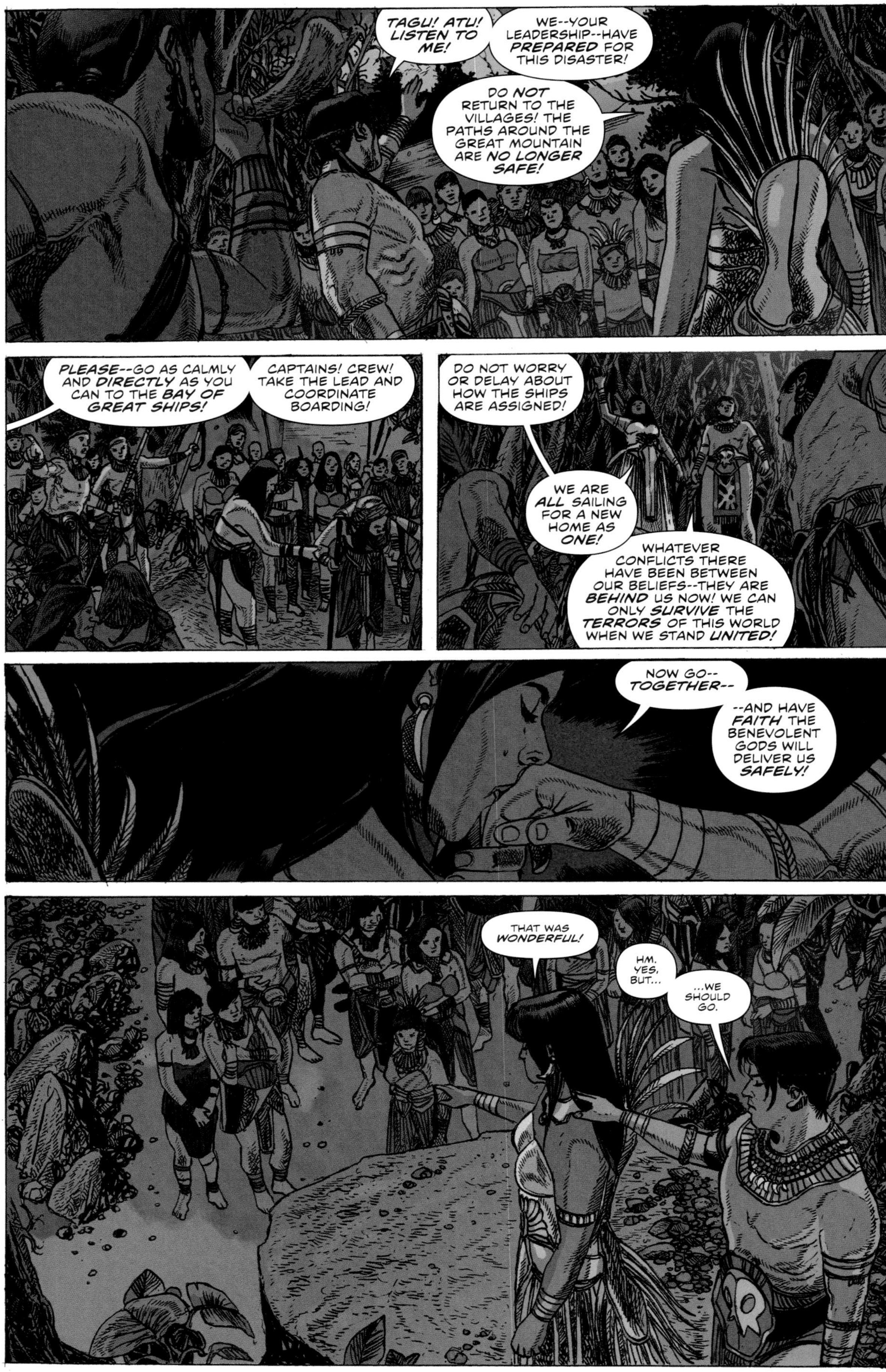
TAGU! ATU! LISTEN TO ME!
WE--YOUR LEADERSHIP--HAVE PREPARED FOR THIS DISASTER!
DO NOT RETURN TO THE VILLAGES! THE PATHS AROUND THE GREAT MOUNTAIN ARE NO LONGER SAFE!
PLEASE--GO AS CALMLY AND DIRECTLY AS YOU CAN TO THE BAY OF GREAT SHIPS!
CAPTAINS! CREW! TAKE THE LEAD AND COORDINATE BOARDING!
DO NOT WORRY OR DELAY ABOUT HOW THE SHIPS ARE ASSIGNED!
WE ARE ALL SAILING FOR A NEW HOME AS ONE!
WHATEVER CONFLICTS THERE HAVE BEEN BETWEEN OUR BELIEFS--THEY ARE BEHIND US NOW! WE CAN ONLY SURVIVE THE TERRORS OF THIS WORLD WHEN WE STAND UNITED!
NOW GO--TOGETHER--
--AND HAVE FAITH THE BENEVOLENT GODS WILL DELIVER US SAFELY!
THAT WAS WONDERFUL!
HM. YES, BUT...
...WE SHOULD GO.

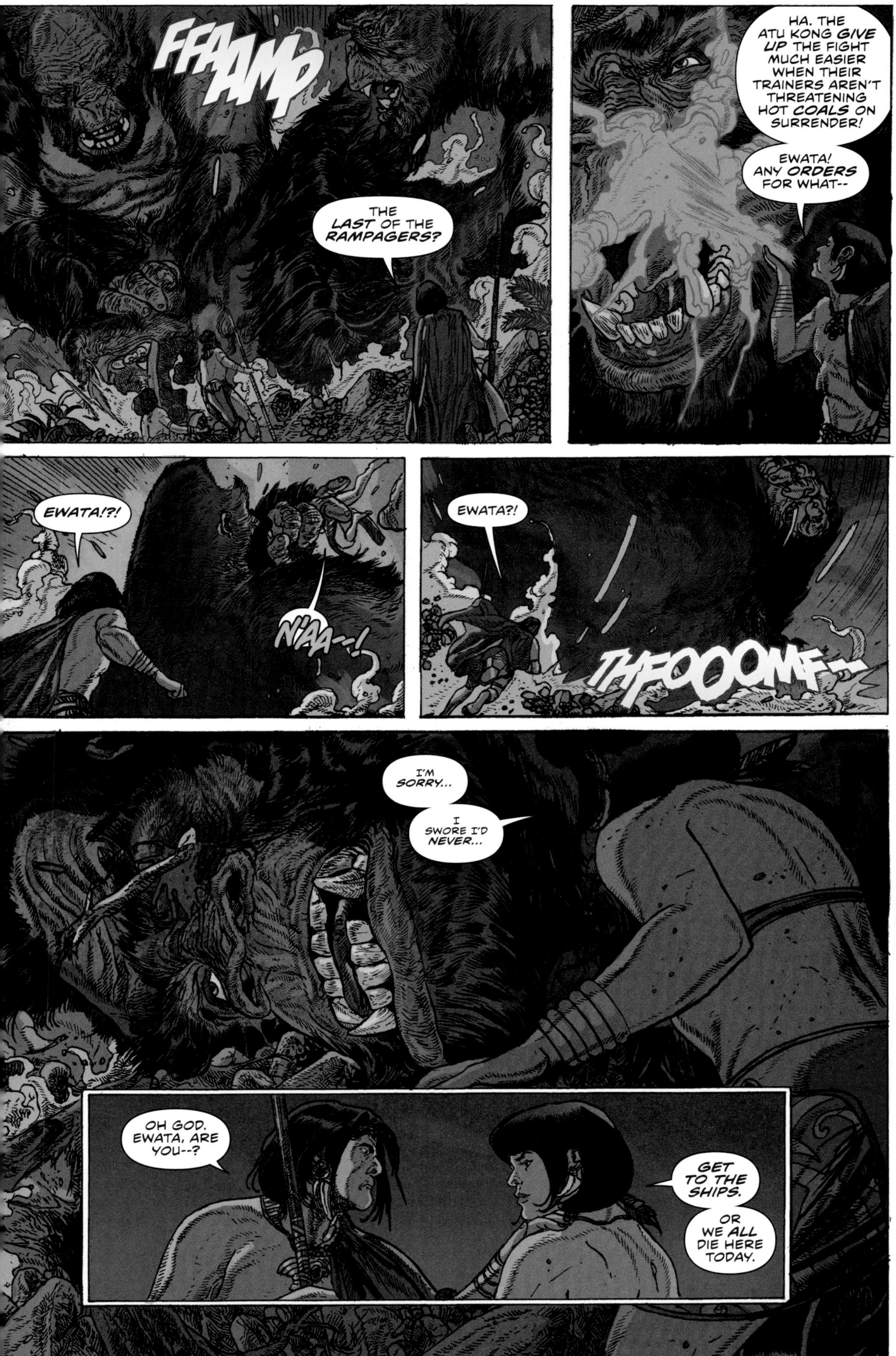
FFAAMP
THE LAST OF THE RAMPAGERS?
HA. THE ATU KONG GIVE UP THE FIGHT MUCH EASIER WHEN THEIR TRAINERS AREN'T THREATENING HOT COALS ON SURRENDER!
EWATA! ANY ORDERS FOR WHAT--
EWATA!?!
NIAA--!
EWATA?!
THFOOOMF--
I'M SORRY...
I SWORE I'D NEVER...
OH GOD. EWATA, ARE YOU--?
GET TO THE SHIPS.
OR WE ALL DIE HERE TODAY.

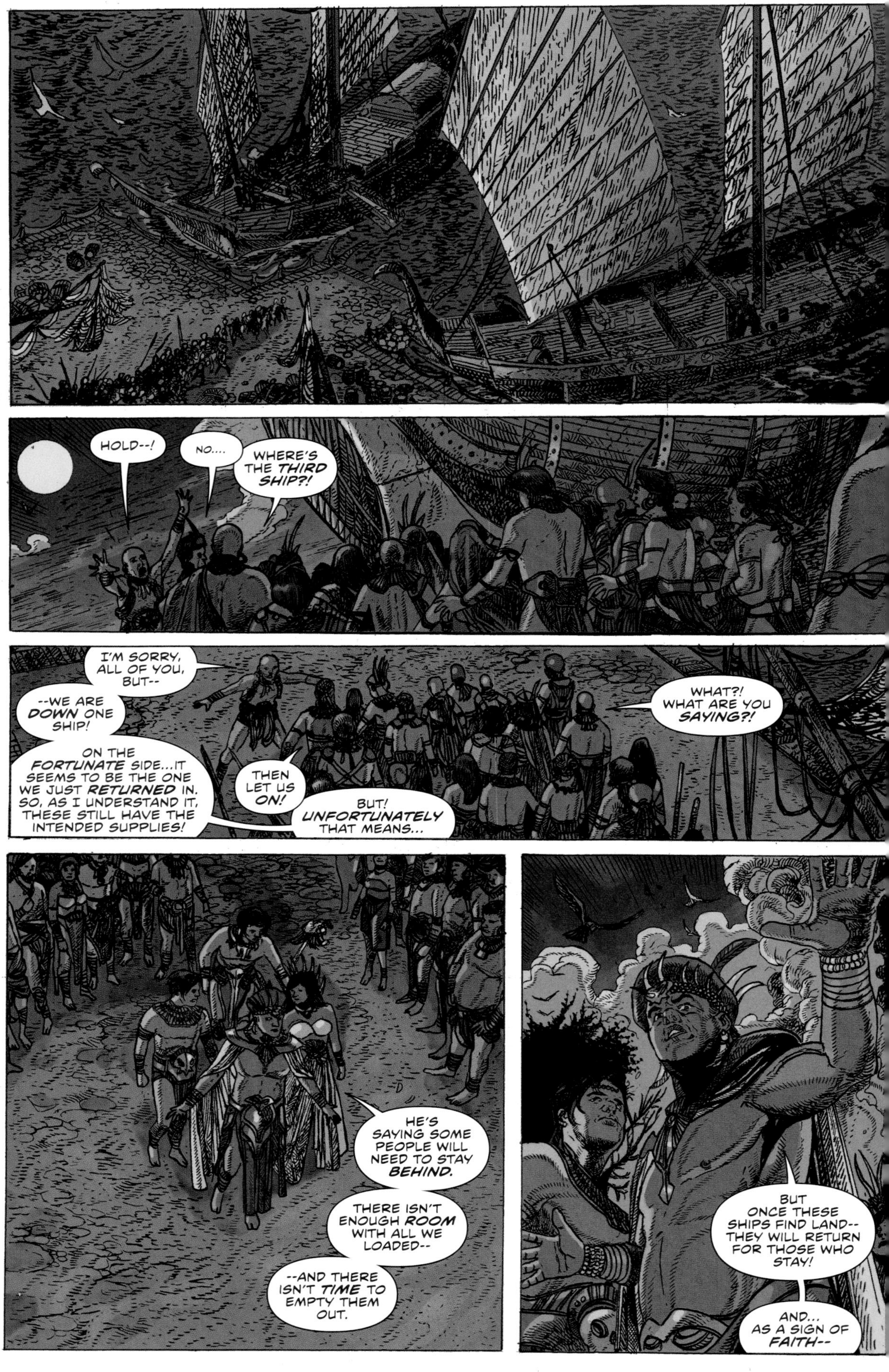
HOLD--!
NO....
WHERE'S THE THIRD SHIP?!
I'M SORRY, ALL OF YOU, BUT--
--WE ARE DOWN ONE SHIP!
ON THE FORTUNATE SIDE...IT SEEMS TO BE THE ONE WE JUST RETURNED IN. SO, AS I UNDERSTAND IT, THESE STILL HAVE THE INTENDED SUPPLIES!
WHAT?! WHAT ARE YOU SAYING?!
THEN LET US ON!
BUT! UNFORTUNATELY THAT MEANS...
HE'S SAYING SOME PEOPLE WILL NEED TO STAY BEHIND.
THERE ISN'T ENOUGH ROOM WITH ALL WE LOADED--
--AND THERE ISN'T TIME TO EMPTY THEM OUT.
BUT ONCE THESE SHIPS FIND LAND--THEY WILL RETURN FOR THOSE WHO STAY!
AND... AS A SIGN OF FAITH--

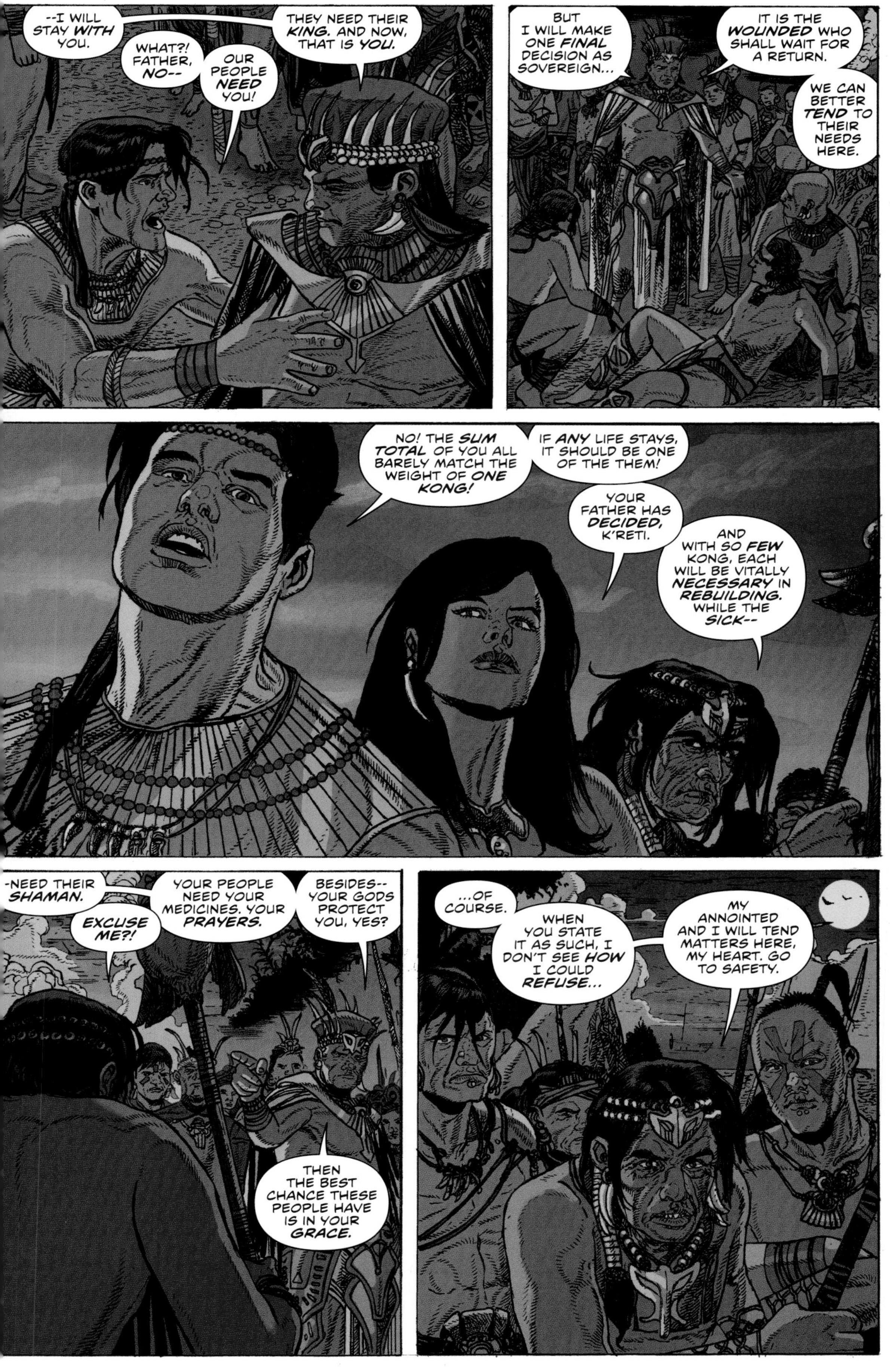
--I WILL STAY WITH YOU.
WHAT?! FATHER, NO--
OUR PEOPLE NEED YOU!
THEY NEED THEIR KING. AND NOW, THAT IS YOU.
BUT I WILL MAKE ONE FINAL DECISION AS SOVEREIGN...
IT IS THE WOUNDED WHO SHALL WAIT FOR A RETURN.
WE CAN BETTER TEND TO THEIR NEEDS HERE.
NO! THE SUM TOTAL OF YOU ALL BARELY MATCH THE WEIGHT OF ONE KONG!
IF ANY LIFE STAYS, IT SHOULD BE ONE OF THE THEM!
YOUR FATHER HAS DECIDED, K'RETI.
AND WITH SO FEW KONG, EACH WILL BE VITALLY NECESSARY IN REBUILDING. WHILE THE SICK--
-NEED THEIR SHAMAN.
EXCUSE ME?!
YOUR PEOPLE NEED YOUR MEDICINES. YOUR PRAYERS.
BESIDES-- YOUR GODS PROTECT YOU, YES?
THEN THE BEST CHANCE THESE PEOPLE HAVE IS IN YOUR GRACE.
...OF COURSE.
WHEN YOU STATE IT AS SUCH, I DON'T SEE HOW I COULD REFUSE...
MY ANNOINTED AND I WILL TEND MATTERS HERE, MY HEART. GO TO SAFETY.

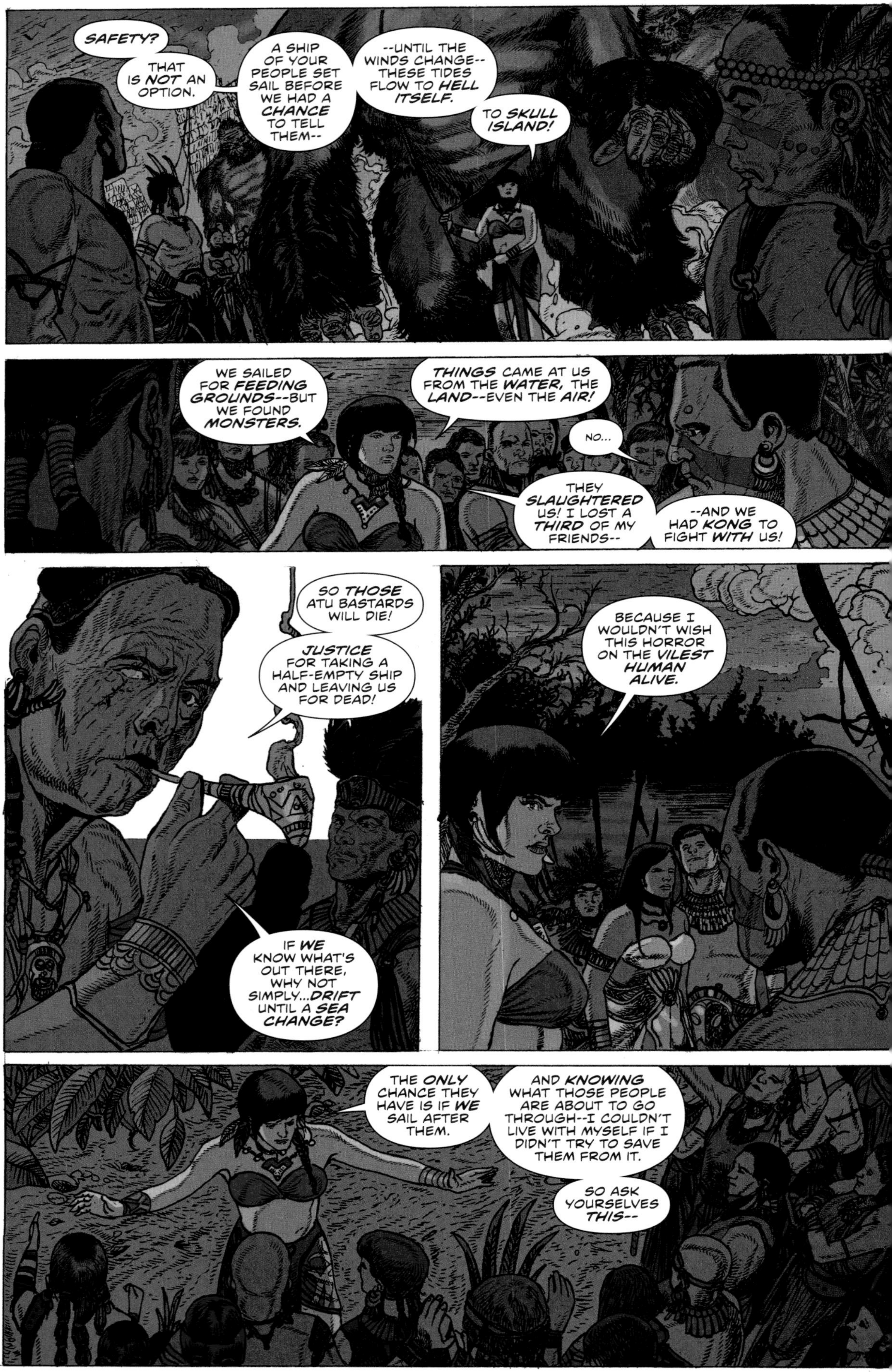
SAFETY?
THAT IS NOT AN OPTION.
A SHIP OF YOUR PEOPLE SET SAIL BEFORE WE HAD A CHANCE TO TELL THEM--
--UNTIL THE WINDS CHANGE-- THESE TIDES FLOW TO HELL ITSELF.
TO SKULL ISLAND!
WE SAILED FOR FEEDING GROUNDS--BUT WE FOUND MONSTERS.
THINGS CAME AT US FROM THE WATER, THE LAND--EVEN THE AIR!
NO...
THEY SLAUGHTERED US! I LOST A THIRD OF MY FRIENDS--
--AND WE HAD KONG TO FIGHT WITH US!
SO THOSE ATU BASTARDS WILL DIE!
JUSTICE FOR TAKING A HALF-EMPTY SHIP AND LEAVING US FOR DEAD!
IF WE KNOW WHAT'S OUT THERE, WHY NOT SIMPLY...DRIFT UNTIL A SEA CHANGE?
BECAUSE I WOULDN'T WISH THIS HORROR ON THE VILEST HUMAN ALIVE.
THE ONLY CHANCE THEY HAVE IS IF WE SAIL AFTER THEM.
AND KNOWING WHAT THOSE PEOPLE ARE ABOUT TO GO THROUGH--I COULDN'T LIVE WITH MYSELF IF I DIDN'T TRY TO SAVE THEM FROM IT.
SO ASK YOURSELVES THIS--

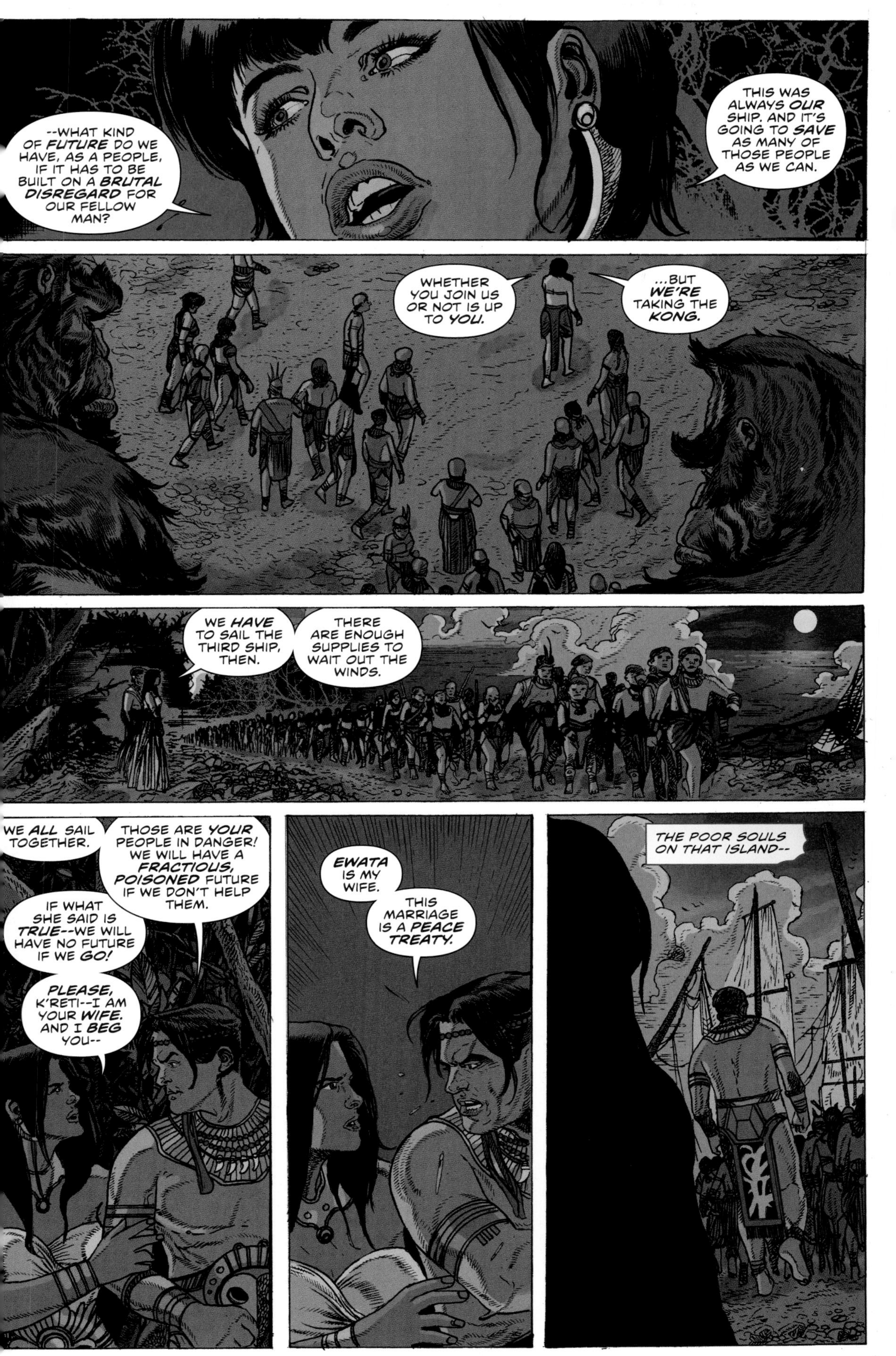
--WHAT KIND OF FUTURE DO WE HAVE, AS A PEOPLE, IF IT HAS TO BE BUILT ON A BRUTAL DISREGARD FOR OUR FELLOW MAN?
THIS WAS ALWAYS OUR SHIP. AND IT'S GOING TO SAVE AS MANY OF THOSE PEOPLE AS WE CAN.
WHETHER YOU JOIN US OR NOT IS UP TO YOU.
...BUT WE'RE TAKING THE KONG.
WE HAVE TO SAIL THE THIRD SHIP, THEN.
THERE ARE ENOUGH SUPPLIES TO WAIT OUT THE WINDS.
WE ALL SAIL TOGETHER.
THOSE ARE YOUR PEOPLE IN DANGER! WE WILL HAVE A FRACTIOUS, POISONED FUTURE IF WE DON'T HELP THEM.
IF WHAT SHE SAID IS TRUE--WE WILL HAVE NO FUTURE IF WE GO!
PLEASE, K'RETI--I AM YOUR WIFE. AND I BEG YOU--
EWATA IS MY WIFE.
THIS MARRIAGE IS A PEACE TREATY.
THE POOR SOULS ON THAT ISLAND--

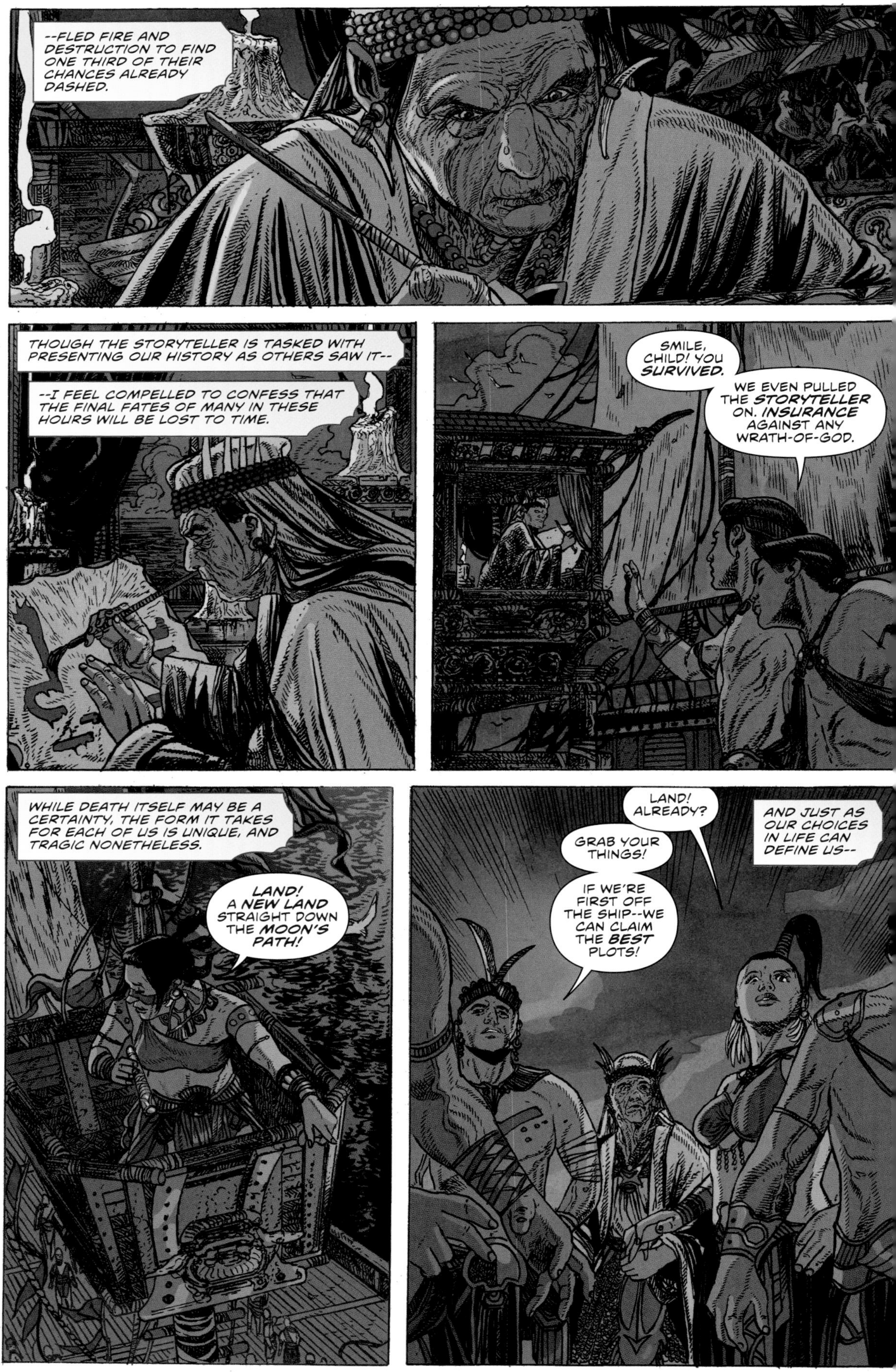
--FLED FIRE AND DESTRUCTION TO FIND ONE THIRD OF THEIR CHANCES ALREADY DASHED.
THOUGH THE STORYTELLER IS TASKED WITH PRESENTING OUR HISTORY AS OTHERS SAW IT--
--I FEEL COMPELLED TO CONFESS THAT THE FINAL FATES OF MANY IN THESE HOURS WILL BE LOST TO TIME.
SMILE, CHILD! YOU SURVIVED.
WE EVEN PULLED THE STORYTELLER ON. INSURANCE AGAINST ANY WRATH-OF-GOD.
WHILE DEATH ITSELF MAY BE A CERTAINTY, THE FORM IT TAKES FOR EACH OF US IS UNIQUE, AND TRAGIC NONETHELESS.
LAND! A NEW LAND STRAIGHT DOWN THE MOON'S PATH!
LAND! ALREADY?
GRAB YOUR THINGS!
IF WE'RE FIRST OFF THE SHIP--WE CAN CLAIM THE BEST PLOTS!
AND JUST AS OUR CHOICES IN LIFE CAN DEFINE US--

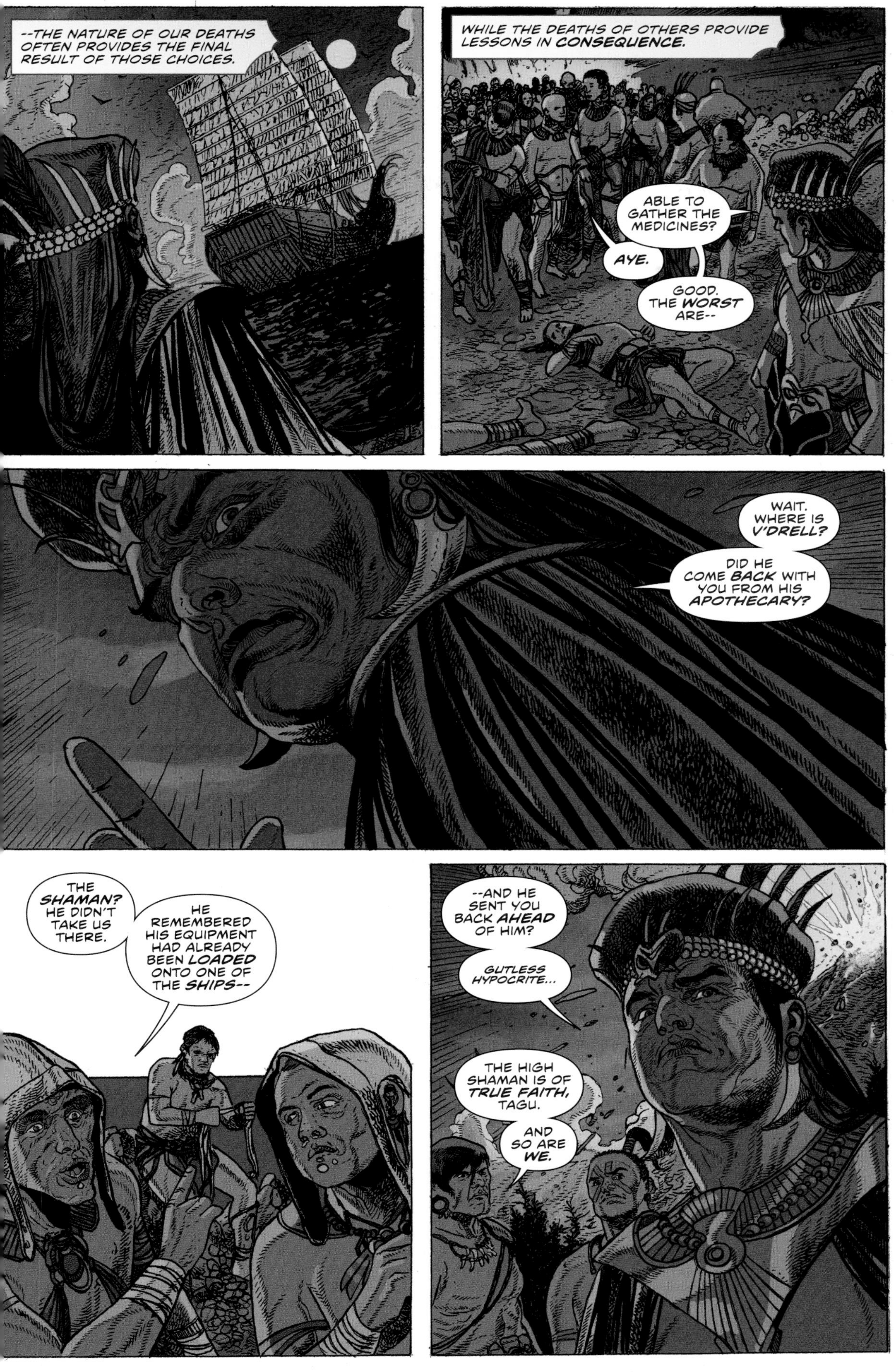
--THE NATURE OF OUR DEATHS OFTEN PROVIDES THE FINAL RESULT OF THOSE CHOICES.
WHILE THE DEATHS OF OTHERS PROVIDE LESSONS IN CONSEQUENCE.
ABLE TO GATHER THE MEDICINES?
AYE.
GOOD. THE WORST ARE--
WAIT. WHERE IS V'DRELL?
DID HE COME BACK WITH YOU FROM HIS APOTHECARY?
THE SHAMAN? HE DIDN'T TAKE US THERE.
HE REMEMBERED HIS EQUIPMENT HAD ALREADY BEEN LOADED ONTO ONE OF THE SHIPS--
--AND HE SENT YOU BACK AHEAD OF HIM?
GUTLESS HYPOCRITE...
THE HIGH SHAMAN IS OF TRUE FAITH, TAGU.
AND SO ARE WE.

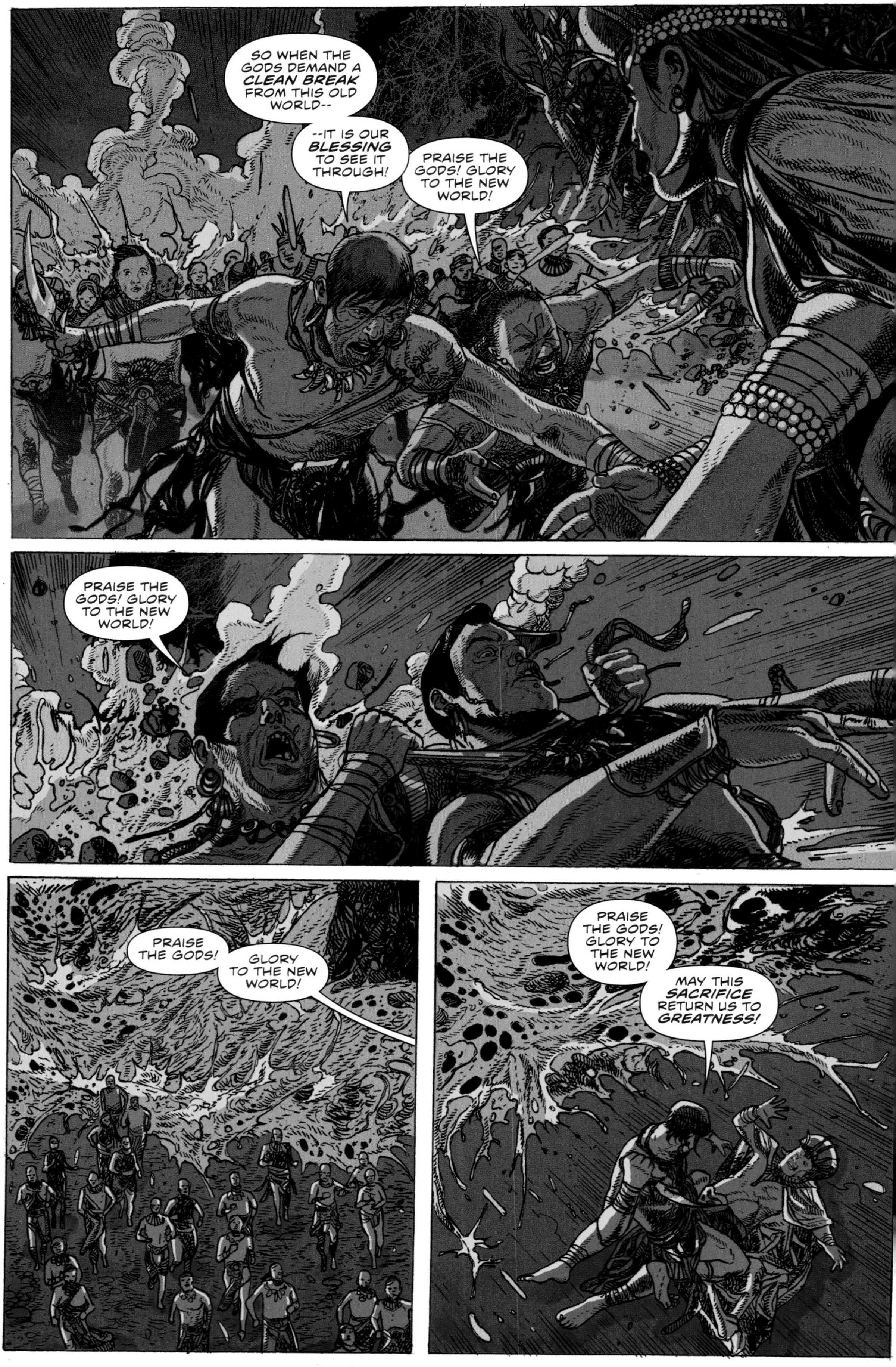
SO WHEN THE GODS DEMAND A CLEAN BREAK FROM THIS OLD WORLD--
--IT IS OUR BLESSING TO SEE IT THROUGH!
PRAISE THE GODS! GLORY TO THE NEW WORLD!
PRAISE THE GODS! GLORY TO THE NEW WORLD!
PRAISE THE GODS!
GLORY TO THE NEW WORLD!
PRAISE THE GODS! GLORY TO THE NEW WORLD!
MAY THIS SACRIFICE RETURN US TO GREATNESS!

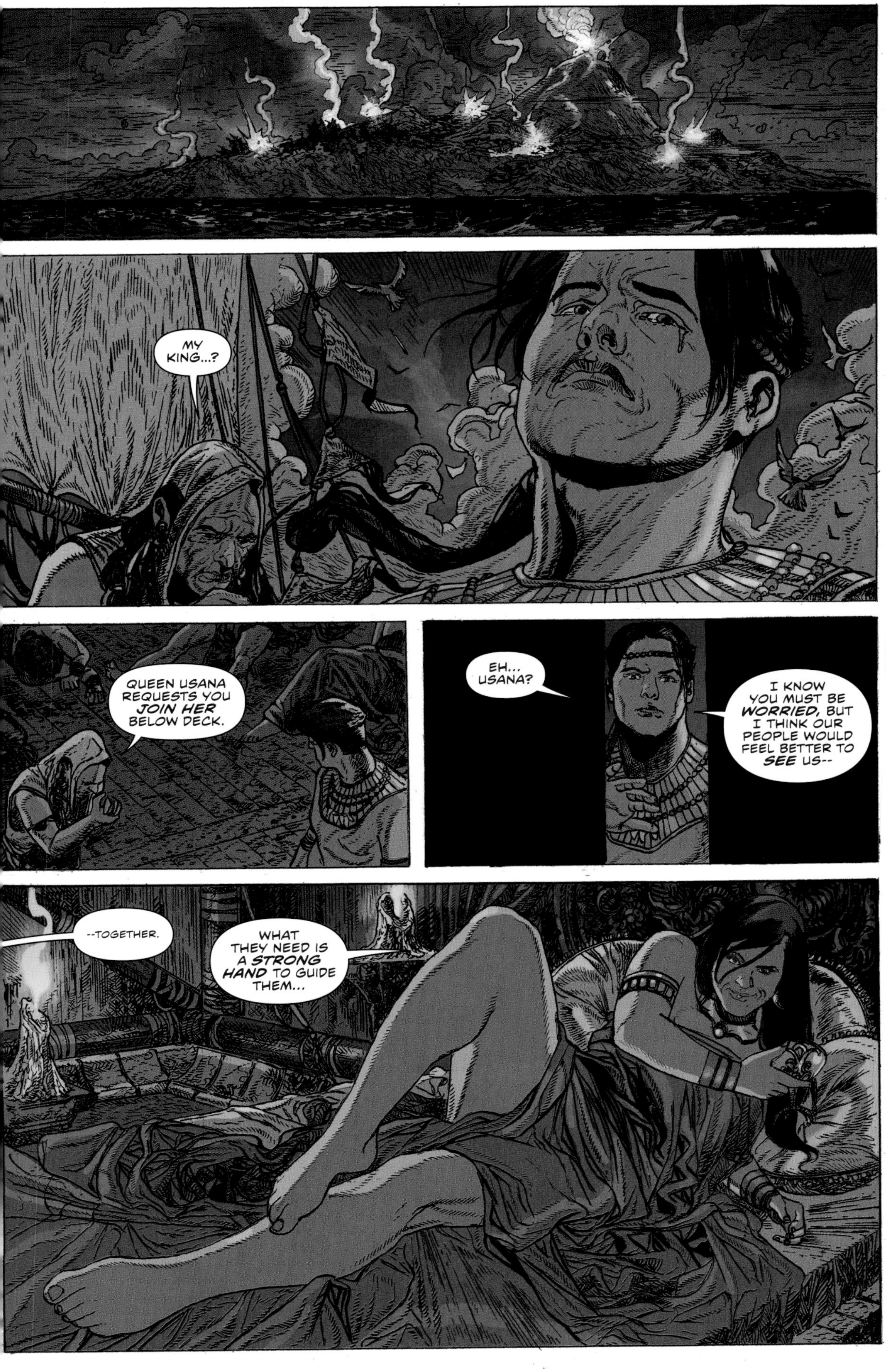
MY KING...?
QUEEN USANA REQUESTS YOU JOIN HER BELOW DECK.
EH... USANA?
I KNOW YOU MUST BE WORRIED, BUT I THINK OUR PEOPLE WOULD FEEL BETTER TO SEE US--
--TOGETHER.
WHAT THEY NEED IS A STRONG HAND TO GUIDE THEM...

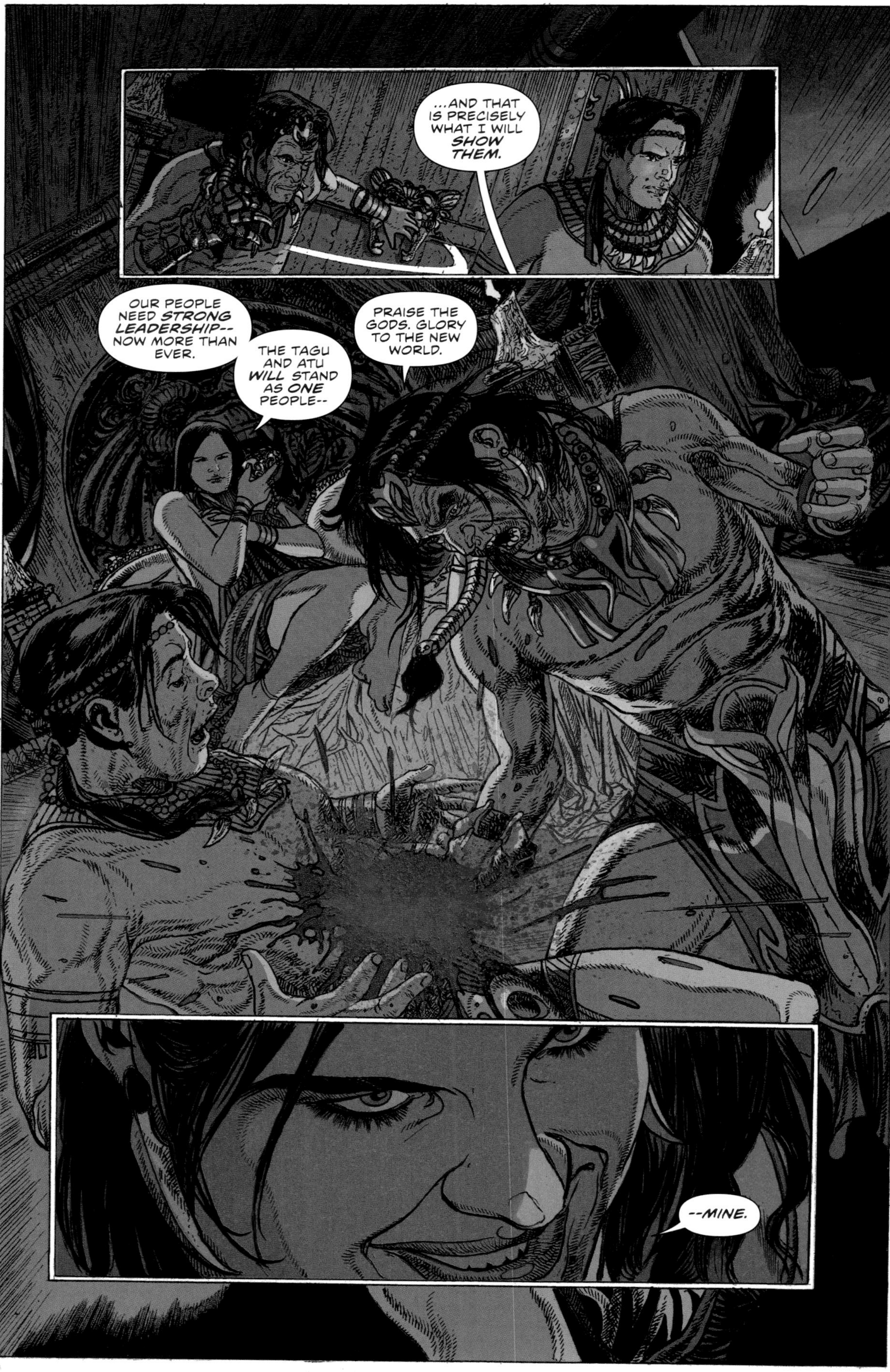
...AND THAT IS PRECISELY WHAT I WILL SHOW THEM.
OUR PEOPLE NEED STRONG LEADERSHIP-- NOW MORE THAN EVER.
THE TAGU AND ATU WILL STAND AS ONE PEOPLE--
PRAISE THE GODS. GLORY TO THE NEW WORLD.
--MINE.

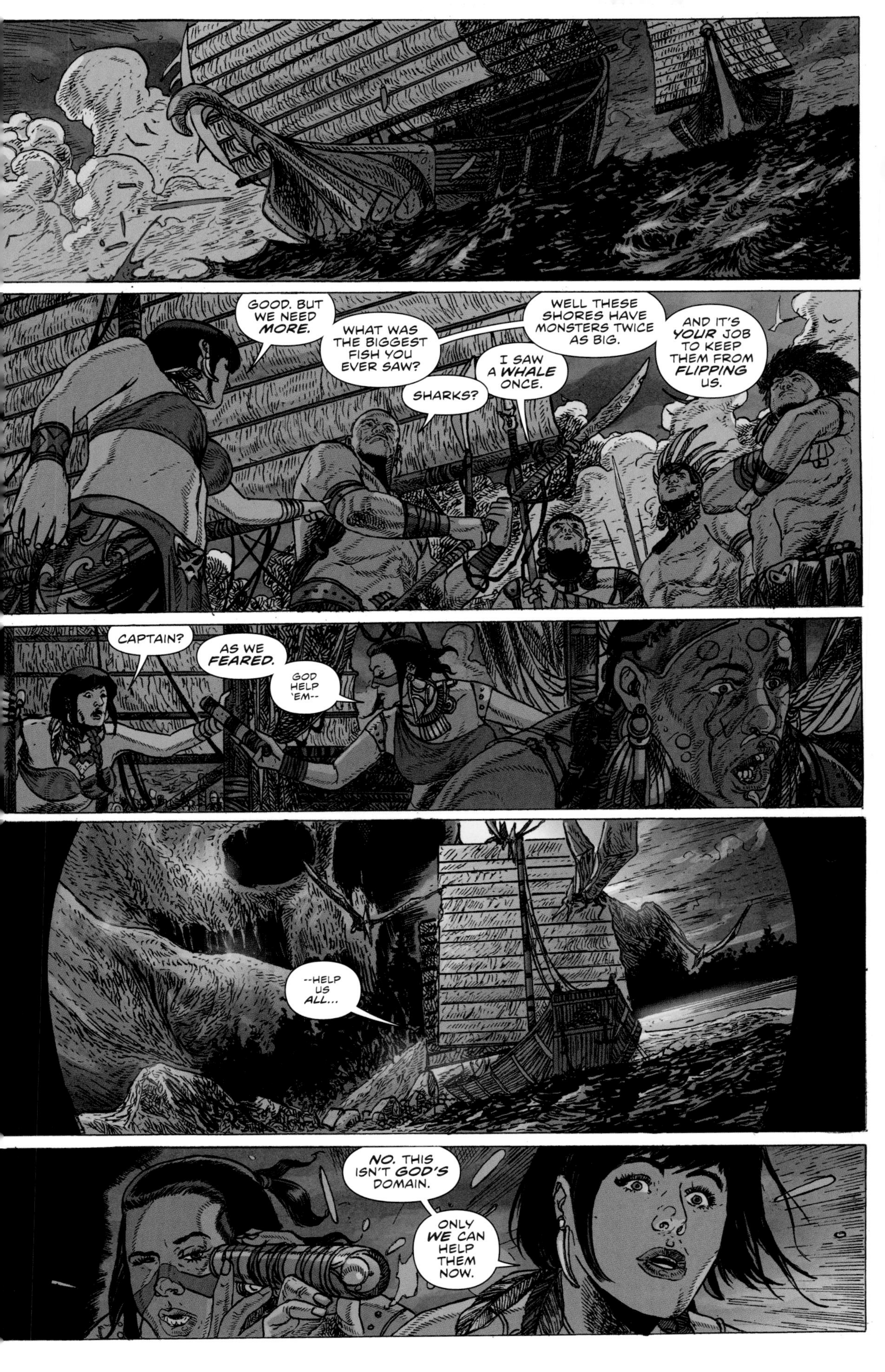
GOOD. BUT WE NEED MORE.
WHAT WAS THE BIGGEST FISH YOU EVER SAW?
WELL THESE SHORES HAVE MONSTERS TWICE AS BIG.
AND IT'S YOUR JOB TO KEEP THEM FROM FLIPPING US.
I SAW A WHALE ONCE.
SHARKS?
CAPTAIN?
AS WE FEARED.
GOD HELP 'EM--
--HELP US ALL...
NO. THIS ISN'T GOD'S DOMAIN.
ONLY WE CAN HELP THEM NOW.

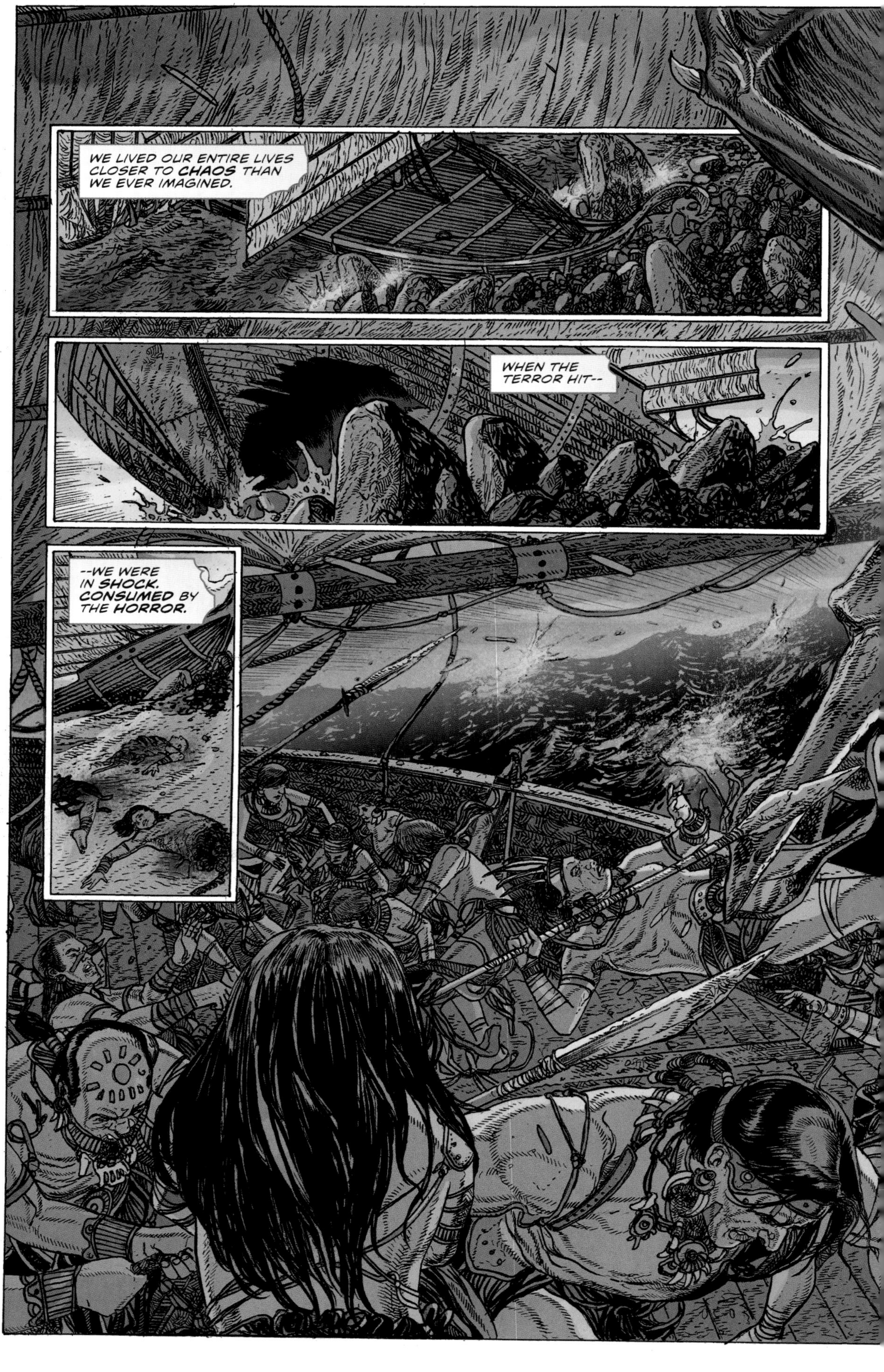
WE LIVED OUR ENTIRE LIVES CLOSER TO CHAOS THAN WE EVER IMAGINED.
WHEN THE TERROR HIT--
--WE WERE IN SHOCK. CONSUMED BY THE HORROR.

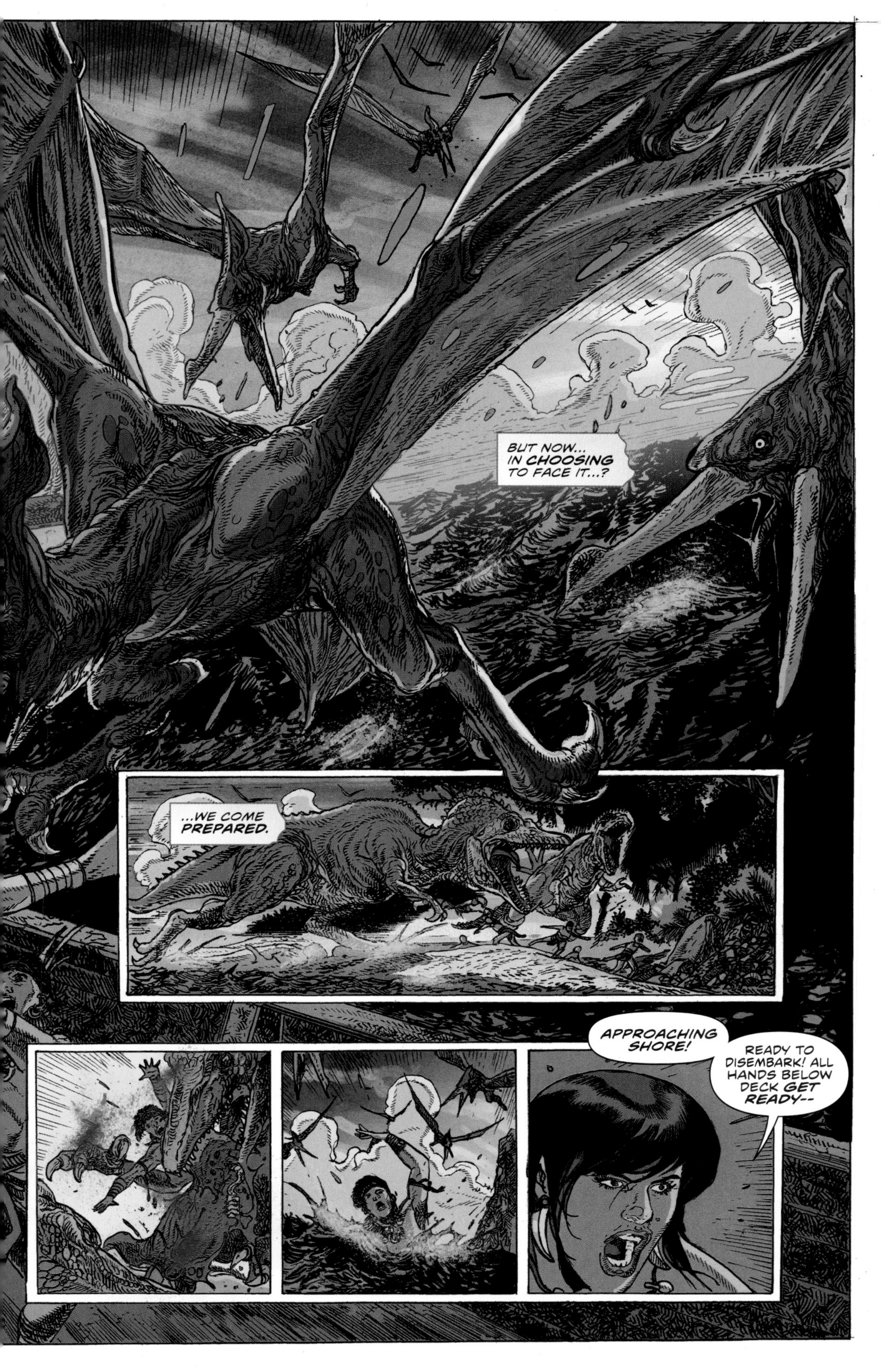
BUT NOW... IN CHOOSING TO FACE IT...?
...WE COME PREPARED.
APPROACHING SHORE!
READY TO DISEMBARK! ALL HANDS BELOW DECK GET READY--

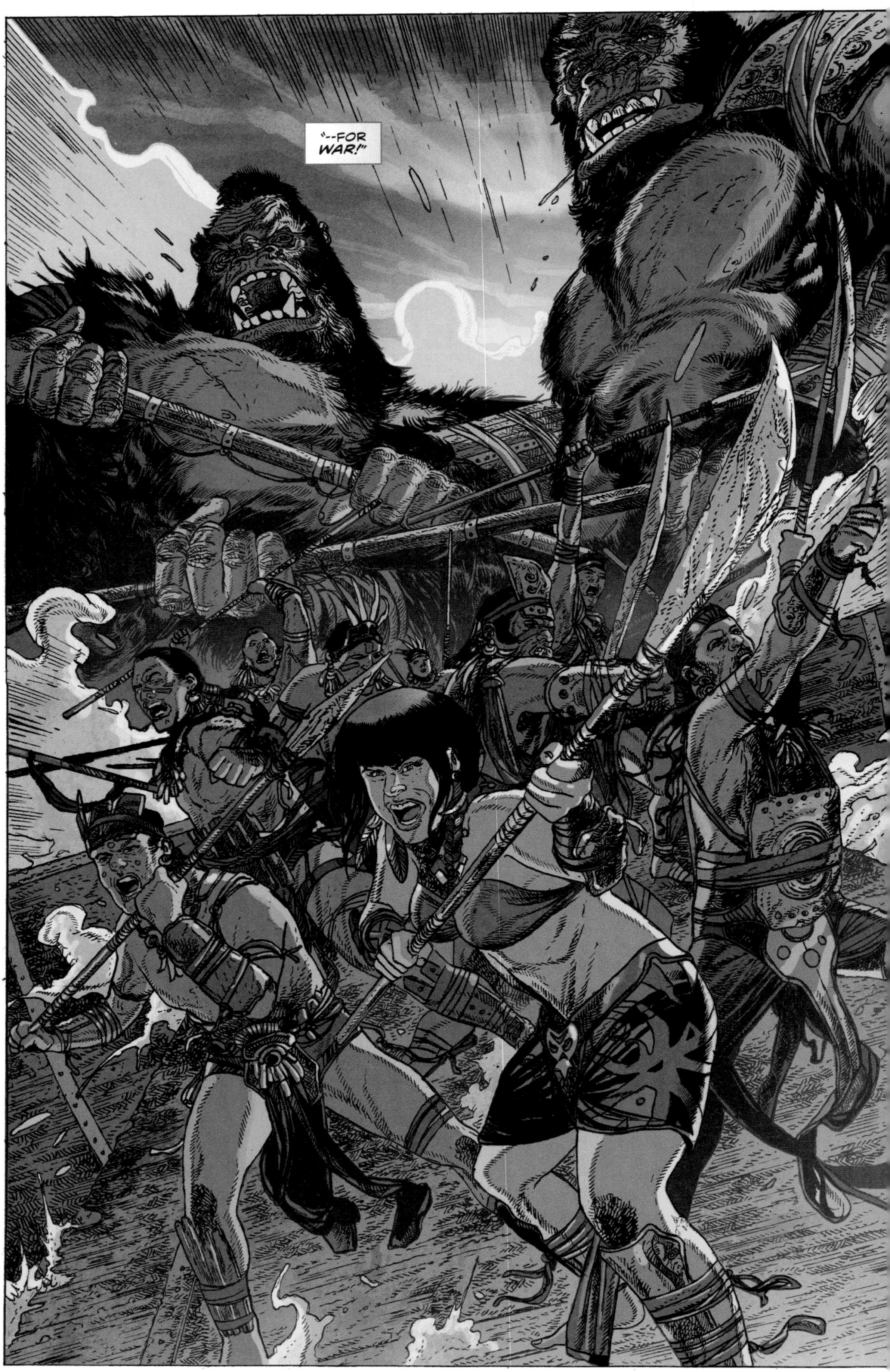
"--FOR WAR!"

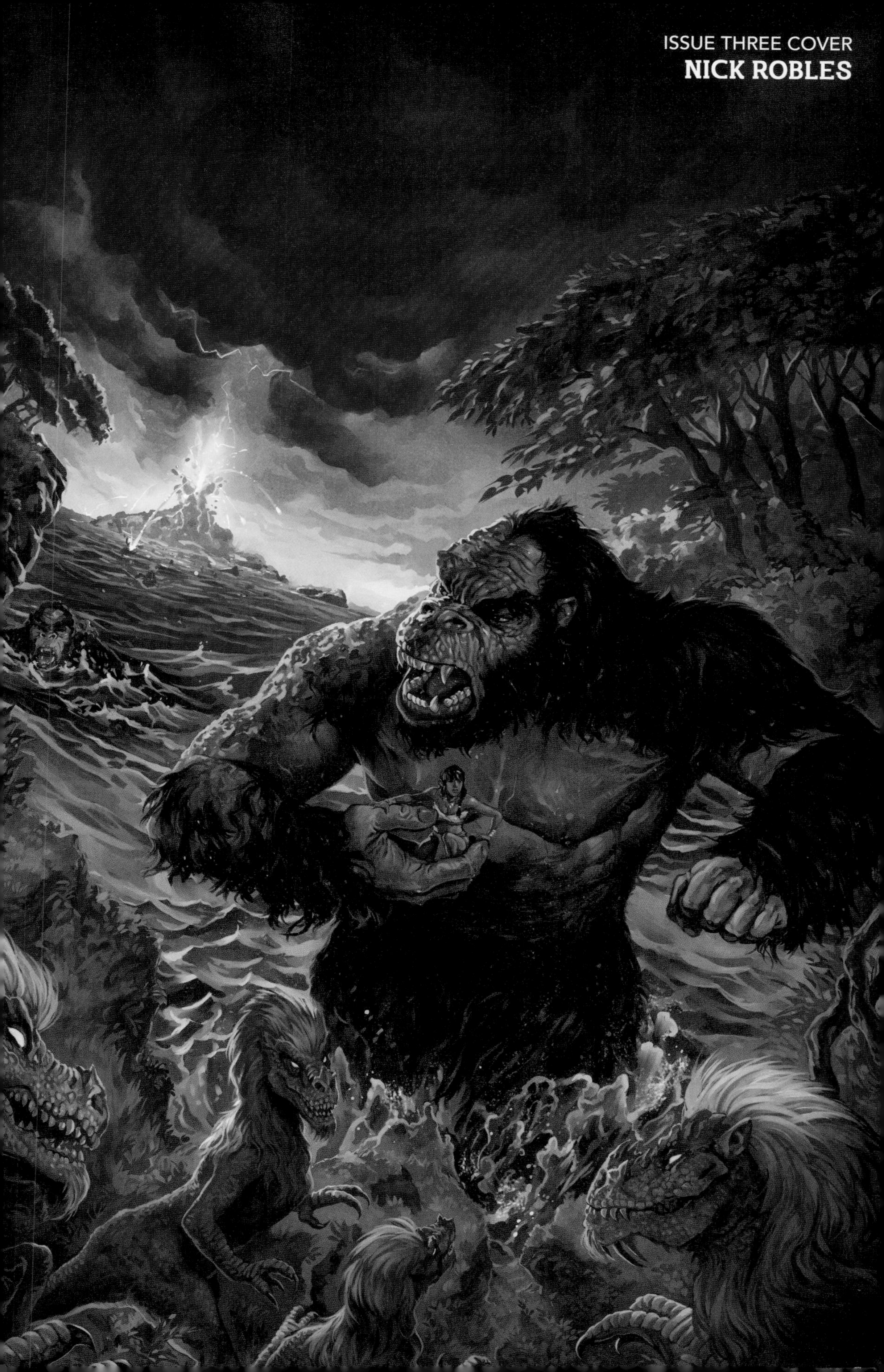

ISSUE THREE COVER
NICK ROBLES

CHAPTER
FOUR

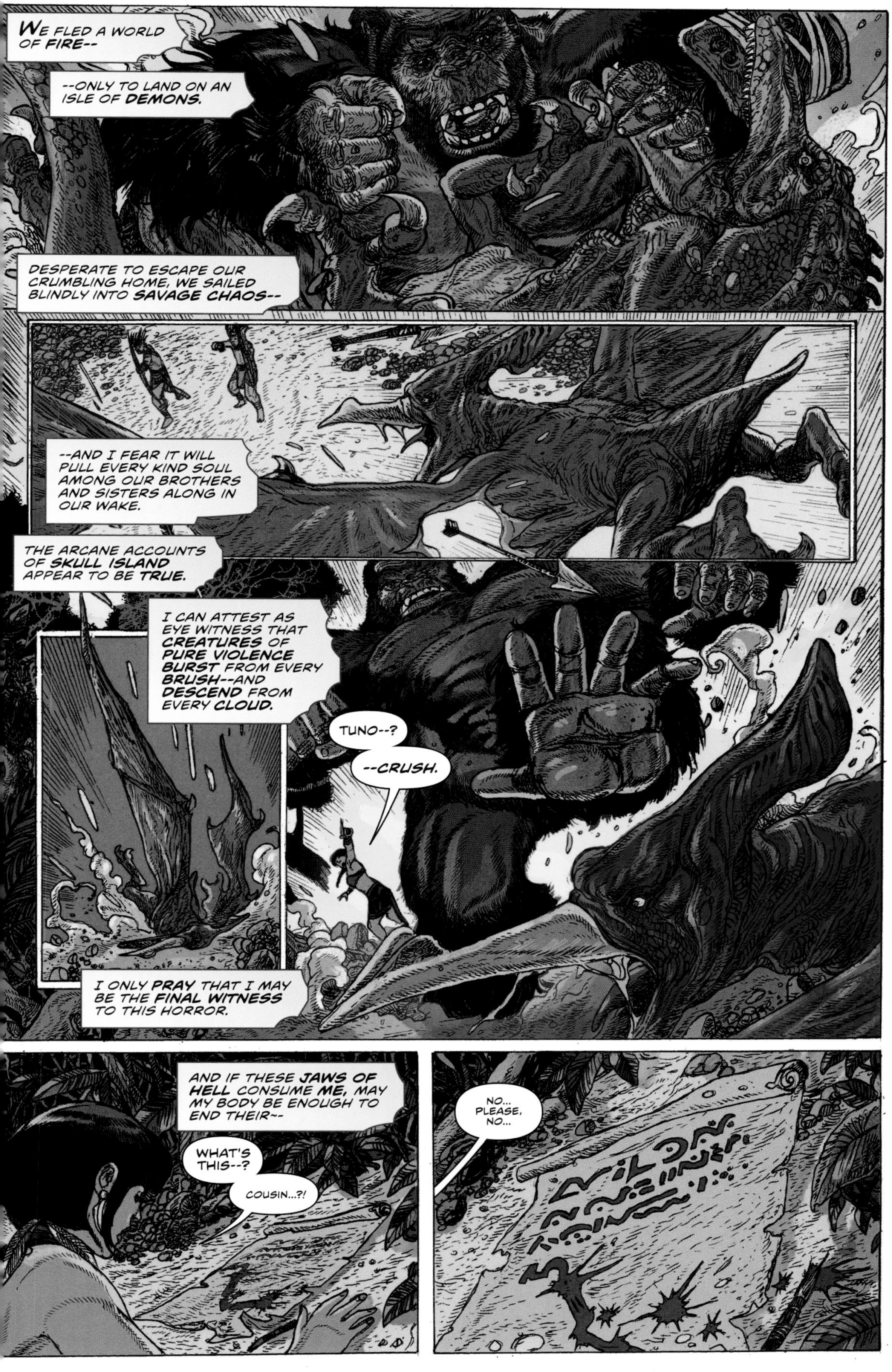
WE FLED A WORLD OF FIRE--
--ONLY TO LAND ON AN ISLE OF DEMONS.
DESPERATE TO ESCAPE OUR CRUMBLING HOME, WE SAILED BLINDLY INTO SAVAGE CHAOS--
--AND I FEAR IT WILL PULL EVERY KIND SOUL AMONG OUR BROTHERS AND SISTERS ALONG IN OUR WAKE.
THE ARCANE ACCOUNTS OF SKULL ISLAND APPEAR TO BE TRUE.
I CAN ATTEST AS EYE WITNESS THAT CREATURES OF PURE VIOLENCE BURST FROM EVERY BRUSH--AND DESCEND FROM EVERY CLOUD.
TUNO--?
--CRUSH.
I ONLY PRAY THAT I MAY BE THE FINAL WITNESS TO THIS HORROR.
AND IF THESE JAWS OF HELL CONSUME ME, MAY MY BODY BE ENOUGH TO END THEIR--
WHAT'S THIS--?
COUSIN...?!
NO... PLEASE, NO...

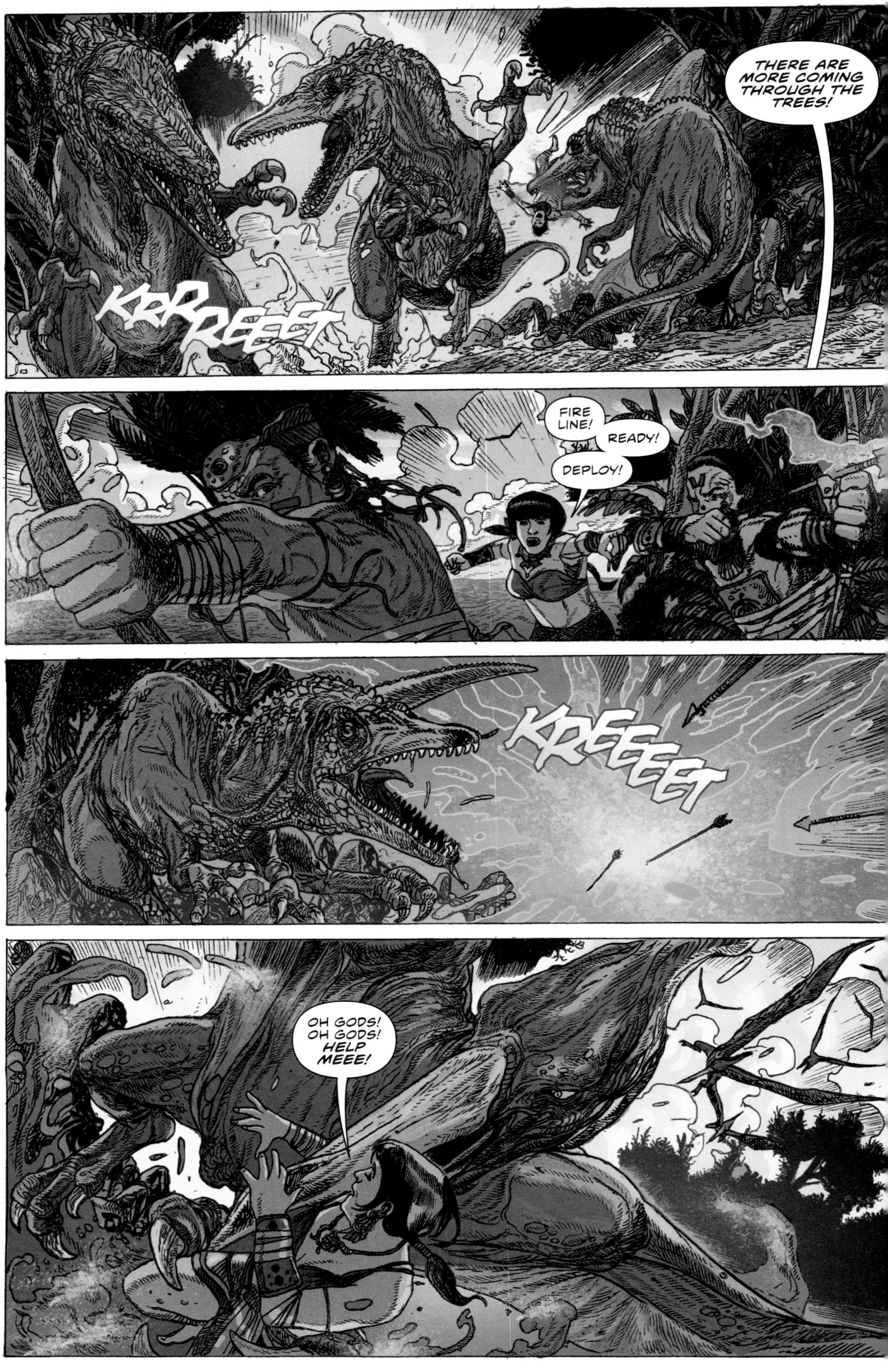
THERE ARE MORE COMING THROUGH THE TREES!
KRRREEEET
FIRE LINE!
READY!
DEPLOY!
KREEEEET
OH GODS! OH GODS! HELP MEEE!

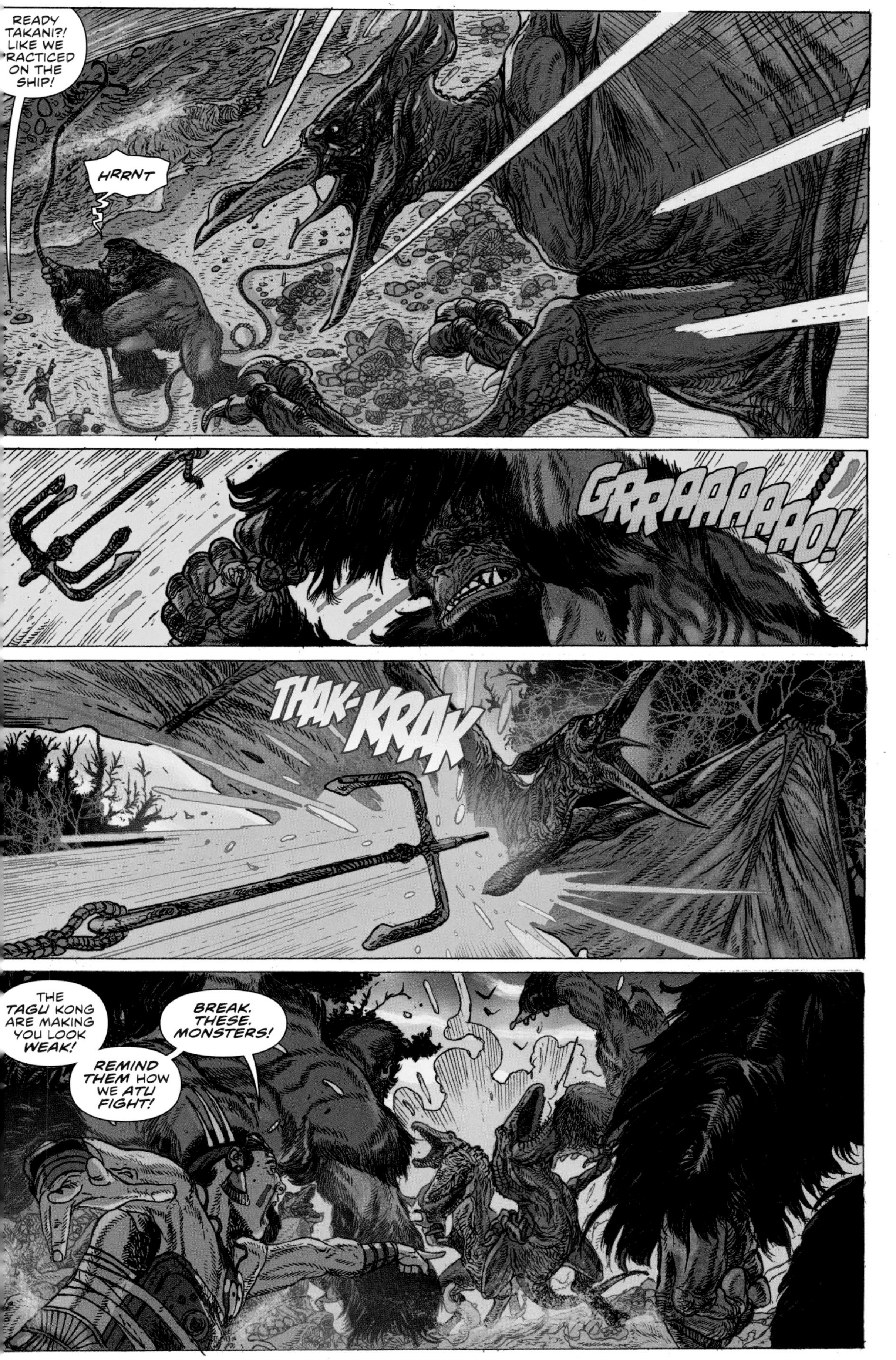

READY TAKANI?! LIKE WE PRACTICED ON THE SHIP!
HRRNT
GRRAAAAAAAO!
THAK-KRAK
THE TAGU KONG ARE MAKING YOU LOOK WEAK!
BREAK. THESE. MONSTERS!
REMIND THEM HOW WE ATU FIGHT!

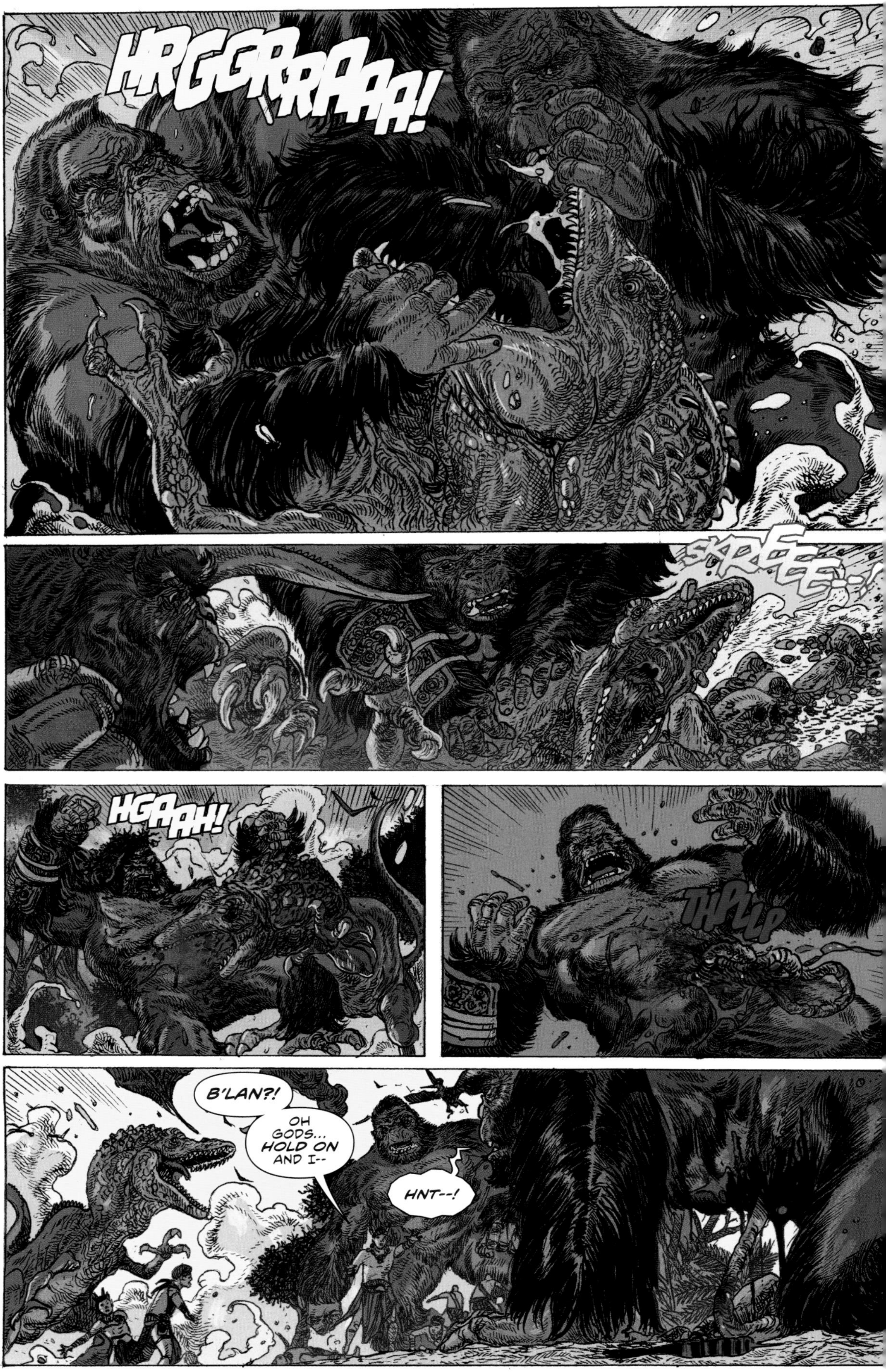
HRGGRRAAAA!
SKREEEE--!
HGAAAH!
THPLLP
B'LAN?!
OH GODS... HOLD ON AND I--
HNT--!

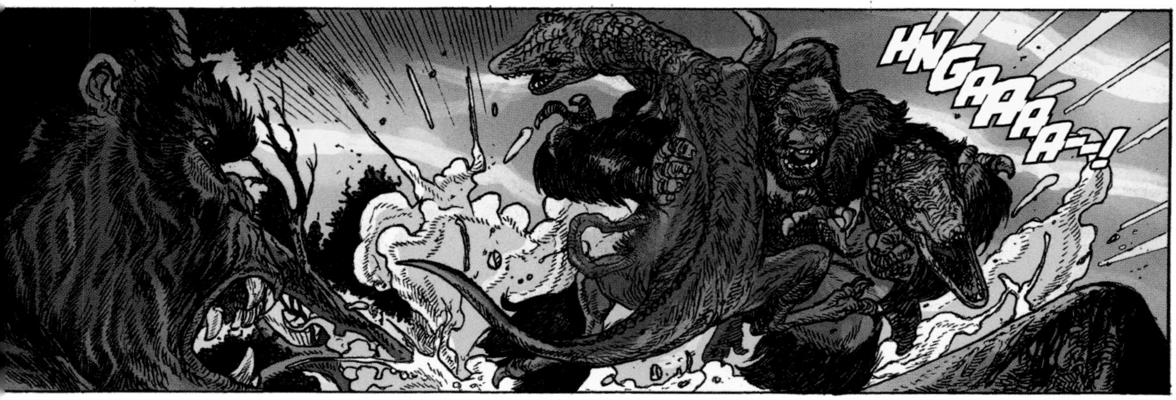
HNGAAAAA~!
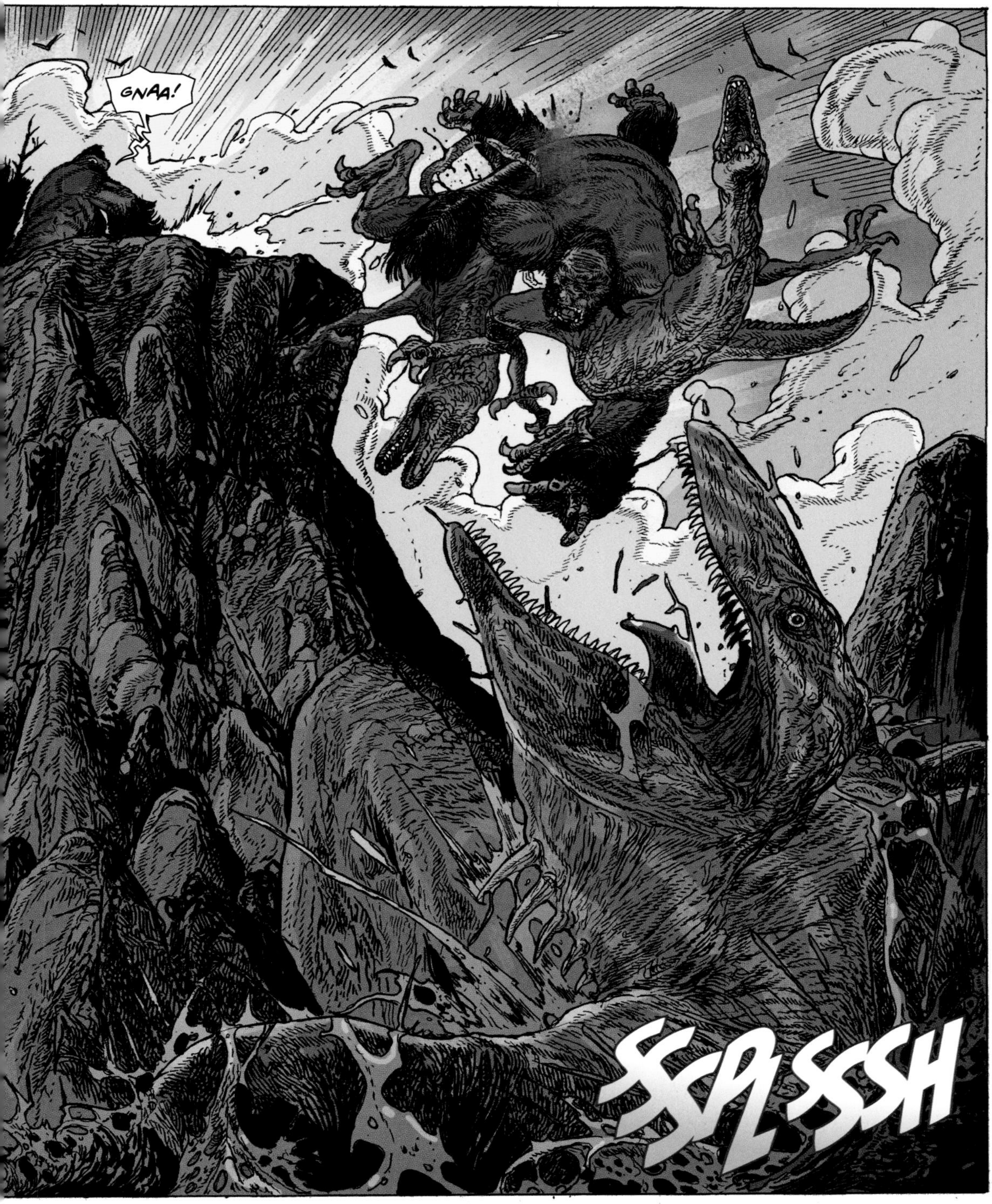
GNAA!
SSPLSSH

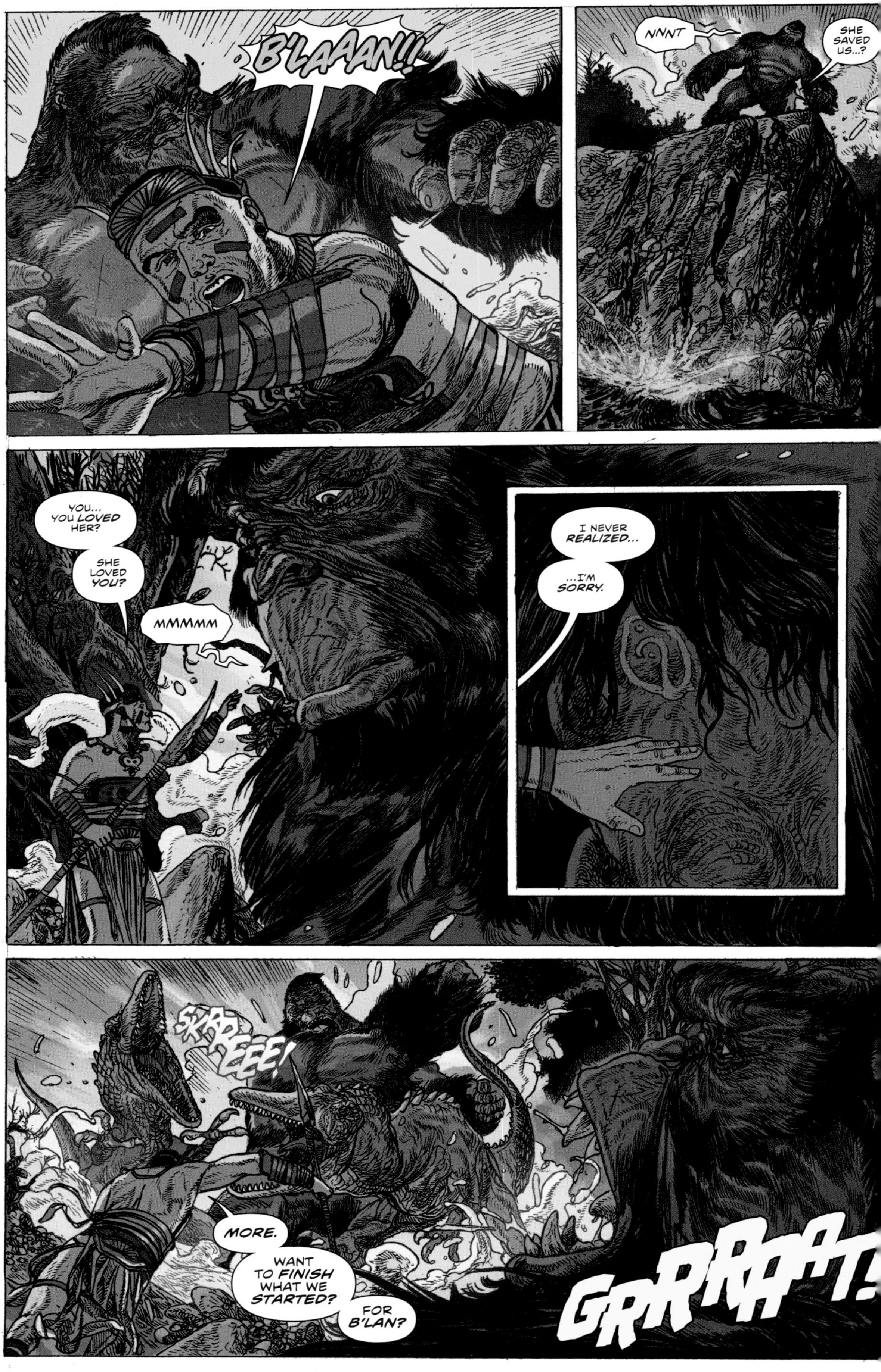
B'LAAAN!!
NNNT
SHE SAVED US...?
YOU... YOU LOVED HER?
SHE LOVED YOU?
MMMMM
I NEVER REALIZED...
...I'M SORRY.
SKREEEE!
MORE.
WANT TO FINISH WHAT WE STARTED?
FOR B'LAN?
GRRRAAT!

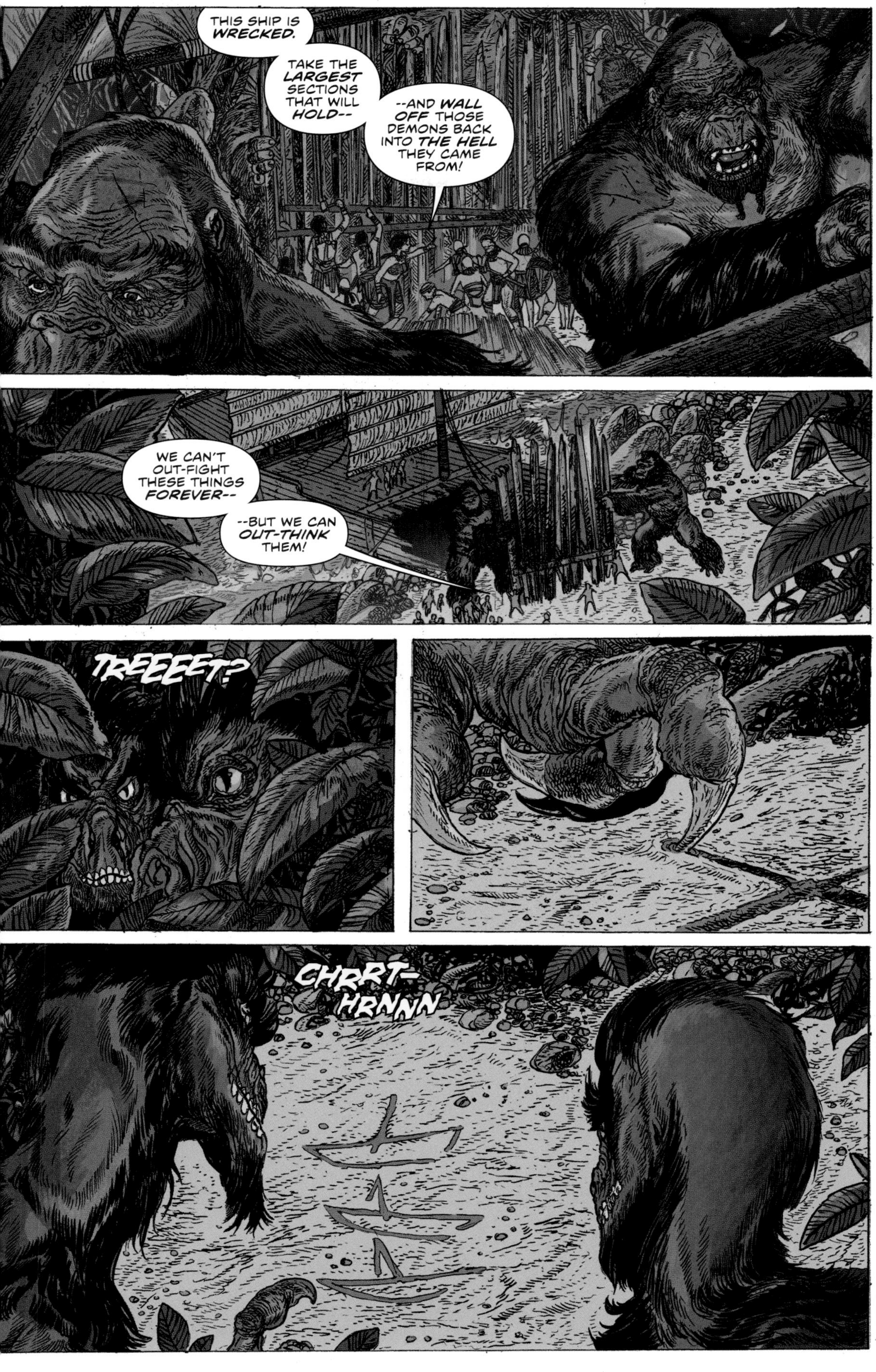
THIS SHIP IS WRECKED.
TAKE THE LARGEST SECTIONS THAT WILL HOLD--
--AND WALL OFF THOSE DEMONS BACK INTO THE HELL THEY CAME FROM!
WE CAN'T OUT-FIGHT THESE THINGS FOREVER--
--BUT WE CAN OUT-THINK THEM!
TREEEEET?
CHRRT-HRNNN

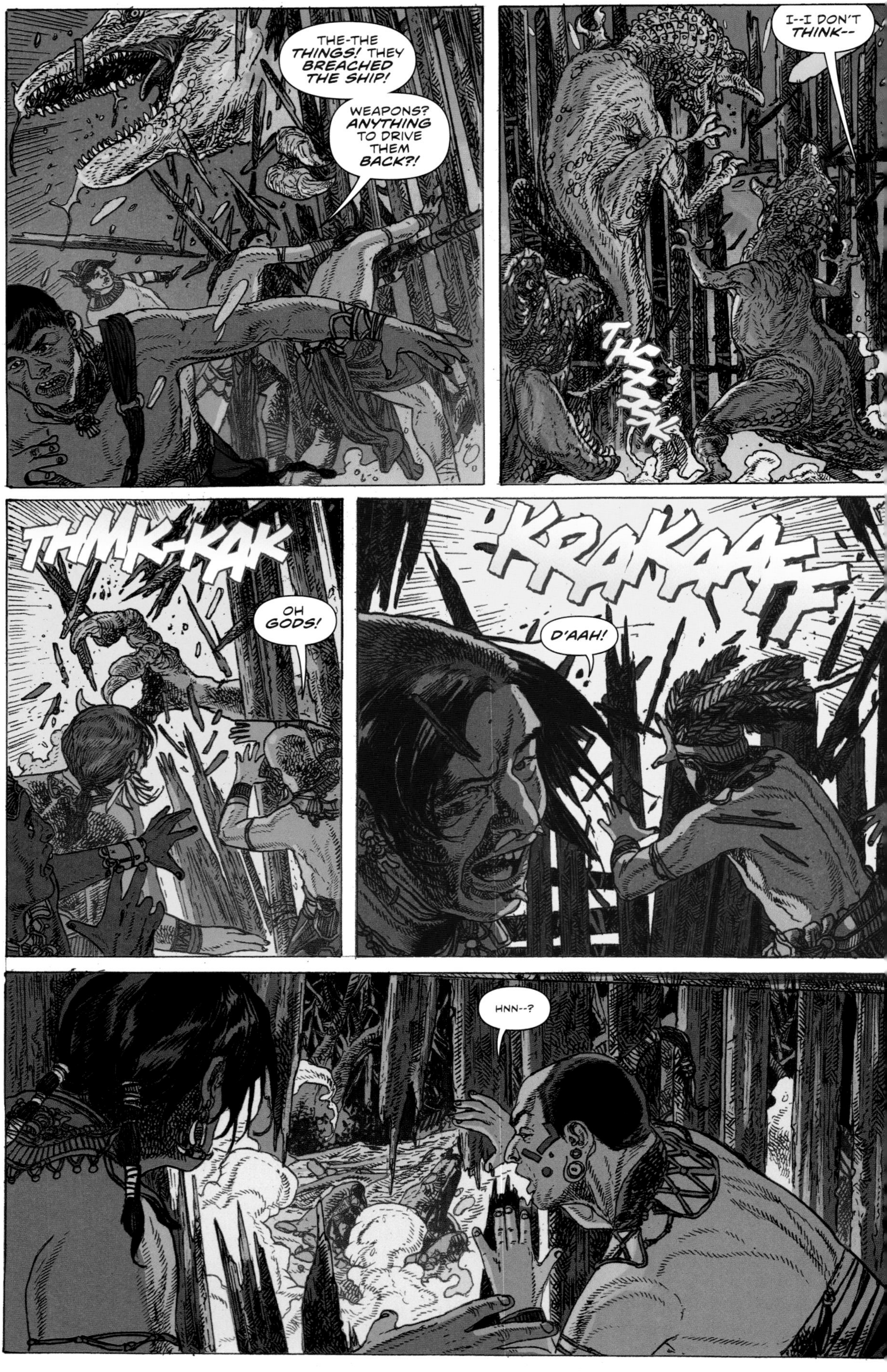
THE-THE THINGS! THEY BREACHED THE SHIP!
WEAPONS? ANYTHING TO DRIVE THEM BACK?!
I--I DON'T THINK--
THMMK
THMK-KAK
OH GODS!
KRAKAAF
D'AAH!
HNN--?

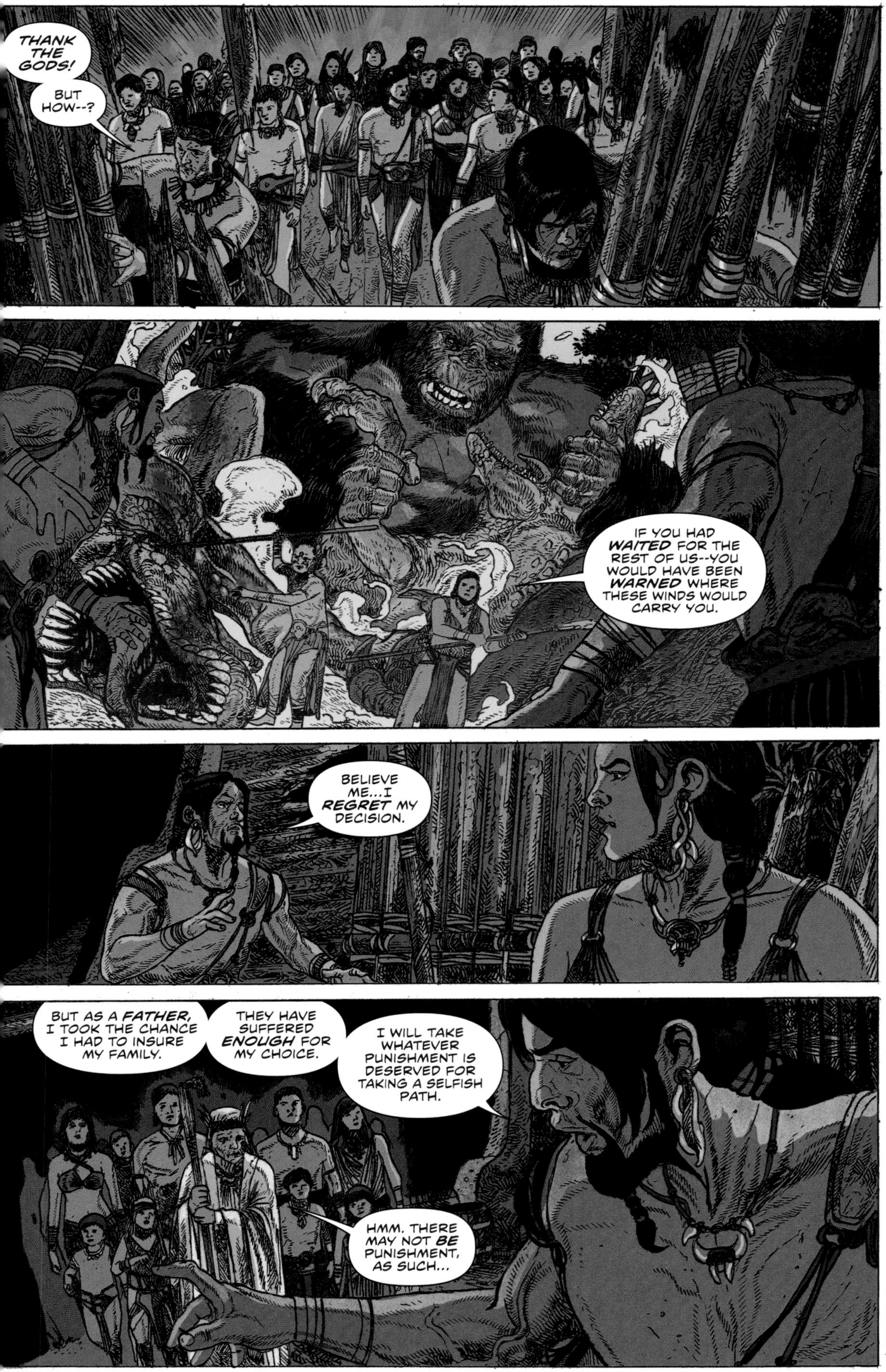
THANK THE GODS!
BUT HOW--?
IF YOU HAD WAITED FOR THE REST OF US--YOU WOULD HAVE BEEN WARNED WHERE THESE WINDS WOULD CARRY YOU.
BELIEVE ME...I REGRET MY DECISION.
BUT AS A FATHER, I TOOK THE CHANCE I HAD TO INSURE MY FAMILY.
THEY HAVE SUFFERED ENOUGH FOR MY CHOICE.
I WILL TAKE WHATEVER PUNISHMENT IS DESERVED FOR TAKING A SELFISH PATH.
HMM. THERE MAY NOT BE PUNISHMENT, AS SUCH...

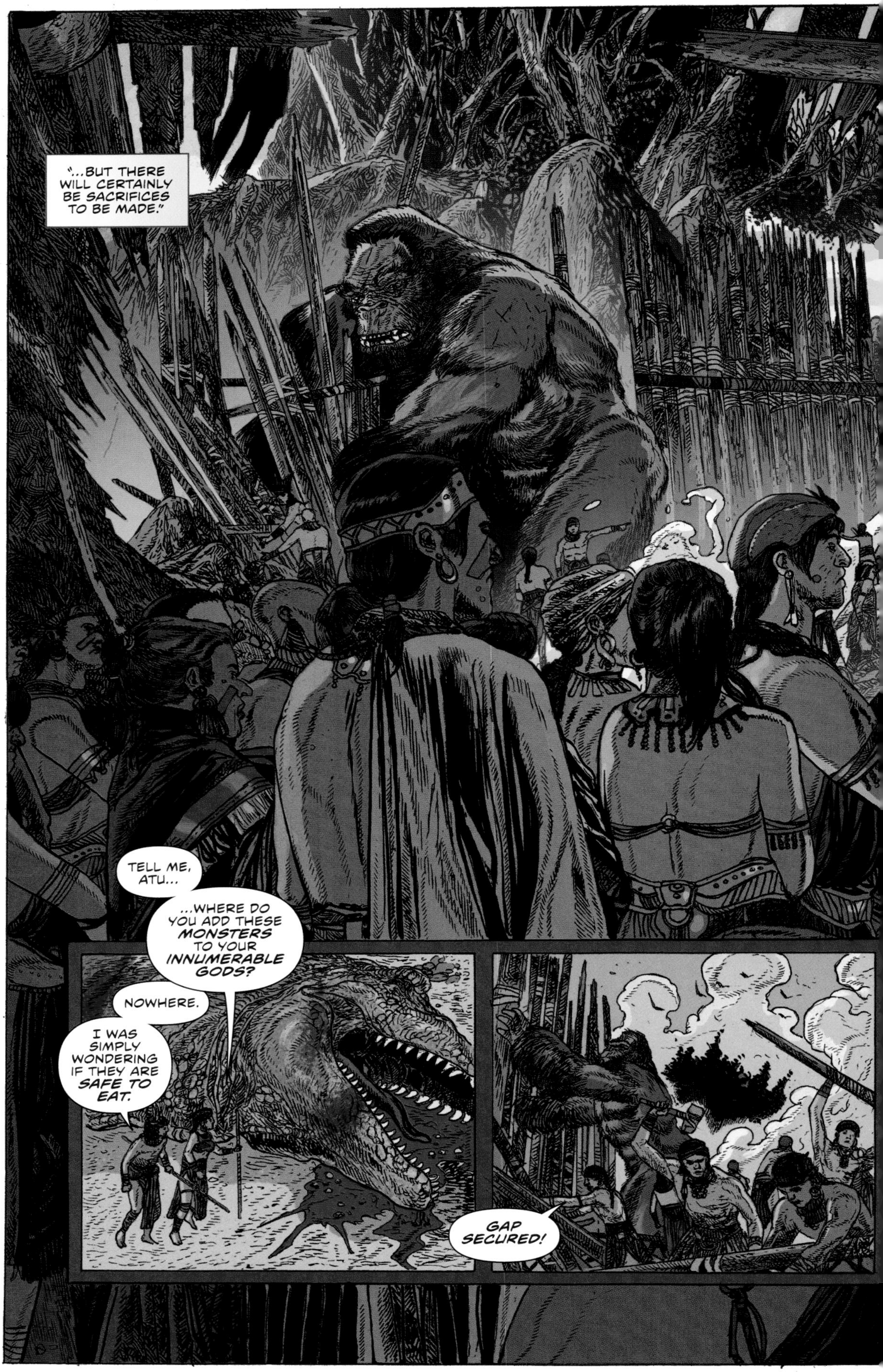
"...BUT THERE WILL CERTAINLY BE SACRIFICES TO BE MADE."
TELL ME, ATU...
...WHERE DO YOU ADD THESE *MONSTERS* TO YOUR *INNUMERABLE GODS?*
NOWHERE.
I WAS SIMPLY WONDERING IF THEY ARE *SAFE TO EAT.*
GAP SECURED!

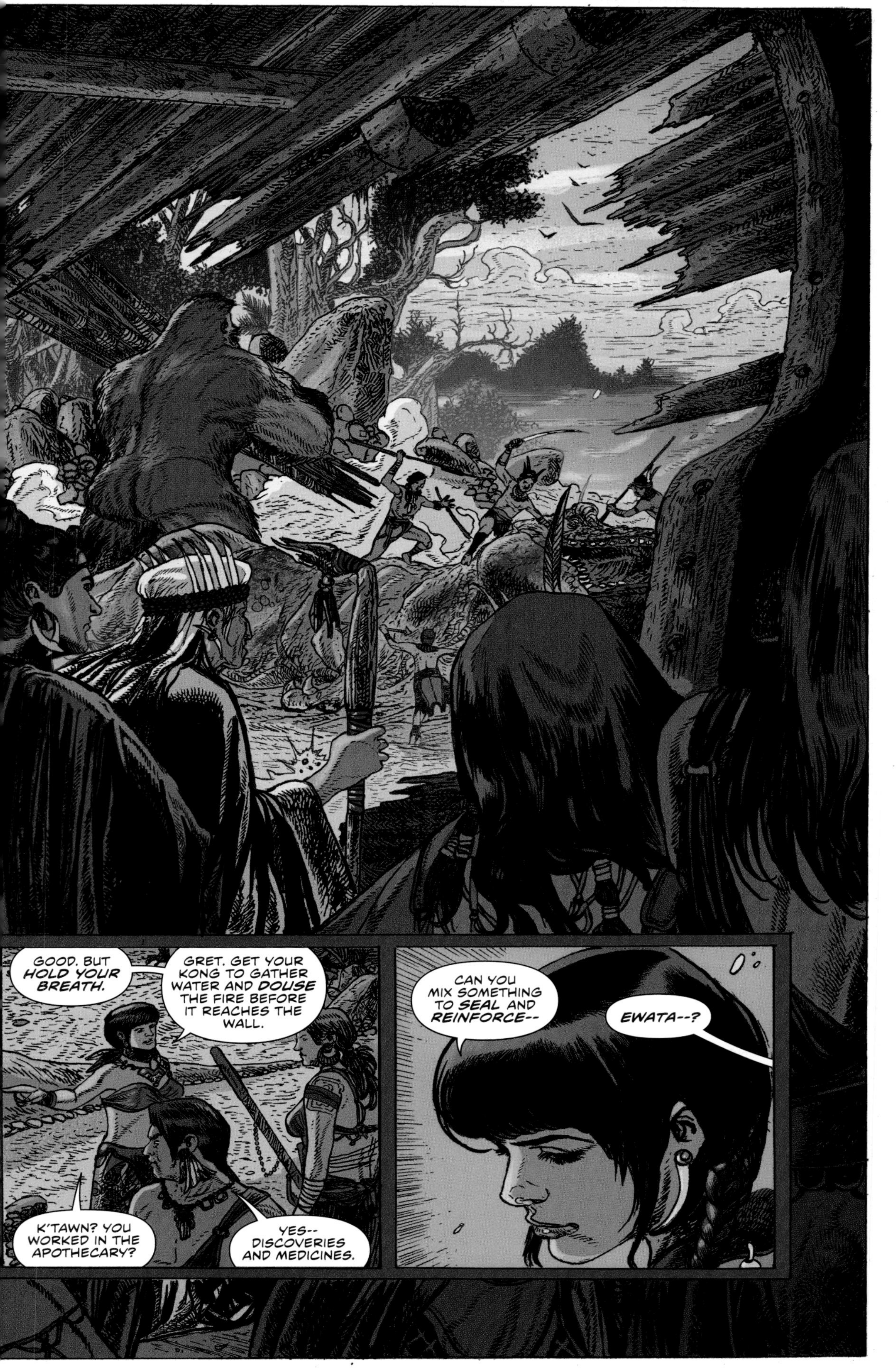

GOOD. BUT *HOLD YOUR BREATH.*
GRET. GET YOUR KONG TO GATHER WATER AND *DOUSE* THE FIRE BEFORE IT REACHES THE WALL.
K'TAWN? YOU WORKED IN THE APOTHECARY?
YES-- DISCOVERIES AND MEDICINES.
CAN YOU MIX SOMETHING TO *SEAL* AND *REINFORCE*--
EWATA--?

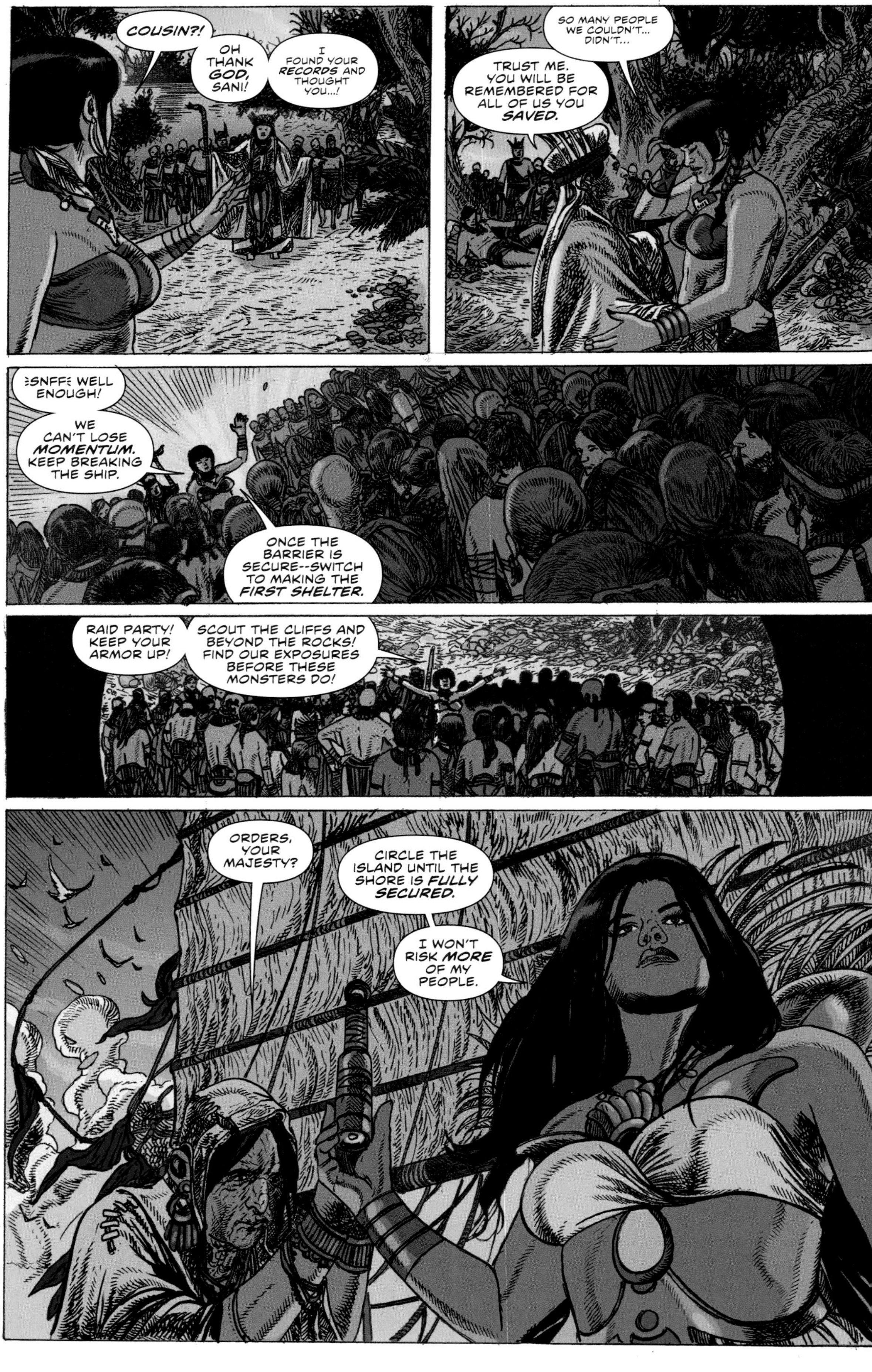
COUSIN?!
OH THANK GOD, SANI!
I FOUND YOUR RECORDS AND THOUGHT YOU...!
SO MANY PEOPLE WE COULDN'T... DIDN'T...
TRUST ME. YOU WILL BE REMEMBERED FOR ALL OF US YOU SAVED.
SNFF WELL ENOUGH!
WE CAN'T LOSE MOMENTUM. KEEP BREAKING THE SHIP.
ONCE THE BARRIER IS SECURE--SWITCH TO MAKING THE FIRST SHELTER.
RAID PARTY! KEEP YOUR ARMOR UP!
SCOUT THE CLIFFS AND BEYOND THE ROCKS! FIND OUR EXPOSURES BEFORE THESE MONSTERS DO!
ORDERS, YOUR MAJESTY?
CIRCLE THE ISLAND UNTIL THE SHORE IS FULLY SECURED.
I WON'T RISK MORE OF MY PEOPLE.

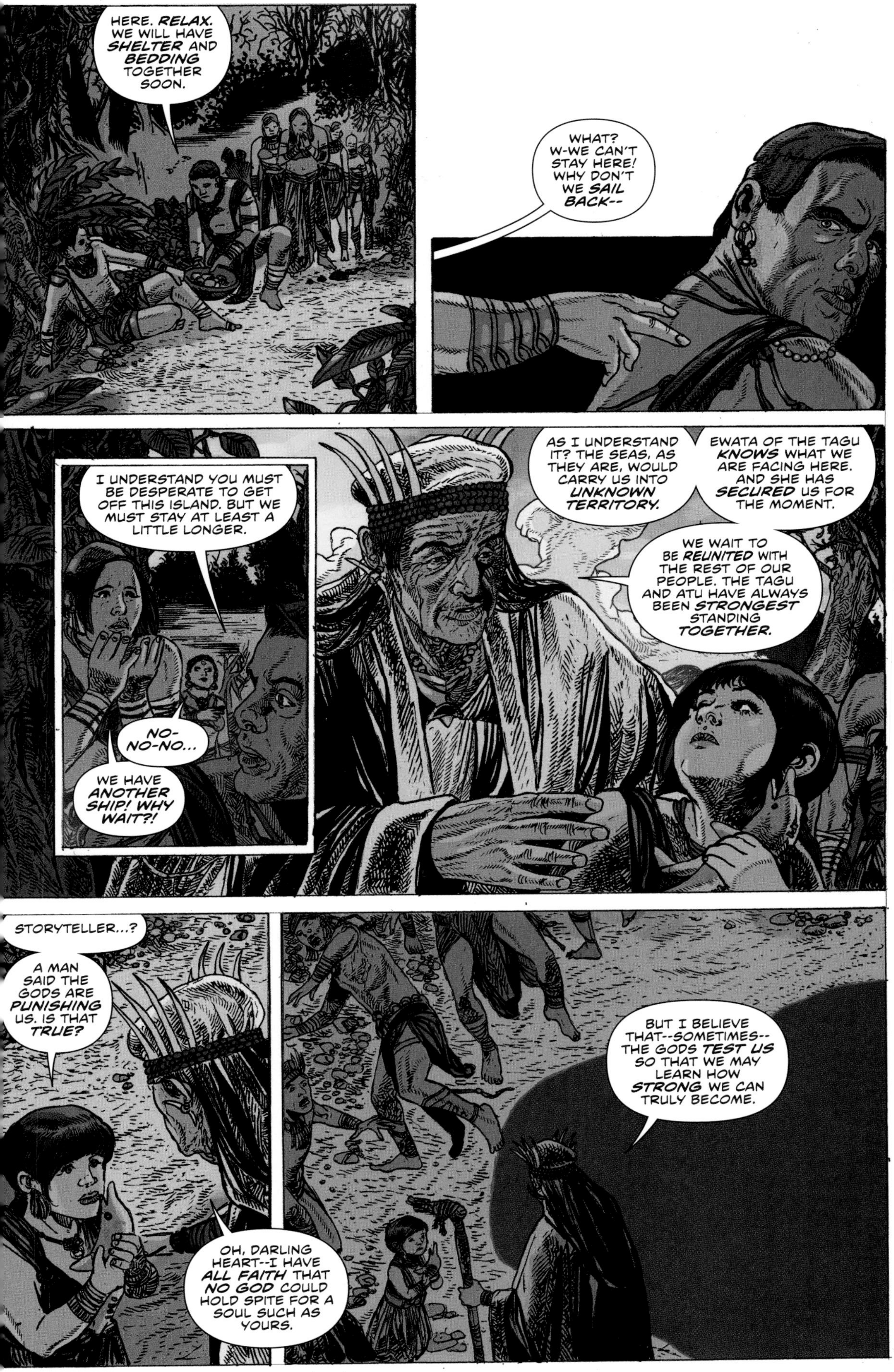
HERE. RELAX. WE WILL HAVE SHELTER AND BEDDING TOGETHER SOON.
WHAT? W-WE CAN'T STAY HERE! WHY DON'T WE SAIL BACK--
I UNDERSTAND YOU MUST BE DESPERATE TO GET OFF THIS ISLAND. BUT WE MUST STAY AT LEAST A LITTLE LONGER.
NO-NO-NO...
WE HAVE ANOTHER SHIP! WHY WAIT?!
AS I UNDERSTAND IT? THE SEAS, AS THEY ARE, WOULD CARRY US INTO UNKNOWN TERRITORY.
EWATA OF THE TAGU KNOWS WHAT WE ARE FACING HERE. AND SHE HAS SECURED US FOR THE MOMENT.
WE WAIT TO BE REUNITED WITH THE REST OF OUR PEOPLE. THE TAGU AND ATU HAVE ALWAYS BEEN STRONGEST STANDING TOGETHER.
STORYTELLER...?
A MAN SAID THE GODS ARE PUNISHING US. IS THAT TRUE?
OH, DARLING HEART--I HAVE ALL FAITH THAT NO GOD COULD HOLD SPITE FOR A SOUL SUCH AS YOURS.
BUT I BELIEVE THAT--SOMETIMES--THE GODS TEST US SO THAT WE MAY LEARN HOW STRONG WE CAN TRULY BECOME.

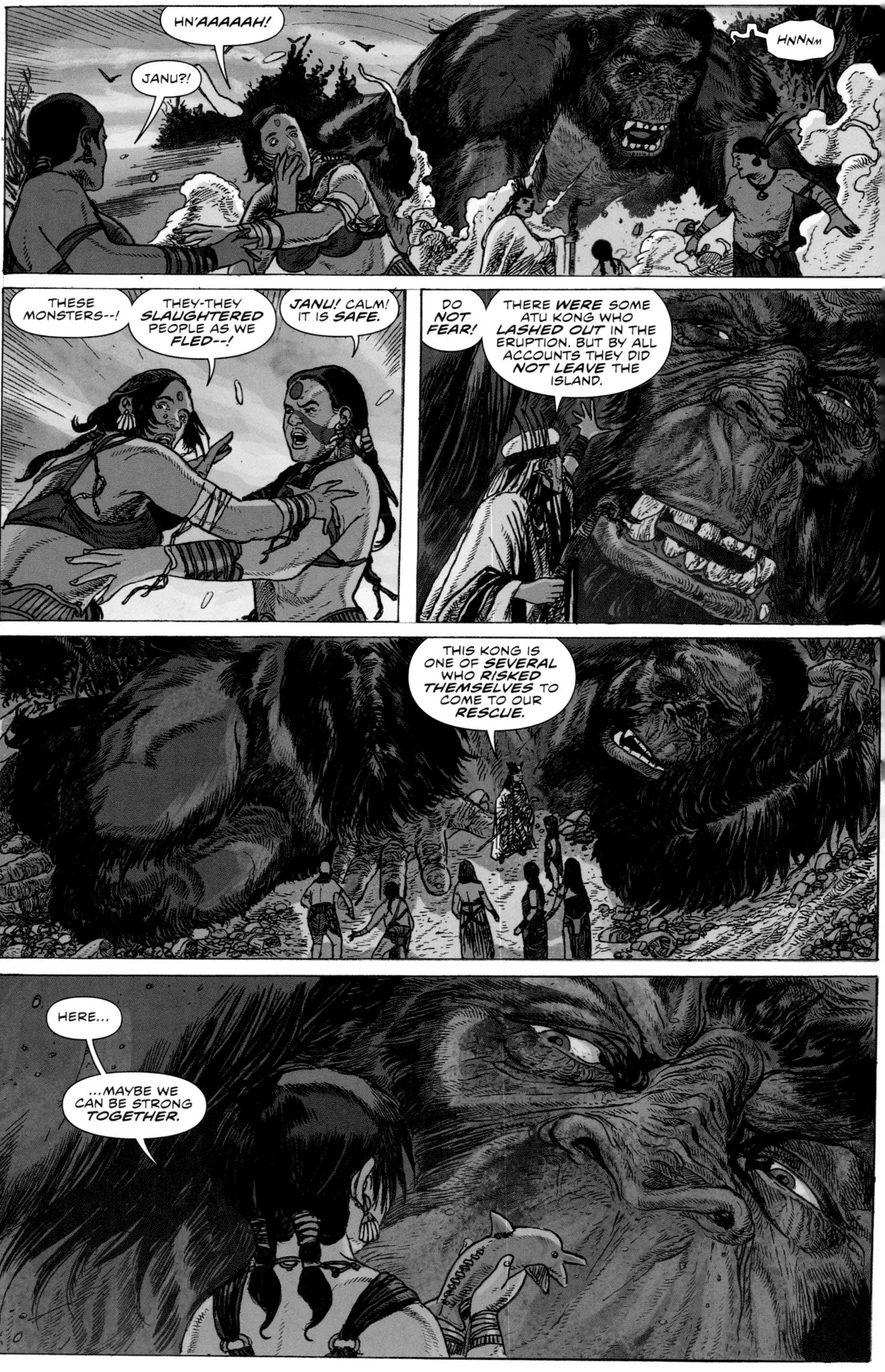
HN'AAAAAH!
JANU?!
HNNNM
THESE MONSTERS--!
THEY-THEY SLAUGHTERED PEOPLE AS WE FLED--!
JANU! CALM! IT IS SAFE.
DO NOT FEAR!
THERE WERE SOME ATU KONG WHO LASHED OUT IN THE ERUPTION. BUT BY ALL ACCOUNTS THEY DID NOT LEAVE THE ISLAND.
THIS KONG IS ONE OF SEVERAL WHO RISKED THEMSELVES TO COME TO OUR RESCUE.
HERE...
...MAYBE WE CAN BE STRONG TOGETHER.

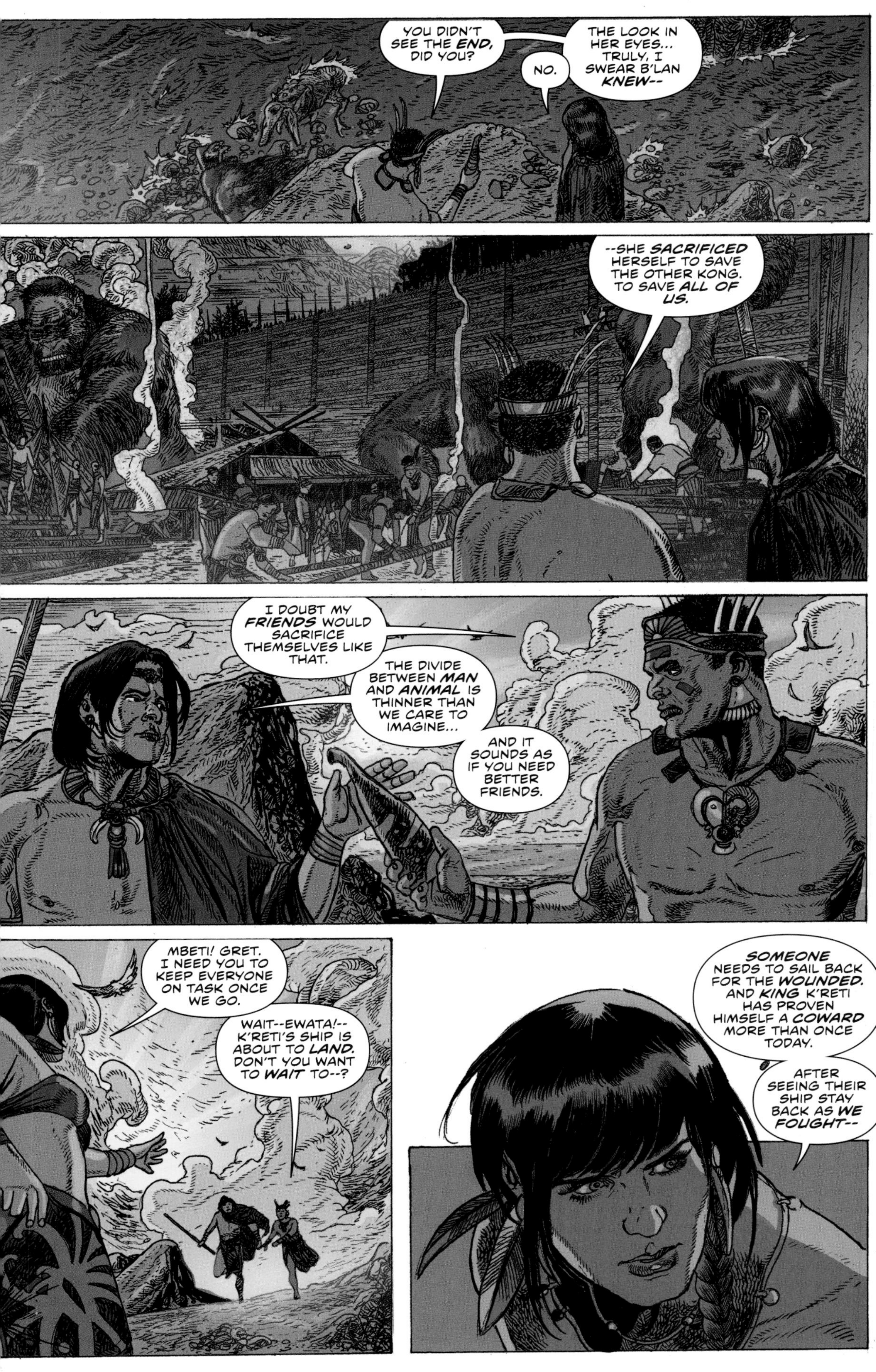

YOU DIDN'T SEE THE END, DID YOU?
NO.
THE LOOK IN HER EYES... TRULY, I SWEAR B'LAN KNEW--
--SHE SACRIFICED HERSELF TO SAVE THE OTHER KONG. TO SAVE ALL OF US.
I DOUBT MY FRIENDS WOULD SACRIFICE THEMSELVES LIKE THAT.
THE DIVIDE BETWEEN MAN AND ANIMAL IS THINNER THAN WE CARE TO IMAGINE...
AND IT SOUNDS AS IF YOU NEED BETTER FRIENDS.
MBETI! GRET. I NEED YOU TO KEEP EVERYONE ON TASK ONCE WE GO.
WAIT--EWATA!--K'RETI'S SHIP IS ABOUT TO LAND. DON'T YOU WANT TO WAIT TO--?
SOMEONE NEEDS TO SAIL BACK FOR THE WOUNDED. AND KING K'RETI HAS PROVEN HIMSELF A COWARD MORE THAN ONCE TODAY.
AFTER SEEING THEIR SHIP STAY BACK AS WE FOUGHT--

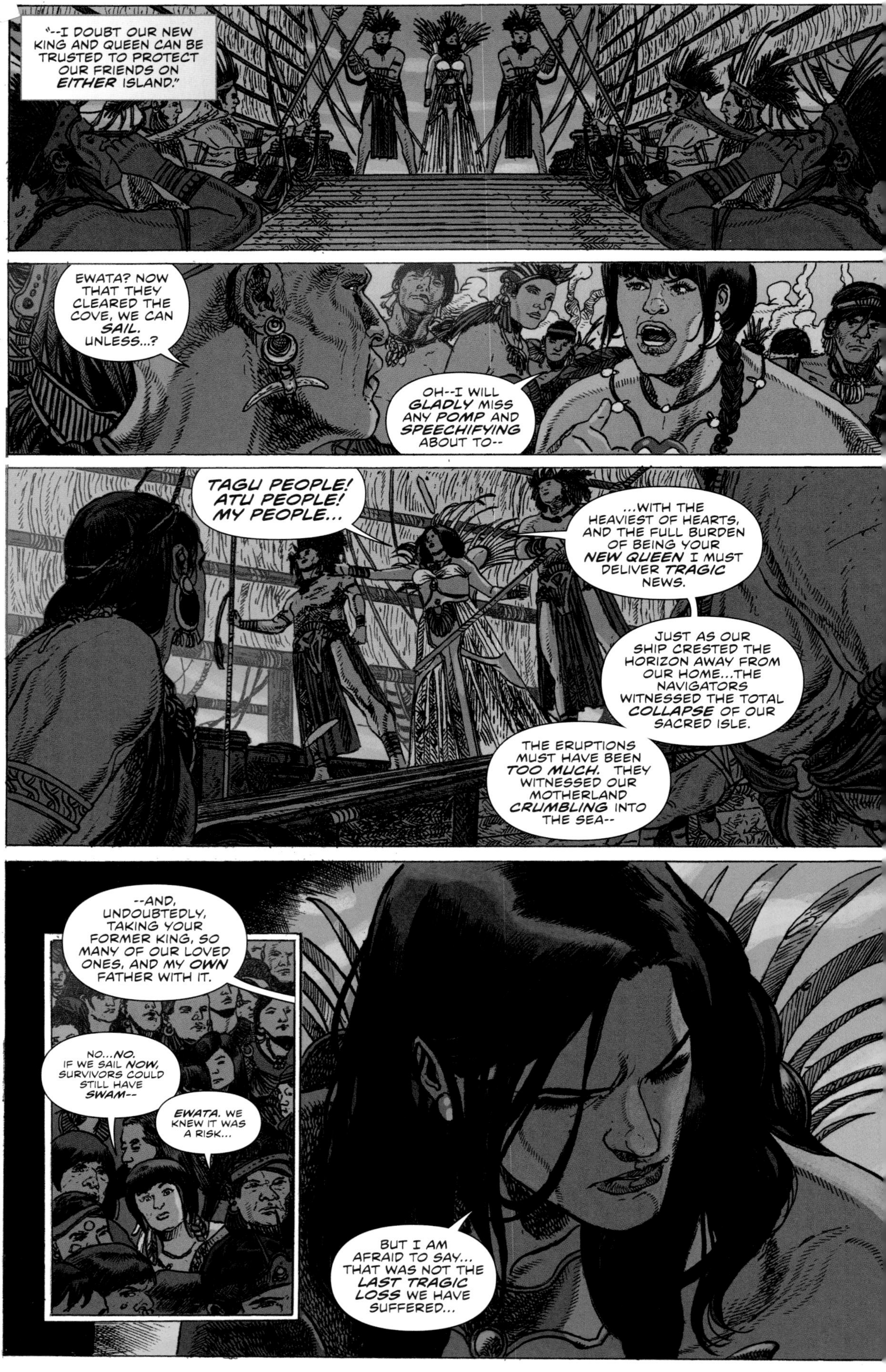
"--I DOUBT OUR NEW KING AND QUEEN CAN BE TRUSTED TO PROTECT OUR FRIENDS ON EITHER ISLAND."
EWATA? NOW THAT THEY CLEARED THE COVE, WE CAN SAIL. UNLESS...?
OH--I WILL GLADLY MISS ANY POMP AND SPEECHIFYING ABOUT TO--
TAGU PEOPLE! ATU PEOPLE! MY PEOPLE...
...WITH THE HEAVIEST OF HEARTS, AND THE FULL BURDEN OF BEING YOUR NEW QUEEN I MUST DELIVER TRAGIC NEWS.
JUST AS OUR SHIP CRESTED THE HORIZON AWAY FROM OUR HOME...THE NAVIGATORS WITNESSED THE TOTAL COLLAPSE OF OUR SACRED ISLE.
THE ERUPTIONS MUST HAVE BEEN TOO MUCH. THEY WITNESSED OUR MOTHERLAND CRUMBLING INTO THE SEA--
--AND, UNDOUBTEDLY, TAKING YOUR FORMER KING, SO MANY OF OUR LOVED ONES, AND MY OWN FATHER WITH IT.
NO...NO. IF WE SAIL NOW, SURVIVORS COULD STILL HAVE SWAM--
EWATA. WE KNEW IT WAS A RISK...
BUT I AM AFRAID TO SAY... THAT WAS NOT THE LAST TRAGIC LOSS WE HAVE SUFFERED...

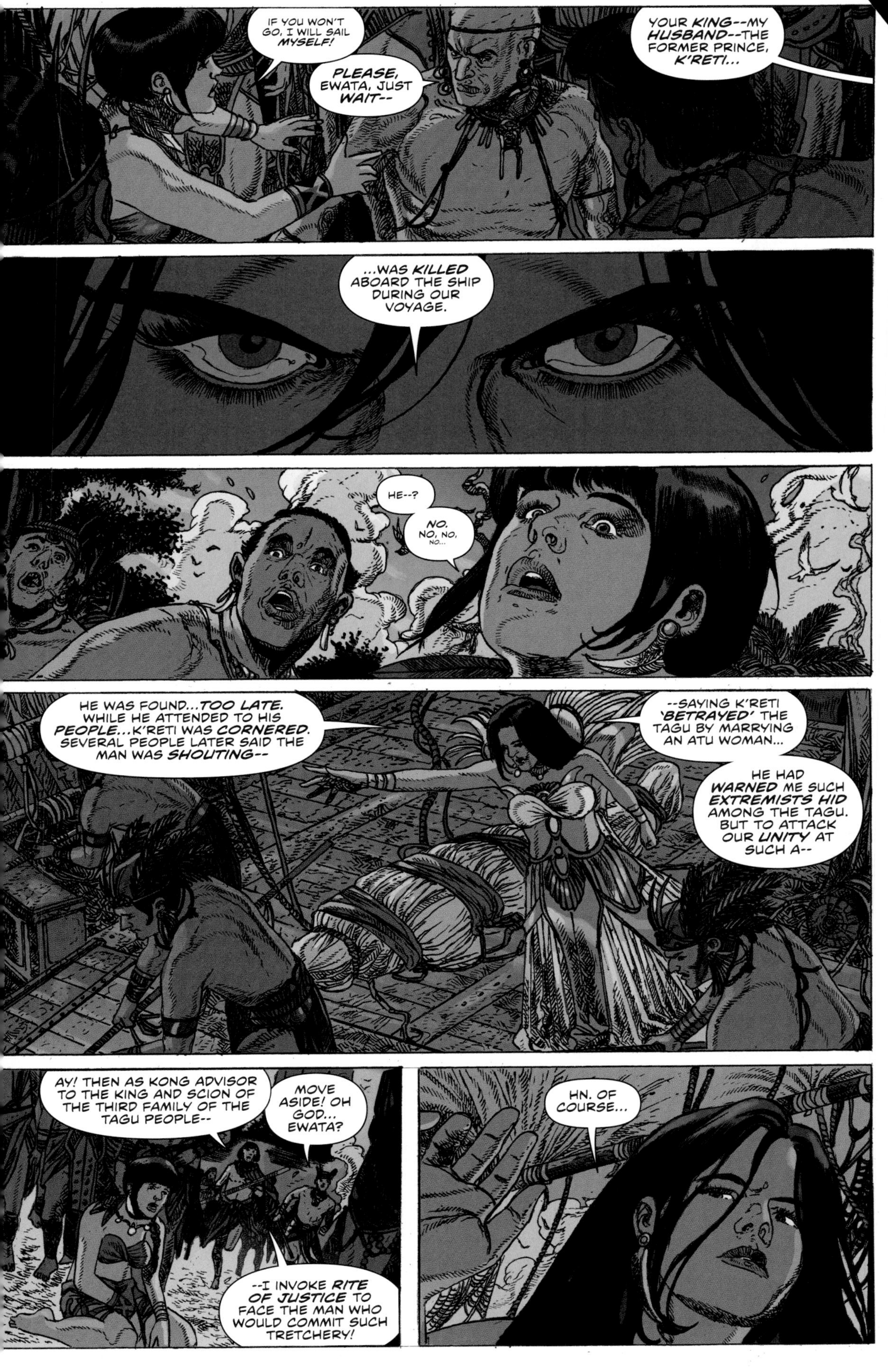
IF YOU WON'T GO, I WILL SAIL MYSELF!
PLEASE, EWATA, JUST WAIT--
YOUR KING--MY HUSBAND--THE FORMER PRINCE, K'RETI...
...WAS KILLED ABOARD THE SHIP DURING OUR VOYAGE.
HE--?
NO. NO, NO, NO...
HE WAS FOUND...TOO LATE. WHILE HE ATTENDED TO HIS PEOPLE...K'RETI WAS CORNERED. SEVERAL PEOPLE LATER SAID THE MAN WAS SHOUTING--
--SAYING K'RETI 'BETRAYED' THE TAGU BY MARRYING AN ATU WOMAN...
HE HAD WARNED ME SUCH EXTREMISTS HID AMONG THE TAGU. BUT TO ATTACK OUR UNITY AT SUCH A--
AY! THEN AS KONG ADVISOR TO THE KING AND SCION OF THE THIRD FAMILY OF THE TAGU PEOPLE--
MOVE ASIDE! OH GOD... EWATA?
--I INVOKE RITE OF JUSTICE TO FACE THE MAN WHO WOULD COMMIT SUCH TRETCHERY!
HN. OF COURSE...

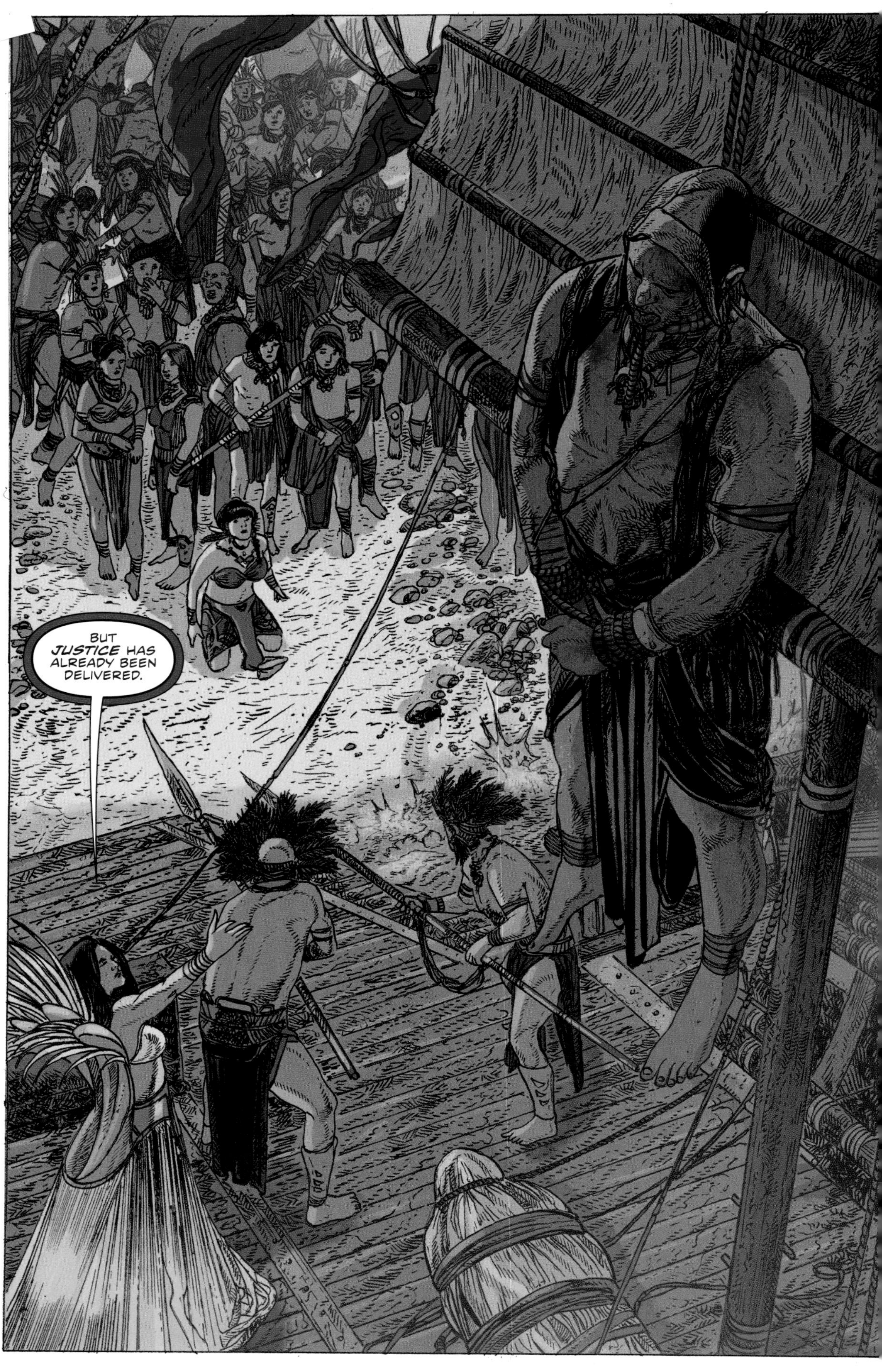
BUT JUSTICE HAS ALREADY BEEN DELIVERED.

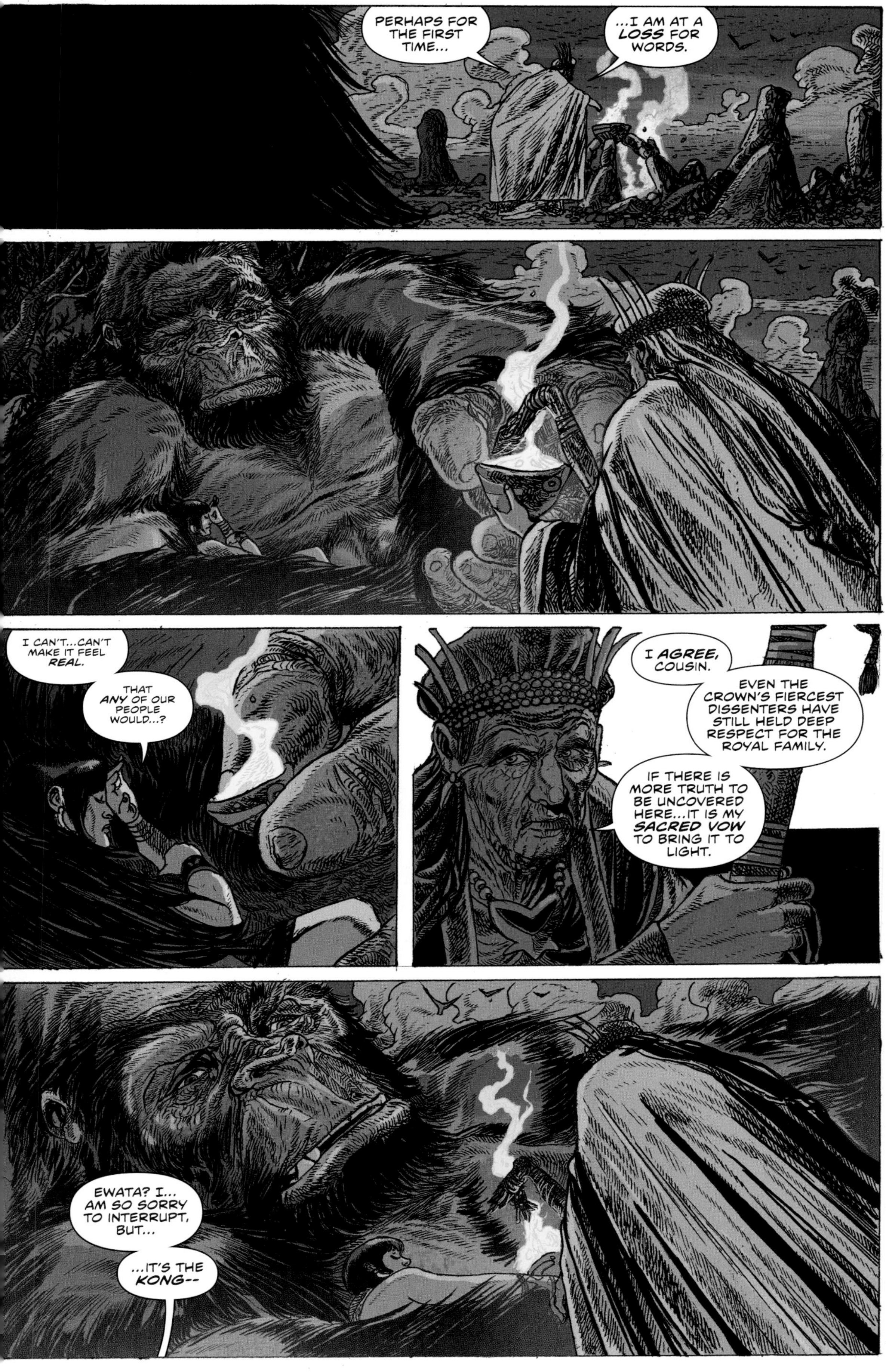
PERHAPS FOR THE FIRST TIME...
...I AM AT A *LOSS* FOR WORDS.
I CAN'T...CAN'T MAKE IT FEEL *REAL.*
THAT *ANY* OF OUR PEOPLE WOULD...?
I *AGREE,* COUSIN.
EVEN THE CROWN'S FIERCEST DISSENTERS HAVE STILL HELD DEEP RESPECT FOR THE ROYAL FAMILY.
IF THERE IS MORE TRUTH TO BE UNCOVERED HERE...IT IS MY *SACRED VOW* TO BRING IT TO LIGHT.
EWATA? I... AM SO SORRY TO INTERRUPT, BUT...
...IT'S THE *KONG--*

HNGGAAA

THEY SEEM... *SCARED*?

ANANI! YOU TRY THE AROMA-TRIGGERS?

YES. BUT *THIS* IS AS CALM AS THEY GOT.

≶SNFF≶ ≶SFFF≶

HRGGGRRR!

SOMETHING IS OUT THERE?

EWATA? WHAT DO YOU *ADVISE*?

THE *FIRST* CREATURES HERE JUST *ATTACKED*. BUT NOW...IF THERE ARE SOME *WAITING--WATCHING US...*?

...MAYBE WE LET THE KONG *KEEP* AT THIS.

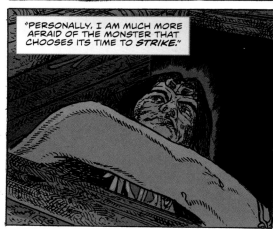

"PERSONALLY, I AM MUCH MORE AFRAID OF THE MONSTER THAT CHOOSES ITS TIME TO *STRIKE*."

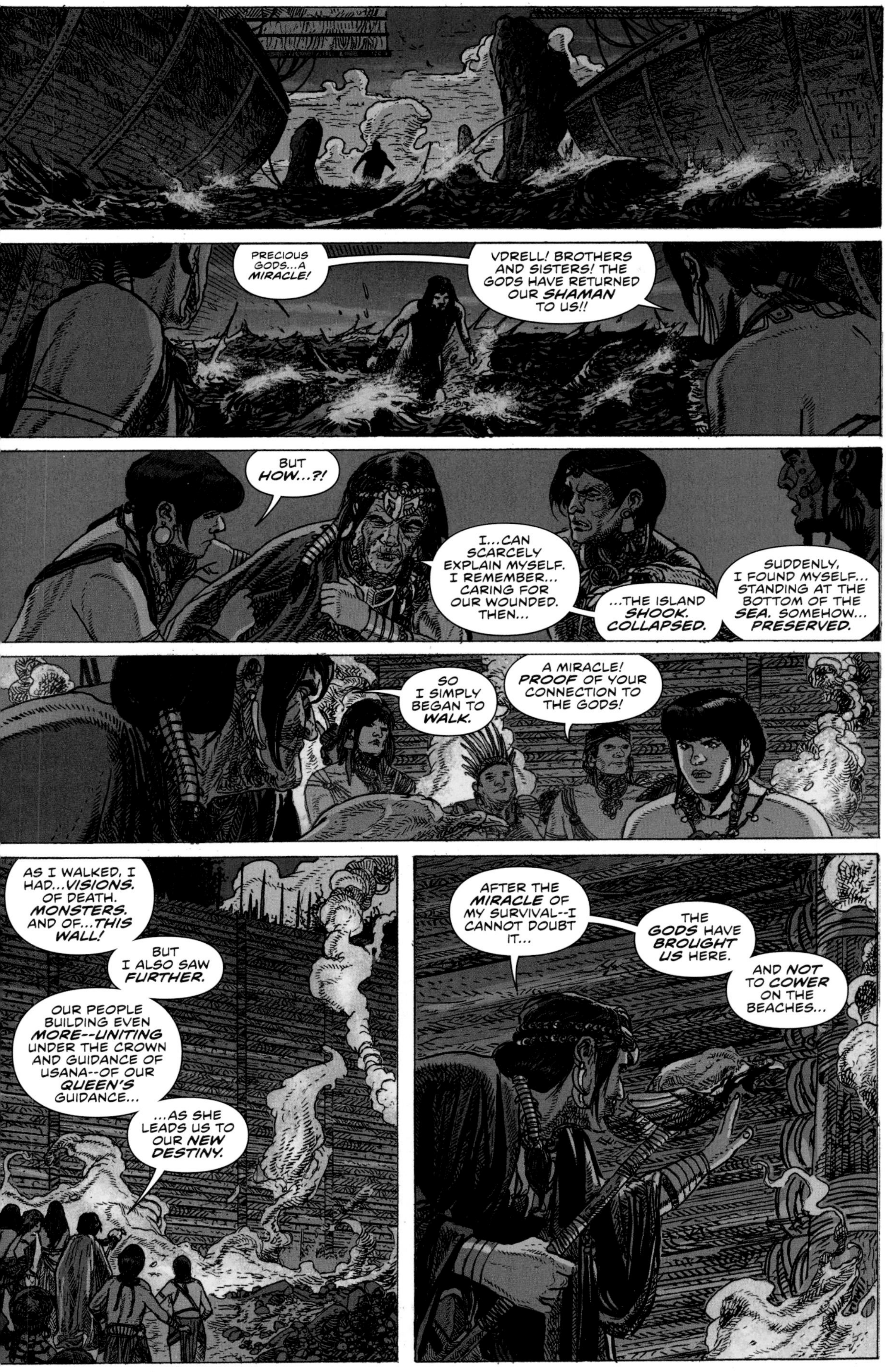

PRECIOUS GODS...A MIRACLE!
VDRELL! BROTHERS AND SISTERS! THE GODS HAVE RETURNED OUR SHAMAN TO US!!
BUT HOW...?!
I...CAN SCARCELY EXPLAIN MYSELF. I REMEMBER... CARING FOR OUR WOUNDED. THEN...
...THE ISLAND SHOOK. COLLAPSED.
SUDDENLY, I FOUND MYSELF... STANDING AT THE BOTTOM OF THE SEA. SOMEHOW... PRESERVED.
SO I SIMPLY BEGAN TO WALK.
A MIRACLE! PROOF OF YOUR CONNECTION TO THE GODS!
AS I WALKED, I HAD...VISIONS. OF DEATH. MONSTERS. AND OF...THIS WALL!
BUT I ALSO SAW FURTHER.
OUR PEOPLE BUILDING EVEN MORE--UNITING UNDER THE CROWN AND GUIDANCE OF USANA--OF OUR QUEEN'S GUIDANCE...
...AS SHE LEADS US TO OUR NEW DESTINY.
AFTER THE MIRACLE OF MY SURVIVAL--I CANNOT DOUBT IT...
THE GODS HAVE BROUGHT US HERE.
AND NOT TO COWER ON THE BEACHES...

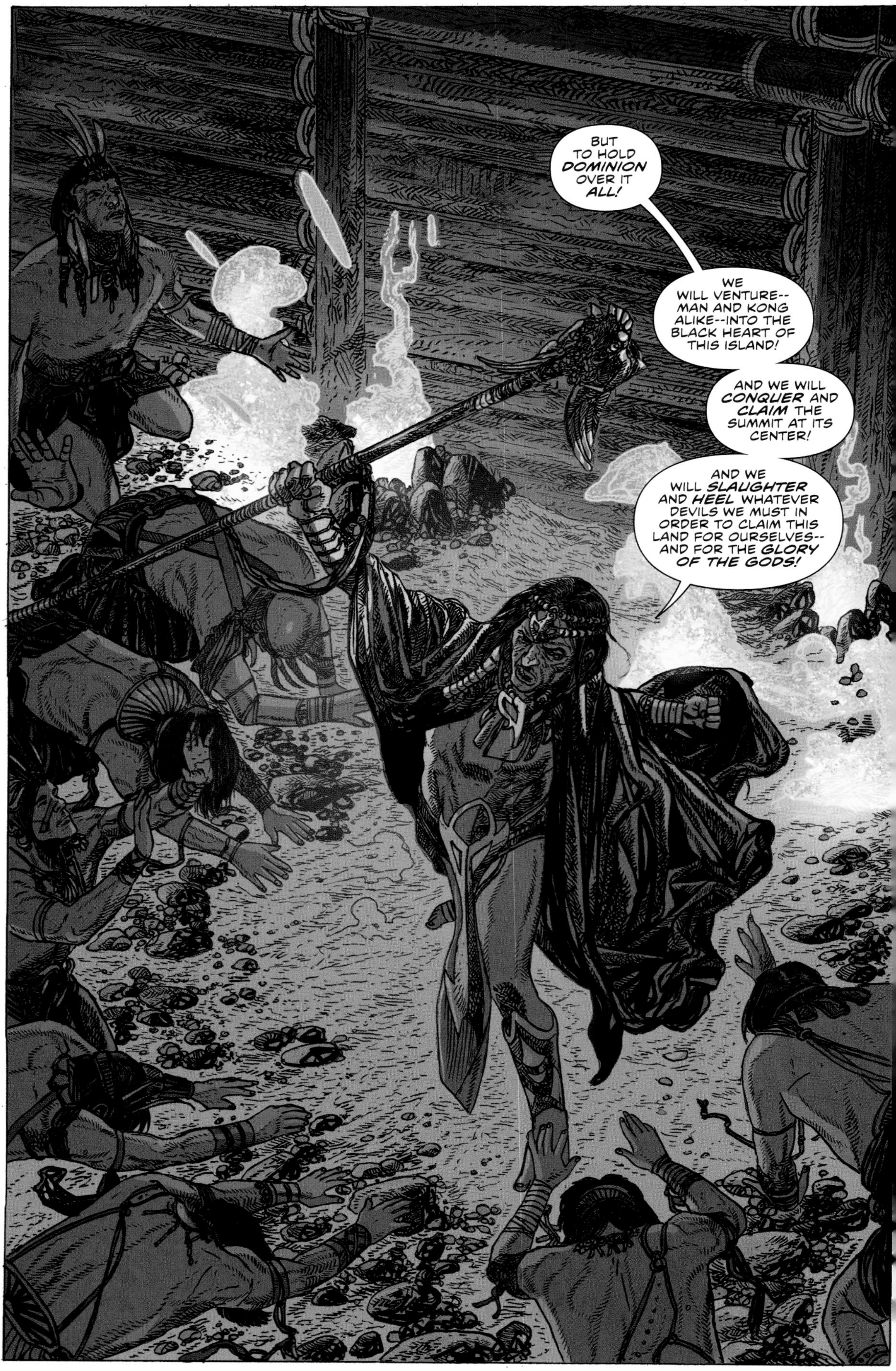
BUT TO HOLD DOMINION OVER IT ALL!
WE WILL VENTURE--MAN AND KONG ALIKE--INTO THE BLACK HEART OF THIS ISLAND!
AND WE WILL CONQUER AND CLAIM THE SUMMIT AT ITS CENTER!
AND WE WILL SLAUGHTER AND HEEL WHATEVER DEVILS WE MUST IN ORDER TO CLAIM THIS LAND FOR OURSELVES--AND FOR THE GLORY OF THE GODS!

ISSUE FOUR COVER
NICK ROBLES

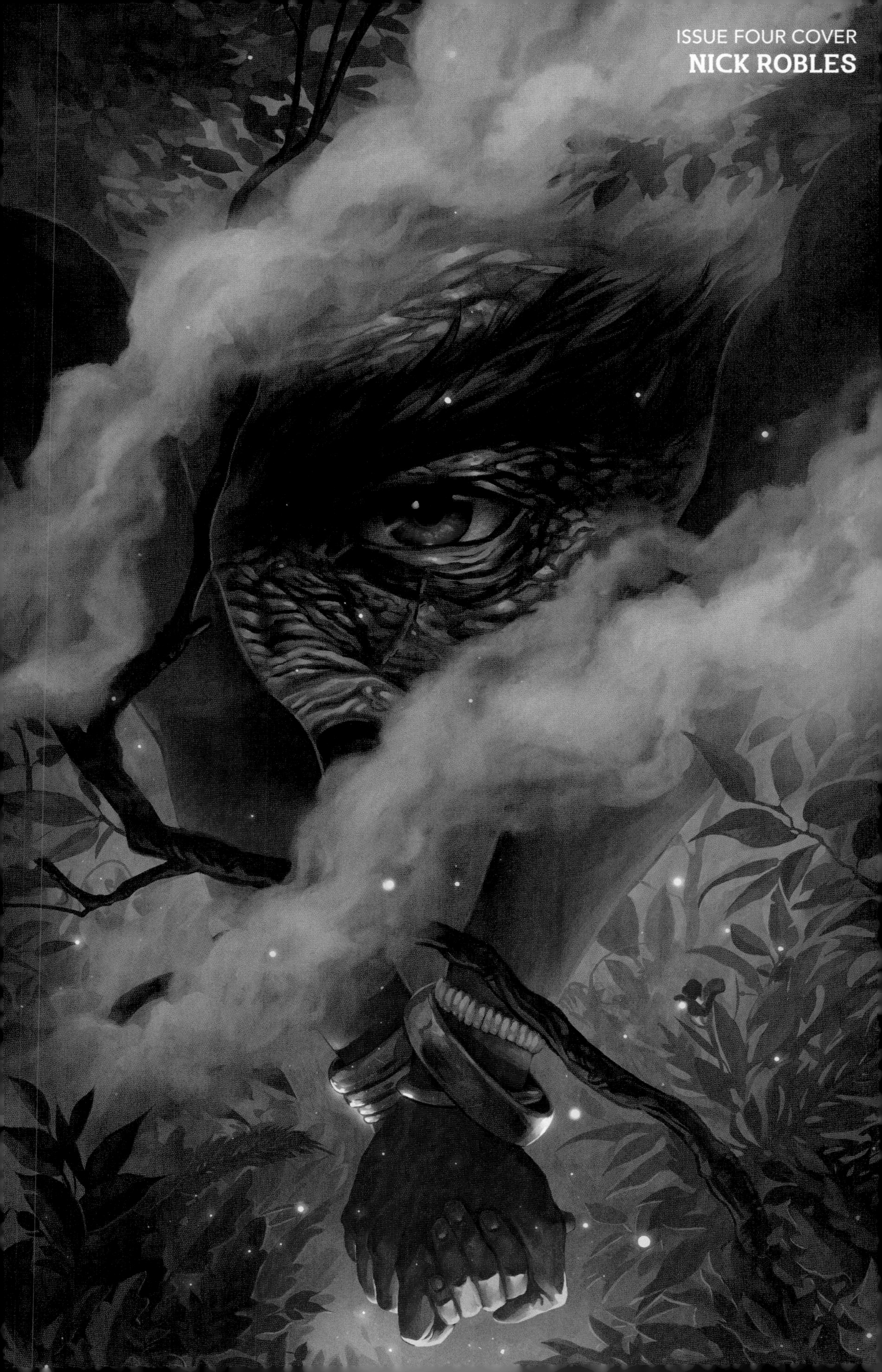

COVER
GALLERY

ISSUE ONE COVER
FELIPE MASSAFERA

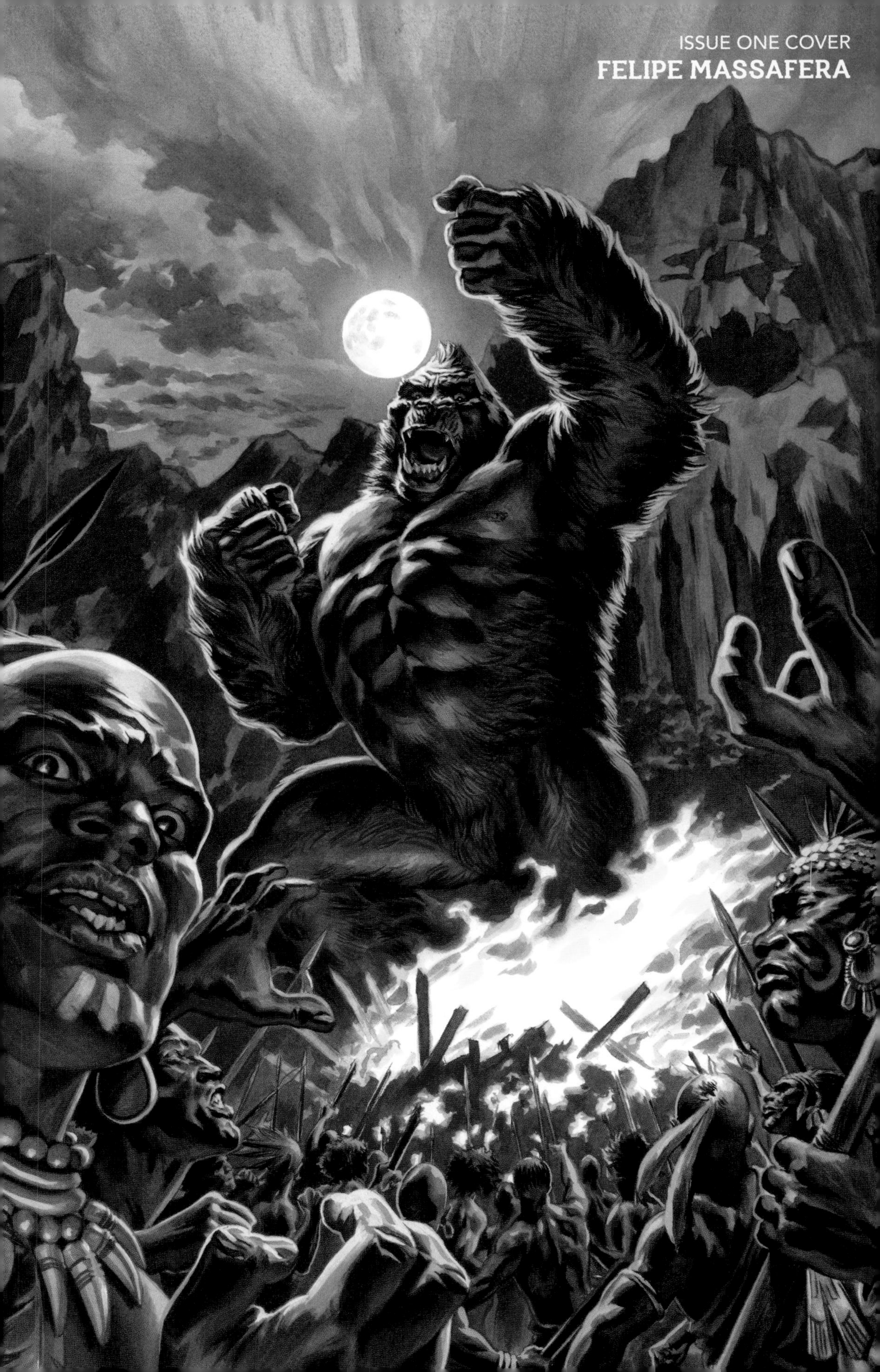

ISSUE ONE COLORING BOOK
VARIANT COVER
CARLOS MAGNO

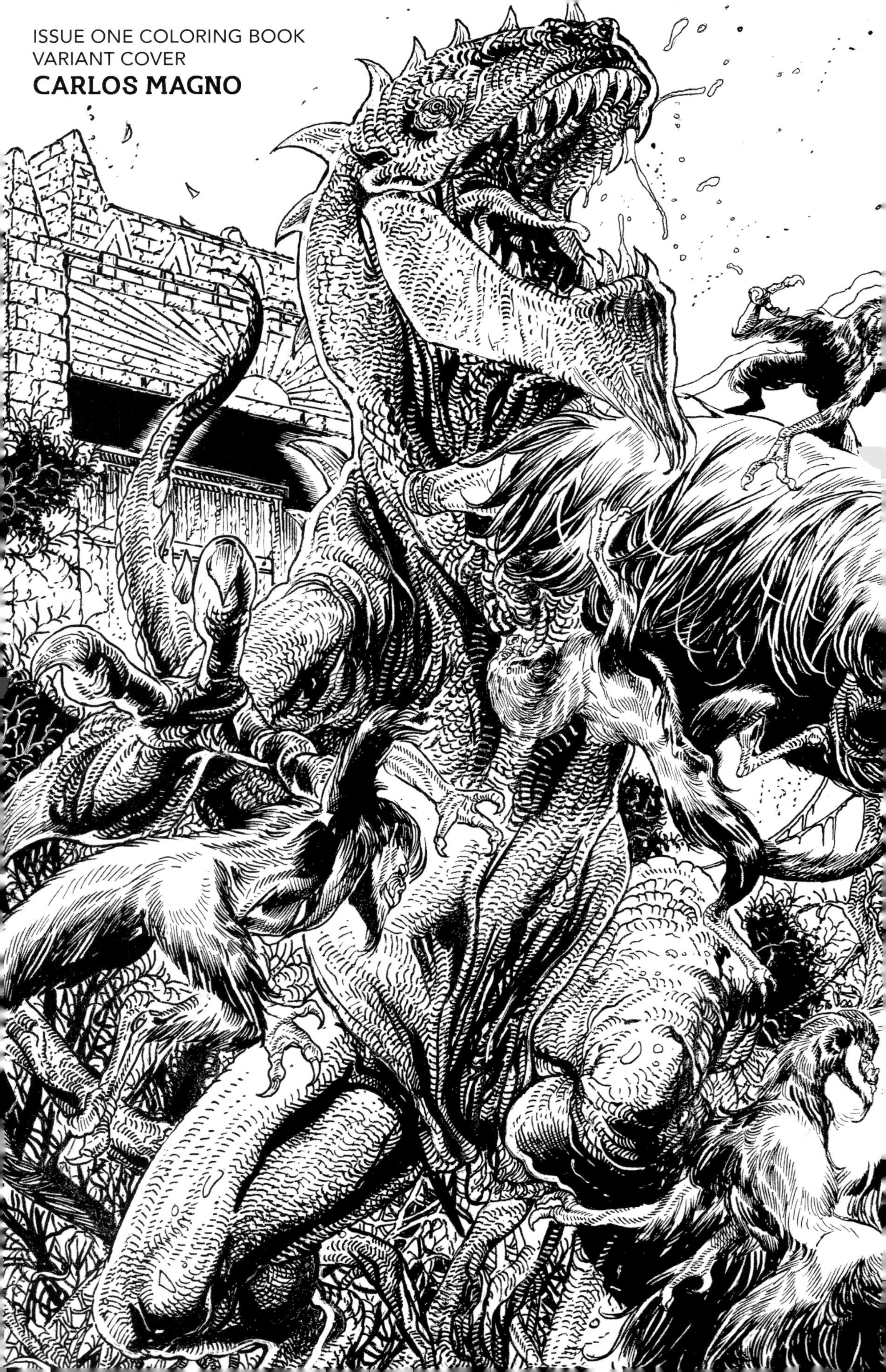

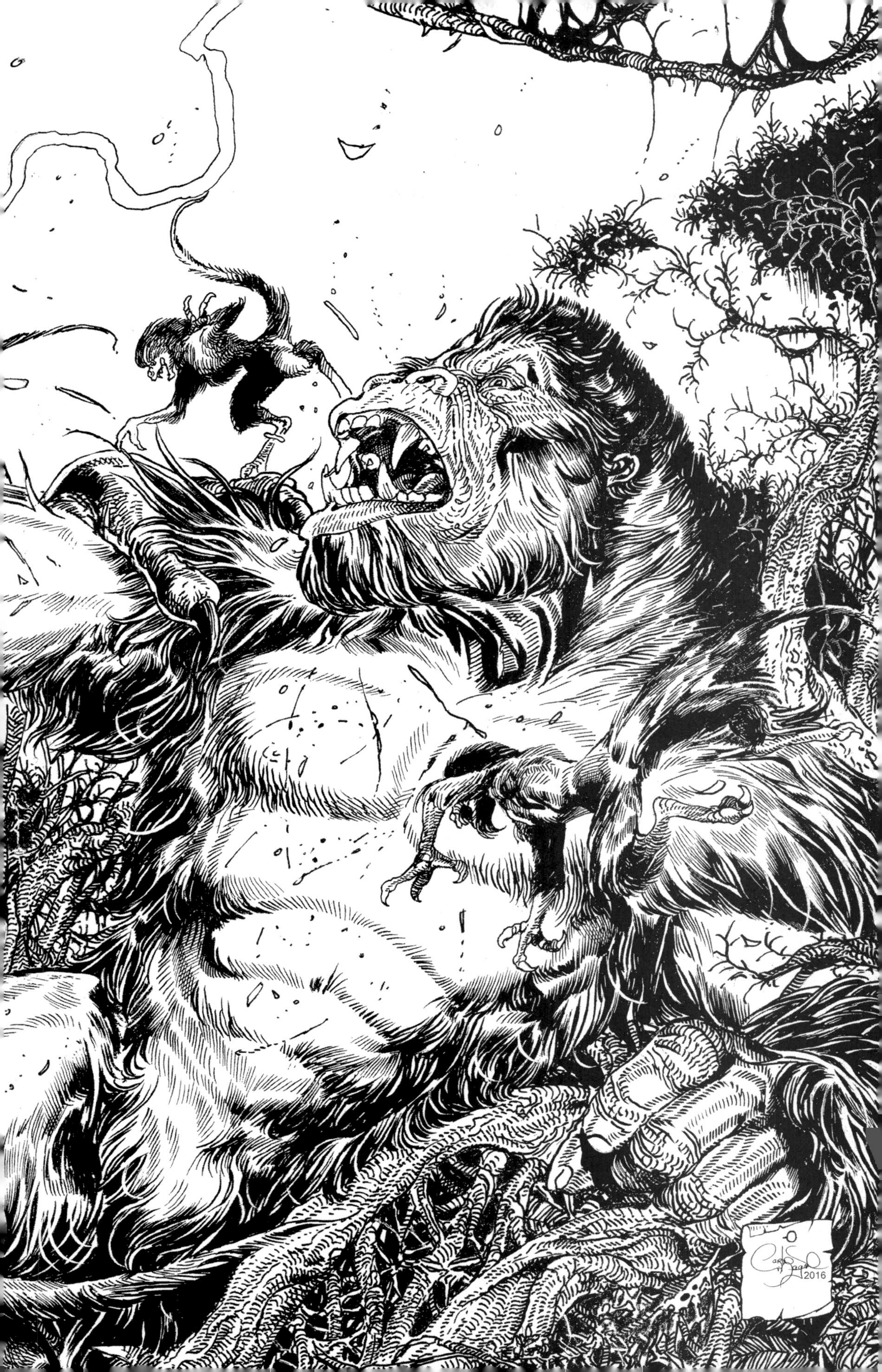
2016

ISSUE ONE MIDTOWN COMICS
EXCLUSIVE COVER
RYAN SOOK

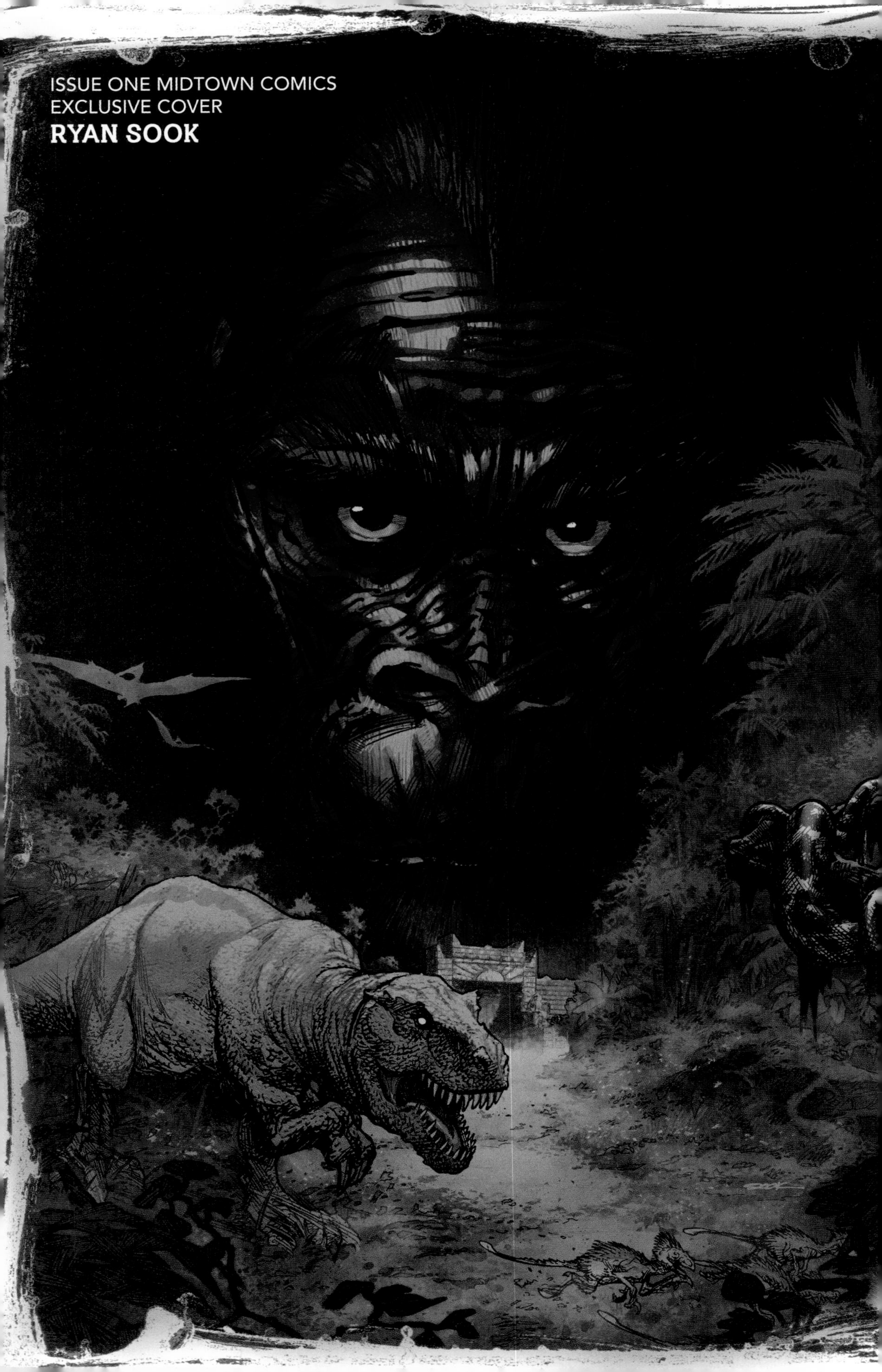

ISSUE ONE GECKO BOOKS & COMICS EXCLUSIVE COVER
PAUL POPE
WITH COLORS BY **JASON WORDIE**

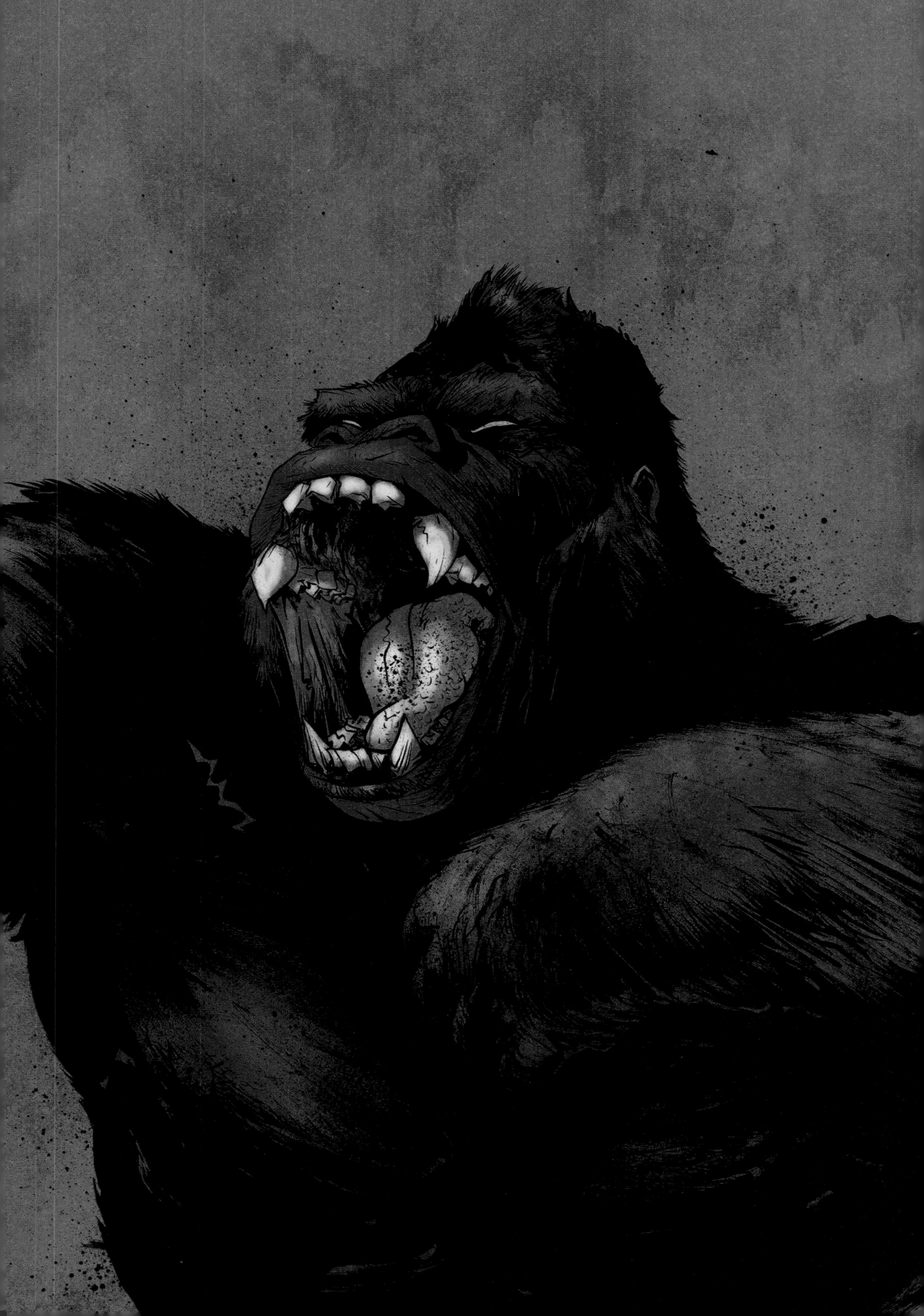

ISSUE ONE BALTIMORE COMIC-CON EXCLUSIVE COVER
DOMINIKE "DOMO" STANTON
WITH COLORS BY **JOHN RAUCH**

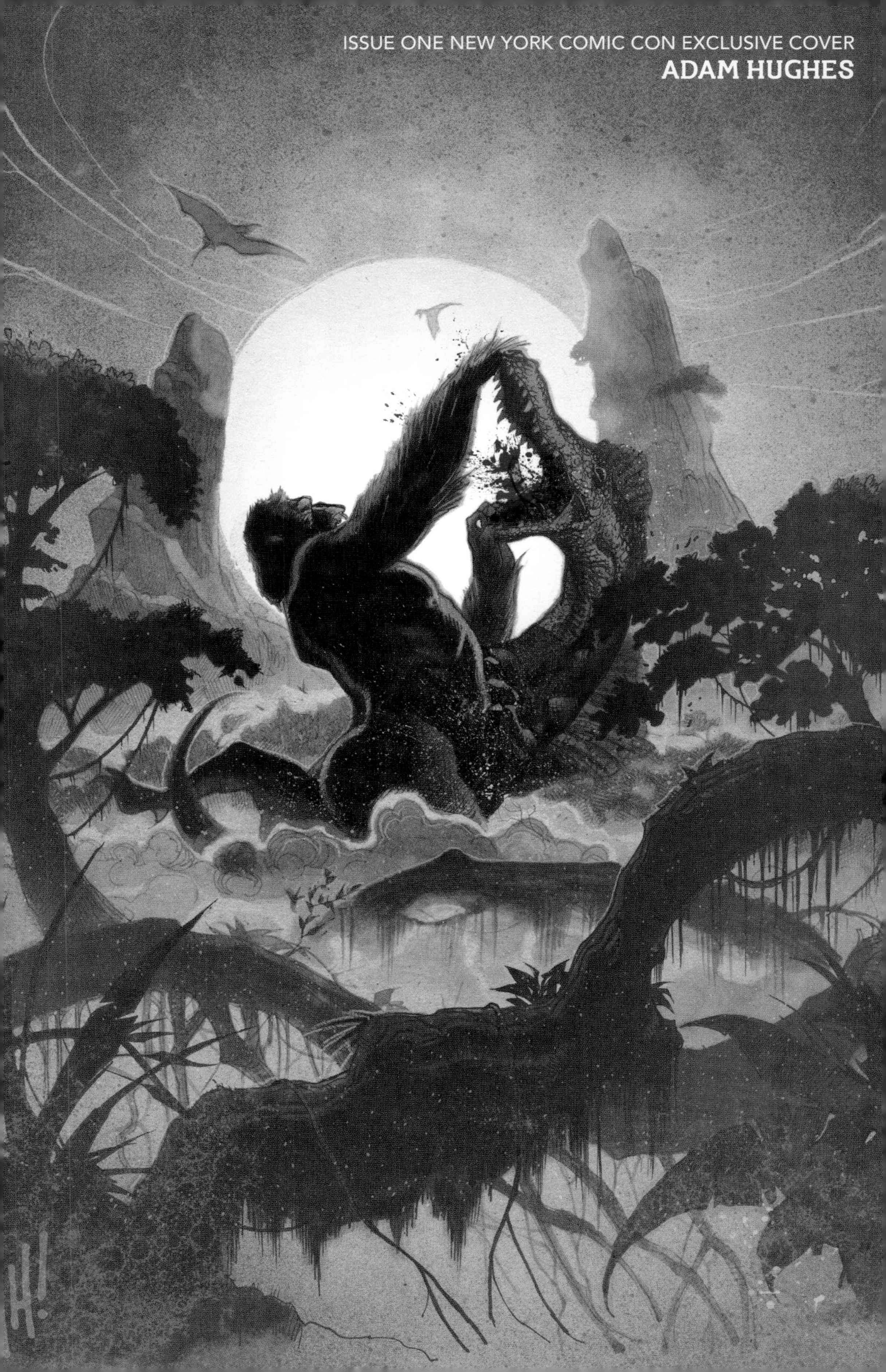

ISSUE ONE NEW YORK COMIC CON EXCLUSIVE COVER
ADAM HUGHES

ISSUE TWO VARIANT COVER

STAN SAKAI

WITH COLORS BY **TOM LUTH**

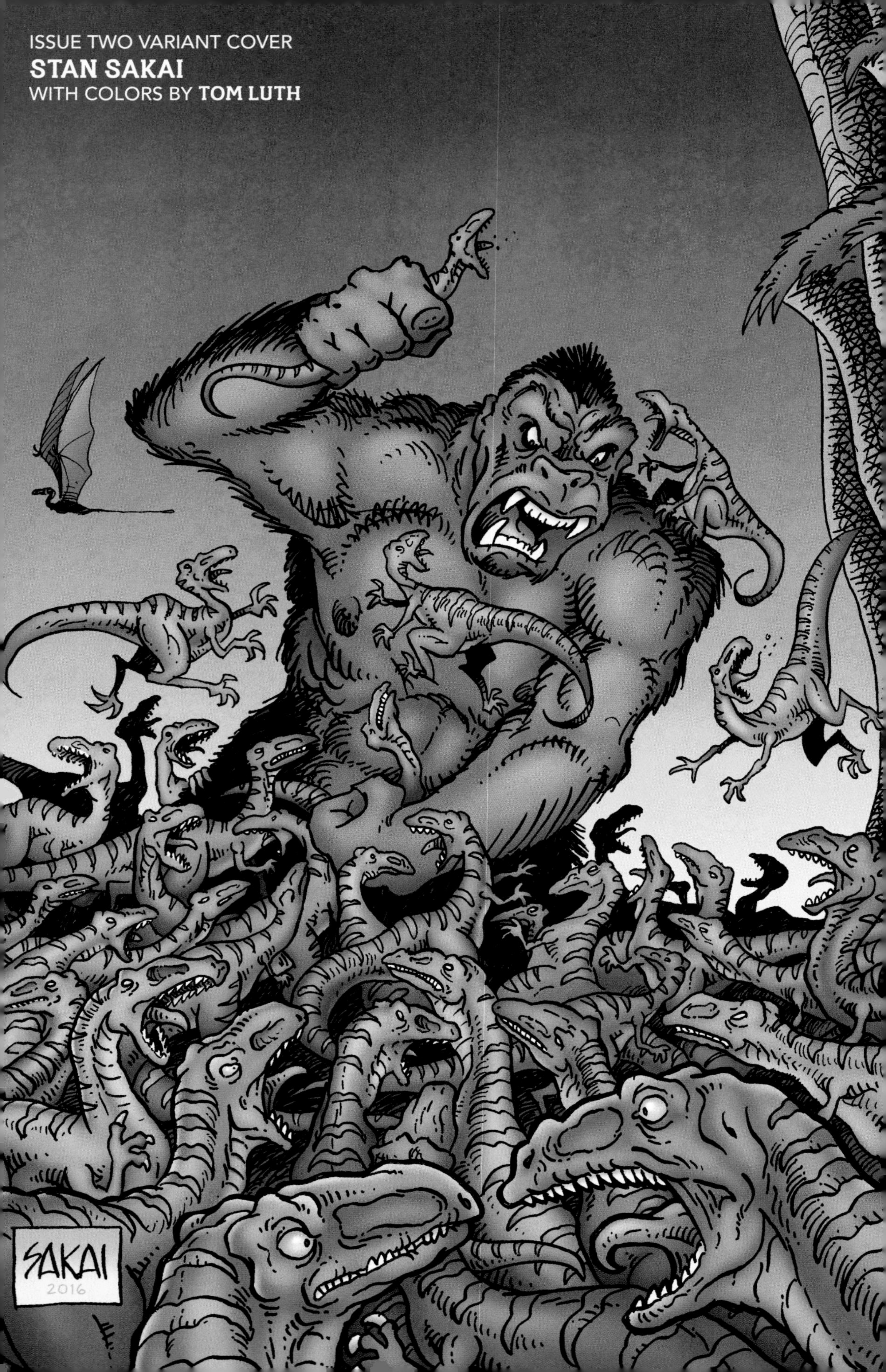
SAKAI
2016

ISSUE THREE VARIANT COVER
TADD GALUSHA

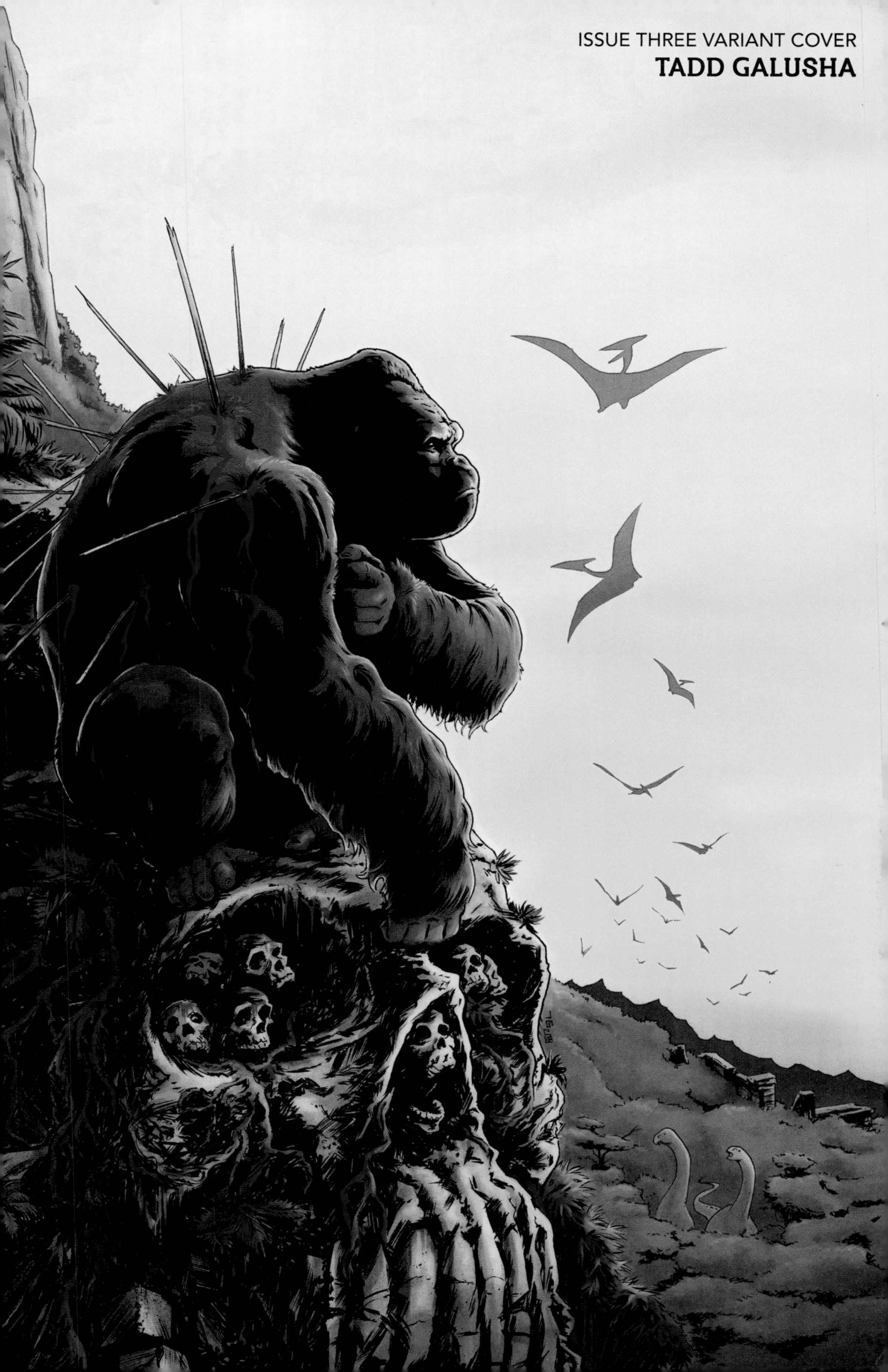

ISSUE FOUR VARIANT COVER

CHRIS BRUNNER

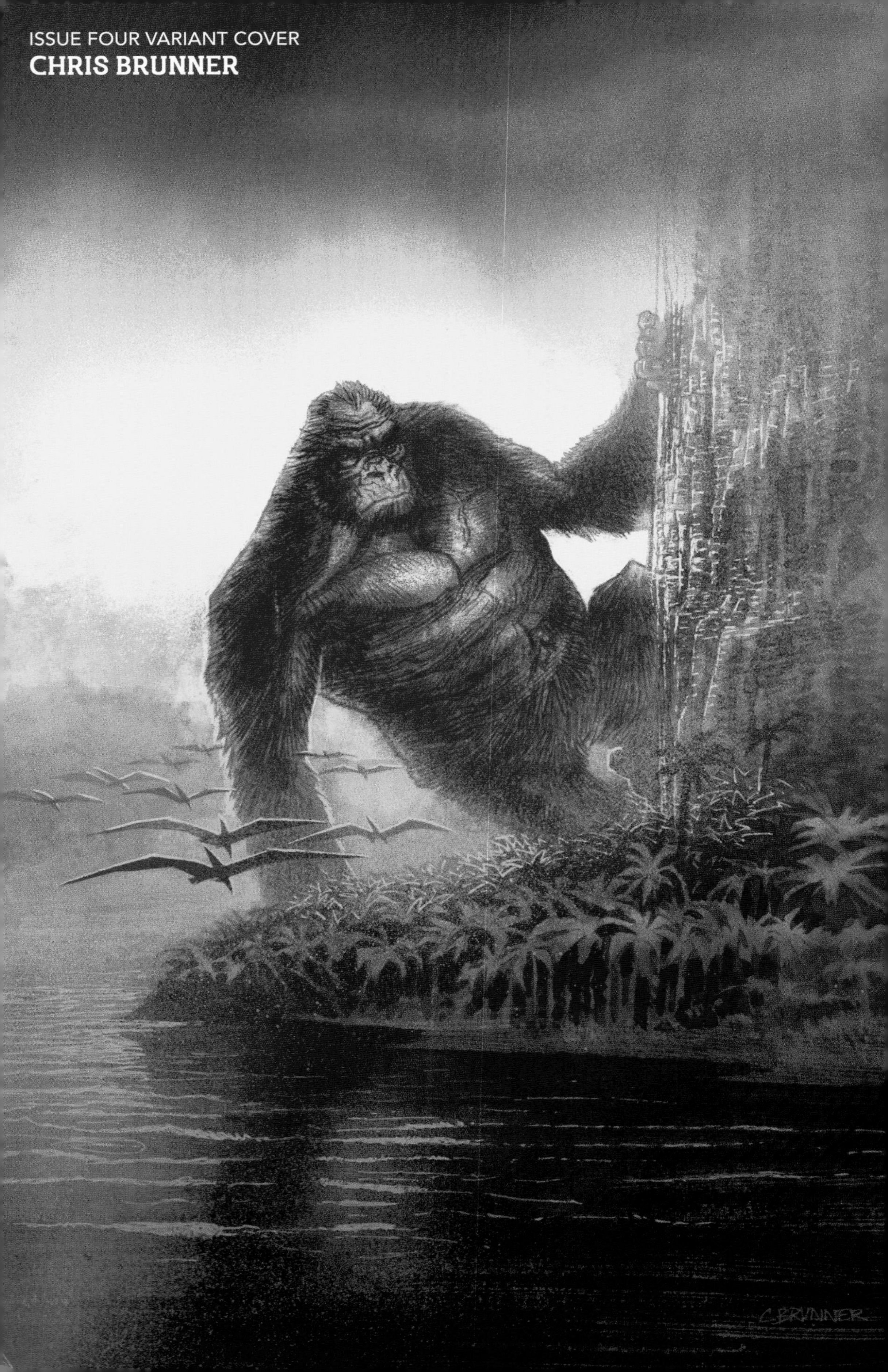
C. BRUNNER

CHARACTER DESIGNS BY **CARLOS MAGNO**

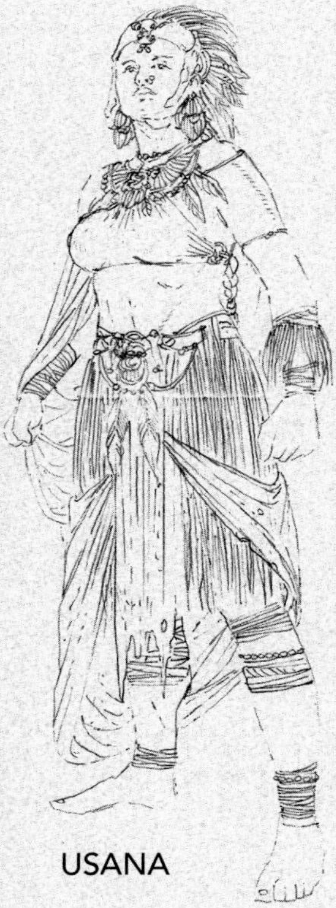

USANA

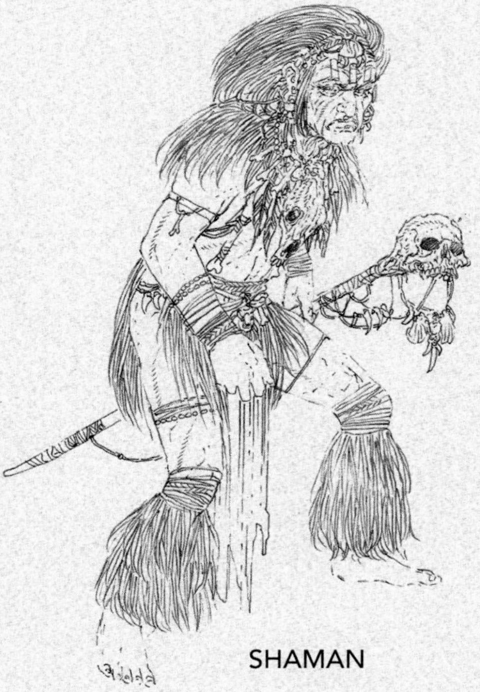

SHAMAN

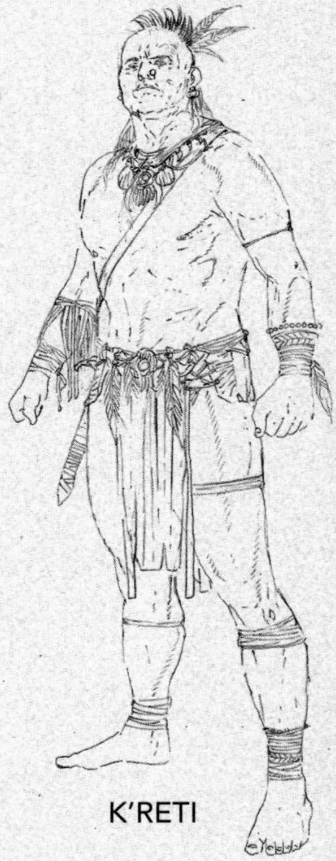

K'RETI

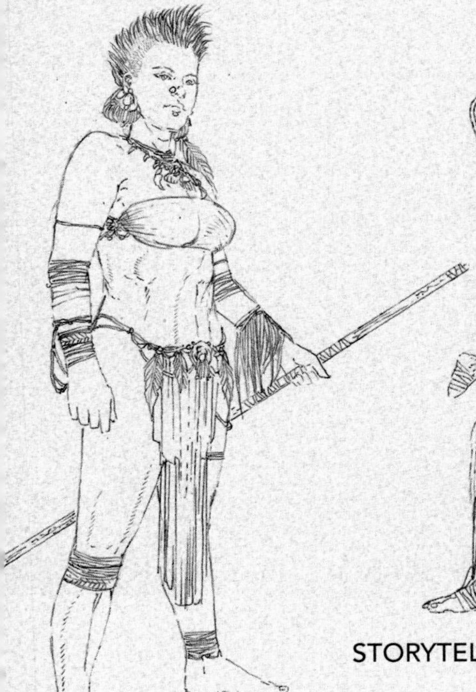

ETAWA

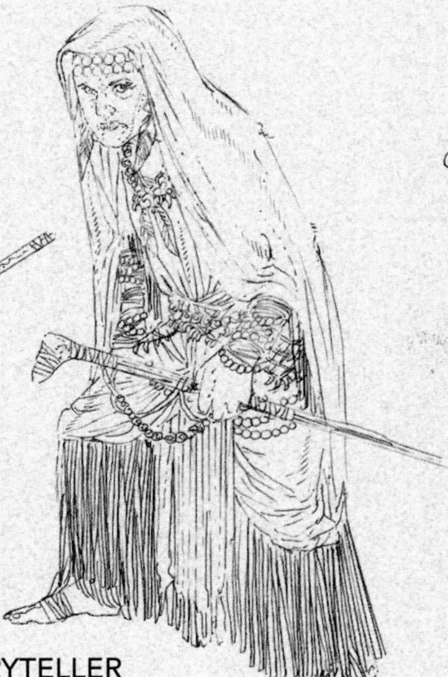

STORYTELLER

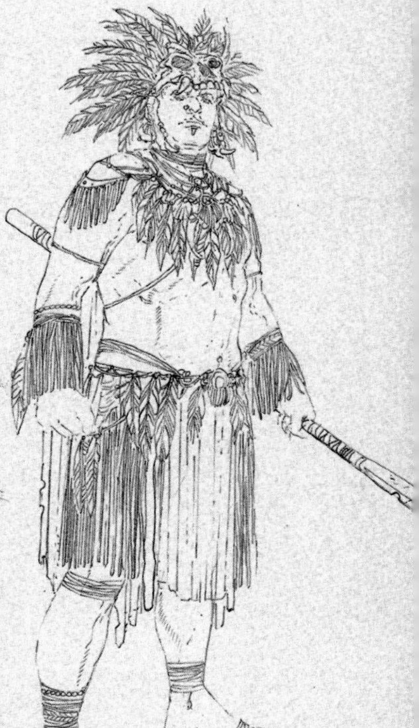

TAGU KING

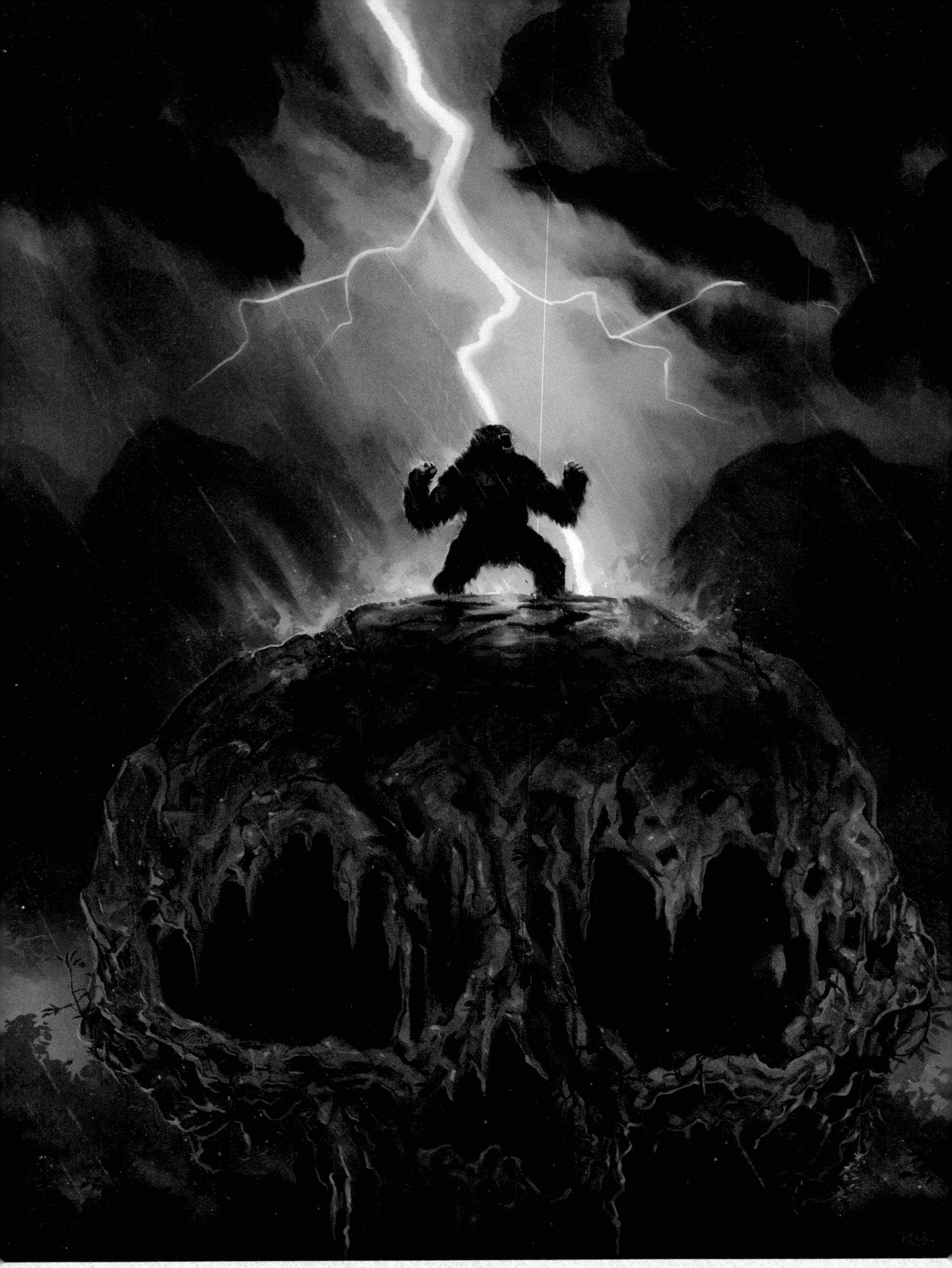

VOLUME TWO
COMING SOON